ANOTHER
TELL ME WHY

ANOTHER
TELL ME WHY

Enlightening Answers to Questions Children Ask

By **ARKADY LEOKUM**

Illustrations by FRANK ALOISE

GROSSET & DUNLAP
A FILMWAYS COMPANY
Publishers · New York

Library of Congress Catalog Card No.: 77-71529

ISBN: 0-448-12954-X (Trade Edition)
ISBN: 0-448-13419-5 (Library Edition)

CONTENTS

Chapter 2
The World We Live In

Chapter 3
The Human Body

Chapter 4
How Things Are Made

Chapter 5
Other Creatures

Chapter 1

HOW IT BEGAN

WHEN WERE FINGERPRINTS FIRST USED FOR IDENTIFICATION?

The fact that human beings had ridges on their fingertips, and that these were different for each person, was known even to prehistoric man! There are ancient Chinese tablets on which fingerprints appear as a way to identify the author of the tablets.

So we can say that fingerprints have been used for personal identification for at least two thousand years. But there is a difference between knowing that man makes individual fingerprints, and organizing this information in a scientific way.

The first important contribution to the science of fingerprinting was made by Marcello Malpighi in 1686. Malpighi, an Italian anatomy professor, studied the ridges of fingertips under a microscope. He saw that these ridges were arranged in patterns of loops and spirals.

Fingerprints were first used officially in Europe to identify prisoners in 1858. A few years later, the first study on the possible use of fingerprints was published. This study described a method of taking prints by using a thin film of printer's ink, a method that is still used today.

In the 1880's Sir Francis Galton, an English scientist, began work on a system for classifying fingerprints. Some years later the system was simplified by Sir Edward Henry, a London police commissioner. Soon after that, fingerprints were being used almost everywhere as a means of identification and crime detection.

Did you know that in many hospitals today the footprints of babies are taken shortly after birth? They are also a means of identification.

HOW DID MOVIES START?

"Movies" is short for "motion pictures," and the development of pictures that seem to move has taken place over many years, thanks to the work of many people.

Way back in the 1800's, experiments were being made using photographs which created the illusion of motion. For example, batteries of cameras were set up to take a series of pictures of a running horse.

In the late 1880's roll film was invented. Then cameras were invented which photographed a series of separate photographs of an action on a strip

of film and then showed them back at the same rate of speed, thus reproducing the action. In fact, these were "movies."

They became quite popular. At first they were only scenes of something that moved: waves on the beach, horses running, children swinging, trains arriving at a station.

The first film which really told a story was produced in the laboratories of Thomas Edison in 1903. It was "The Great Train Robbery," and it caused a nationwide sensation. It was exhibited in black lightproof tents.

The first permanent motion-picture theater in the United States opened in November, 1905, in Pittsburgh, Pennsylvania. The owners called it a nickelodeon. Soon nickelodeons were opened all over the country and everybody began to go to the movies.

Most of the first films were made in New York and New Jersey and it wasn't until 1913 that films began to be made in Hollywood.

WHEN DID HORSE RACING BEGIN?

Using horses for racing seems to be one of the oldest sports enjoyed by man. Races between horses were run in very ancient times. They were held in Egypt, Babylonia, and Syria. Homer described a Greek chariot race that took place about eight centuries before the birth of Christ.

But modern horse racing as we know it originated in England, and it had to do with the development in England of the thoroughbred horse. There were horse races in England as early as the 12th century, but it was in the late 17th and early 18th centuries that the breeding of horses for sport really began.

Eastern horses were brought to England from Arabia, Turkey, and Persia. Stallions from these countries were bred to English mares. Three of these stallions were very important. They were called the Darley Arabian, the Godolphin Arabian, and the Byerly Turk. The lineage of every modern registered thoroughbred traces back to all three in the male line!

During the 18th century horse racing became an important English sport. The Jockey Club was established in 1751. And in 1793 the first issue of the "General Stud Book," which lists the lineage of thoroughbreds, was issued.

Horse racing has long been known as the "sport of kings." This is because English royalty has owned and raced champion horses, and because royalty and wealthy people in other countries have been involved with the sport.

In the United States, horse races were held in the early 17th century, even before the development of the thoroughbred.

16

WHEN WERE JOKES AND RIDDLES FIRST TOLD?

Riddles have been asked since very ancient times. Today, we consider riddles as a form of amusement, but long ago people took riddles very seriously.

Ancient oracles often answered questions and gave advice in the form of riddles. Kings used riddles to send each other secret messages. These serious riddles were also called enigmas.

Greeks and Romans held riddle contests at their feasts and gave prizes to the winners. According to some legends, a man's life sometimes depended on his giving the correct answer to a riddle.

Riddles even appear in the Bible. At Samson's wedding feast, a riddle contest was held and the Queen of Sheba asked King Solomon a number of riddles.

Jokes are as old as the spoken word. In every country in the world and in every age in history, people have told funny stories to make one another laugh.

In the Middle Ages in Europe the court jesters, or fools, amused the king and his court with jokes and tricks. At first, court jesters sang of brave deeds, or gestes. But as time went by they became tellers of jokes and funny stories.

Jokes told by jesters began to appear in collections, or jestbooks. One of the best-known English jestbooks was "Tarlton's Jests," which appeared about 1611. So you see how long ago people were collecting jokes. The most famous joke-teller in history is Joe Miller, an English actor who lived from 1684 to 1738.

WHO INVENTED THE ELEVATOR?

The idea of the elevator was invented by no one man; it was developed over a long period of time. This is because the mechanical principles of elevators had been in use for centuries.

The ancient Greeks knew how to lift objects, using pulleys and winches. A pulley is a grooved wheel that a rope can slide over. A winch is a machine that has a broad wheel, or drum, with a rope fastened to it. By turning the drum with a crank, the rope can be wound up on the drum or let out. By running the rope over a pulley, it can be made to raise or lower a load.

In the 17th century, a "flying chair" was invented. It was designed to carry people to the top floors of buildings and was operated by a system of weights and pulleys. The chair and its machinery were outside the building. The "flying chair" never became popular.

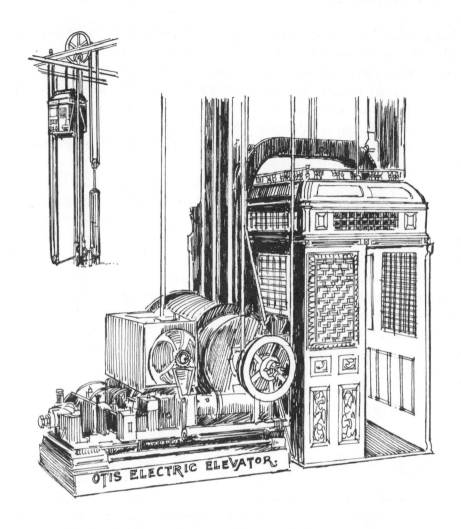

OTIS ELECTRIC ELEVATOR.

During the first half of the 19th century, elevators were already in existence, but they were mostly used for freight. Steam power was used to turn the hoisting drums of these elevators.

What people were afraid of was that the rope holding the elevator might snap and the elevator would go crashing down. Then Elisha Otis invented a safety device that prevented this from happening, and elevators became popular. Also, at this time hydraulic power (fluid under pressure) began to be used to raise and lower elevators.

The electric elevator, which is what is used today, was developed by the German engineer, Werner von Siemens.

WHEN WERE HOUSES FIRST BUILT?

Man began to build a home, a shelter for himself and his family, thousands and thousands of years ago. The kinds of homes people built long ago depended almost completely upon the climate in which they lived, the building materials that were close at hand, and the dangers they faced in their daily lives. So we cannot say such and such a "house" was the first ever built.

For example, when the stone ax was invented thousands of years ago, wood began to play an important part in home-building. So early man was already building himself houses of wood.

On the other hand, in ancient times, people living in warm climates found that grass houses were easy to make and comfortable to live in. So all over the wet, hot grasslands of Africa and on some of the islands of the South Pacific, houses were made of grasses, leaves, or vines that grew nearby.

Thousands of years ago people who lived in hot, dry climates found a way to make fine walls for their homes. They plastered a sticky mixture of clay or mud over house walls of loosely woven twigs. The mud plaster dried hard in the sun and stuck firmly to the house walls.

The ancient Egyptians are believed to have been among the first to discover how to make bricks. In Mesopotamia primitive people later developed a way of making the sun-dried bricks harder and stronger. They placed the molded bricks in a hot fire and "burned" them. Later on, the ancient Assyrians found out how to burn a glaze onto their bricks. Such bricks have lasted for thousands of years.

WHERE WAS THE FIRST THEATER?

Theater as we know it first developed in Greece as part of religious observance. The stage was simply a circle of turf on which the worshipers danced around the altar of Dionysus. The spot was usually at the foot of a hill so that the spectators on the slopes could watch the dancing.

This started the tradition of Greek theaters—semicircles of seats built into a hillside. In fact, the word "theater" is of Greek origin and means "a place for seeing."

A theater built in Athens about 500 B.C. had a circular place, called the orchestra, where the performance was given. Erected behind the circle of the orchestra was a dignified-looking stage building. It was used as a dressing place for the performers. This "skene" (from which comes the word "scene") served as a background for the action of the play. Very little scenery was used by the Greeks, and no artificial lighting was needed, because the plays were presented in the daytime.

The first permanent stone theater was built in Rome in 52 B.C. The theaters of the Romans were similar to those of the Greeks, except that they were built on level ground. The Romans were the first to fill the orchestra with seats and present the play on a raised stage behind which was the "skene."

After the Roman world turned Christian, no theaters were built for about a thousand years. The first modern theater was the Teatro Farnese at Parma, Italy. It was built in 1618 or 1619. Its stage, instead of projecting far out into the orchestra, was built into one of the walls. A curtain was used to separate the stage from the auditorium, so that changes of scenery could be made out of sight of the audience.

WHEN WAS THE FIRST FIRE DEPARTMENT?

Long ago there were no regular firemen. If a house caught fire, everybody became a fire fighter. People formed bucket brigades to fight fires. They stood in line to make a human chain from the burning house to the river or well. They passed buckets of water along from hand to hand for those up front to pour on the flames.

modern magazines, began to print cartoons that expressed opinions on events of the day, and this was the beginning of political cartoons which appear in our daily newspapers today.

One of the greatest political cartoonists was the Frenchman Honore Daumier (1808-1879). He made bitter attacks on people in power and corruption in government. In fact, he was sent to jail for six months because of a cartoon he drew that made fun of the king.

Today, almost everybody recognizes the popular humorous cartoons that appear in many of our papers.

WHEN WAS OIL FIRST USED AS FUEL?

Crude oil is called petroleum. The rocks in which petroleum is found lie deep underground. The oil is reached by drilling below the earth's surface.

In some places petroleum seeps to the surface of the ground through cracks. These seepages, or oil springs, were easy for men to locate. And this crude oil from surface seepages was known to most ancient peoples. Some oil was burned in lamps and torches.

The real history of oil began in the 19th century. The Industrial Revolution brought a need for better lamp fuels to light the new factories. In the United States oil lay close to the surface in many regions and it was often used as medicine.

The first man who thought of drilling for oil was a New York lawyer named George Bissell. He sent a sample of Pennsylvania crude oil to a scientist at Yale University, Benjamin Silliman. Silliman reported that petroleum yielded many useful products: lamp oils, lubricating oils, illuminating gas, paraffin wax for candles, and others. Silliman's report convinced businessmen that there was money to be made in oil.

Bissell hired a man named Edwin Drake to drill for oil near Titusville, Pennsylvania. On August 27, 1859, they struck oil. The news spread quickly. Men rushed to buy or lease land where oil might be found, and the oil rush was on. Oil fever spread to other parts of the United States, to Canada, and to Europe. New uses for petroleum products were found, including its use as fuel, and the demand for oil increased. Today, the search for new oil fields is still going on all over the world.

WHY ARE LONDON POLICEMEN CALLED "BOBBIES"?

The idea of a police system to protect a city originated in London. In 1737 a law was passed creating a police system with 68 men. But as the city grew and poverty increased, looting and rioting were soon out of control in London.

In 1829 Sir Robert Peel formed the London Metropolitan Police, with headquarters in Scotland Yard. The new recruits wore top hats and tailcoats. But this new force that Peel had created was much larger, better trained, and more highly disciplined than any other police force had ever been.

The rioting in London was soon controlled, but before long it spread to other areas. As a result, in 1835 all towns and cities in England were empowered to form their own police departments. From Sir Robert Peel's name came the familiar nickname "bobby" for the English policeman.

In the 1830's a group of people from New York City made a study of the British police system. As a result, in 1844 New York became the first city in the United States to establish a day-and-night police force similar to Peel's.

Before long other cities followed New York's example.

Why are American policemen known as "cops" or "coppers"? Some people believe that the name comes for the eight-pointed copper star once worn by New York policemen. Others believe that the name was taken from the initial letters of the words "constable on patrol."

WHY IS THE NUMBER 13 CONSIDERED UNLUCKY?

The idea that the number 13 is unlucky is a superstition. There are many different kinds of superstitions, based on things in nature, charms, spirits, objects, colors, accidents, and so on.

But there is probaaly no superstition that has as many people observing it, in one way or another, all over the world, as the one that 13 is unlucky. Hotels don't have a 13th floor—the count goes from 12 to 14. Hotel rooms don't have a 13. Many people would never have 13 persons at a dinner table.

Yet the strange thing is that there is no single, accepted explanation for the origin of the superstition about 13. There are many different ideas about the origin of it.

Some experts say 13 was unpopular from the time when man learned to count. By using his ten fingers and two feet as units, he came up with the number 12. But beyond that—13—was unknown and frightening to him.

Among religious circles, the 13 superstition is traced back to the Last Supper, at which were Christ and the twelve Disciples—thirteen in all. Other people go back to the story of the Valhalla banquet in Greek mythology, to which twelve gods were invited. Loki, the Spirit of Strife and Mischief, intruded, making thirteen. As a result, Balder, the favorite of the gods, was killed.

Another strange thing about 13 is that his number was regarded as lucky by the ancient Chinese and Egyptians.

WHO FIRST MADE BREAD WITH YEAST?

The action of yeast in moist, warm dough is called leavening. The yeast cells convert the starch of the dough into sugar, which they then digest. As they do this they give off carbon dioxide as a waste product. The gas is trapped in the dough, forms larger and larger bubbles, and makes the dough rise.

Wild yeast spores are almost always present in the air and will land naturally on the dough. The first people to discover the value of yeast were the Egyptians. They tried baking with fermented dough and liked the lighter, tastier bread. Bread that rises with the aid of wild yeast, however, may turn out differently each time. This is because different kinds of yeast may fall on it.

The Egyptians discovered a way to control this. Each time they baked they set aside some of the leavened dough to mix with the next batch. In this way they could be sure of using the same kind of yeast.

Around 1000 B.C. Phoenician traders carried the art of making leavened bread to the Greeks, who became the master bakers of antiquity. The Greeks had over 70 different recipes for bread.

The Romans turned baking into a large-scale industry and passed many laws governing the quality of bread. The bakers were so proud of the superior taste of their bread that each baker marked his loaves with his name, just as bakeries put their brand name on the wrappers today.

During the Middle Ages, only rich people ate white bread. Dark, often sour, rye bread was what most of the people ate.

WHO WERE THE FIRST BARBERS?

There have been barbers since very ancient times—so long ago, in fact, that we can't possibly know who the first barbers were. The first records of barbers in history go back to ancient Egypt. Later on, in ancient Greece and Rome, barbershops were favorite meeting places where men discussed affairs of the day.

Everybody knows what the barber's pole looks like. Those red-and-white stripes have something to do with work that barbers did in olden days. In ancient times, doctors didn't want to have anything to do with surgery. So it was the barbers who performed surgery on patients. They did bloodletting (letting a patient bleed so that the "bad blood" or "sick blood" would leave the body). They treated wounds, and some of them even extracted teeth.

The barber's pole of red-and-white stripes goes back to those days. The red stands for blood, and the white for bandages.

In England the barbers were chartered as a guild as far back as 1462. In 1540, their guild was merged with the guild of surgeons. But about this time, the king of England forbade the barbers who cut hair and gave shaves to practice surgery.

In the next two hundred years, the work of the barber was separated more and more from that of the surgeon, and in time all they were allowed to do was give haircuts.

By the way, the word "barber" comes from the Latin word "barba," which meant "beard." So their work of trimming beards may have been more important than cutting hair.

HOW DID ANIMALS GET THEIR NAMES?

The names of animals, like the names of so many other things, didn't originate in one particular way. The names developed in many different ways, from many different sources.

For example, a strange name like "hippopotamus" is actually a descriptive name. In Greek, "hippos" means "horse" and "potamus" means "river." So the hippopotamus was a "river horse." "Rhinoceros" came from two Greek words, "rinos," the nose, and "keras," a horn. That's just what this creature has: a horn on the nose! "Leopard" is from the Latin "leopardus"—which meant a "spotted lion."

Some names of animals that we use are based on names used in other places. "Camel" comes from the Arabic "gamel," and "giraffe" from the Arabic

"zirafoh," meaning "long neck." The name "ox" is an Icelandic term which became "oxa" in Anglo-Saxon. And "cow" also comes from Iceland, where the name was "ku." The name "bull" comes from the Anglo-Saxon verb "belan," which meant to roar, to bellow.

"Deer" comes from the Anglo-Saxon "deor," which meant "a wild animal." We get our name "cat" from the French "chat," which came from the Latin "gata." "Mouse" comes from the Anglo-Saxon "mus." The name "poodle" has an interesting origin. It comes from the German "pudel," short for "pudelhund," which meant "a dog that splashes in water." The duck is so named because this bird "ducks" in the water, from an old English word "duce," a "diver".

These are only a few names with explanations of how they started. But you can see that animals got their names in many different ways.

WHEN DID WOMEN START CURLING THEIR HAIR?

Men and women have dressed and done things to their hair as far back as there are any records of human beings. An interesting thing is that dressing the hair was not a mark of "civilization." Primitive and savage races all over the world have always paid a great deal of attention to their hair.

It seems that, even in ancient times, curled hair was considered more attractive than straight hair. Artificial means were used to curl the hair, and it was done by both men and women. Men also curled their beards.

With the coming of civilization, methods of arranging and dressing the hair became more varied. During the Renaissance curling irons, henna for dyeing, and silk floss wigs were popular all over Europe.

In fact, men were so fond of wearing long hair arranged in all kinds of fashions that King Henry VIII of England issued an order for all men to wear only short hair. But he allowed them to grow nice beards and to curl their mustaches. When James I came to the throne of England (1603), men again grew long hair and curled it.

The custom of short hair for men became definitely established in the 19th century. But for hundreds of years women had worn long hair because they were taught that hair was the "crowning glory" of their appearance. It is interesting to note that, despite this, bobbing the hair was actually a fad at the court of Louis XIV and was also popular at the court of James I of England.

WHEN WAS SURFING FIRST DONE?

Surfing is the sport of riding ocean waves on a long, narrow surfboard. The sport is enjoyed at beaches all over the world and has become so popular that we tend to think of it as a new thing.

But surfing is actually quite old. It apparently originated in the Pacific islands hundreds of years ago. When Captain James Cook discovered Hawaii in 1788, surfing was already a very popular sport among the Hawaiians.

The Hawaiians held surfing contests and the winners who won prizes were acclaimed by the people. The islanders used boards 14 to 18 feet long which were about 150 pounds in weight.

About 1957 a big change took place in surfing that helped make it popular. Lightweight boards began to be used. These boards, which are about 10 feet long and weigh as little as 22 pounds, have made it possible for women and even children to take up surfing. The new boards are generally made of foam plastic, coated with fiberglass and resin. A surfboard is the only special equipment the sport requires.

When riding a wave, surfers stand on the board and maneuver right and left. The surfer must first take his board out past the surf line—the point where the waves begin to break. Kneeling or lying prone on his board, he waits for a set, or series of swells, to form. When the wave he wants to ride comes up behind him, he paddles quickly toward shore with his hands. As the wave moves beneath him, the board first rises with it, then slides down the unbroken front of the wave. Having "caught" the wave, the surfer stands, one foot forward, and steers away from the breaking part of the wave.

WHEN WAS THE FIRST PLASTIC MADE?

In making a plastic, the chemist starts with the molecule. The chemist causes molecules to form a long chain, the links being the molecules. The new "long-chain" molecule acts differently from the single molecule. The whole process is called polymerization, and it is by polymerization that new materials are made.

Chemists knew about and had worked with plastics as early as the mid-1800's. Vinyl chloride was polymerized in 1838, styrene in 1839, acrylics in 1843, and polyester in 1847. But at that time there was no particular need for these synthetic materials.

In 1870, looking for a substitute for ivory, John Hyatt and his brother Isiah Hyatt discovered Celluloid. This was a new, tough, easily made and shaped material, and resisted many chemicals. It stimulated chemists to think about developing additional synthetic materials.

In 1909 the Belgian-American chemist Leo Baekeland discovered phenol-formaldehyde. This was the first of a type of plastics called thermosetting plastics. Baekeland was actually trying to invent a substitute for shellac. Instead, he produced a dark syrup that would harden when heated. The new material was not dissolved by ordinary solvents; it could be molded into any shape, it did not conduct electricity, and it was inexpensive.

Baekeland named the new material Bakelite, after himself. This plastic was the first entirely synthetic material to be produced in large quantities. It opened the way to the development of a whole world of new plastics.

WHY DO WE HAVE APRIL FOOLS' DAY?

Some customs, holidays, and traditions are very hard to trace to their beginnings. We just do it and can't explain why. April Fools' Day, and how it originated, has been explained in several ways, but no one is quite sure.

First of all, there is a day like our April Fools' Day in nearly all parts of the world. It is a day when practical jokes are played on friends and neighbors, like sending them on foolish errands or tricking them into doing silly things.

It is believed that our April Fools' Day started with the French. When the calendar was reformed, the first nation to adopt the reformed calendar was France. Charles IX ordered, in 1564, that the year should begin with the 1st of January. Until then, New Year's visits and the exchange of New Year's gifts has been associated with the 1st of April.

Now, after Charles issued his decree, all this became associated with the 1st of January. But there were many people who objected to the change and refused to go along with it. The other people made fun of them for this.

They did it this way: they sent them mock gifts, they pretended to be visiting them, they invited them to mock New Year's celebrations—all on the 1st of April. In other words, they were April Fools—people who still felt April 1st was the beginning of the new year. Also, the custom of fooling somebody on this day started with the mock gifts and celebration they had with these people.

HOW WERE WORDS MADE?

The words of the English language originated in many different ways from many different sources, but Greek and Latin supplied most of the words used in English today. A single Latin word like "manus" ("hand"), for example, is the source of "manufacture," "manicure," "manipulate," "emancipate," and so on.

The Latin word "scribere" ("to write") gives us "scribble," "scripture," "subscription," and many others. The Greek word "autos," meaning "self," gives us "autobiography," "automobile," "autograph," "automatic," and so on.

Many words are formed simply by putting part of a word in front of the root (called a prefix) or adding to the end of a root (a suffix). For example: bi- ("two") makes "bicycle" and "bisect." And: -able ("fitness for") makes "lovable" and peaceable."

The English language includes words borrowed from many other languages. The English language began early in the Christian era with the dialects of such tribes as the Angles, Jutes, and Saxons. Viking invaders from Scandinavia added to it. And at the time of the Norman Conquest (1066) William the Conqueror's invaders brought many thousands of French and Latin terms into the language.

Later, as English explorers and traders ranged over the world, they borrowed many words from the peoples with whom they traded. For example, from India came such words as "madras," "bungalow," "punch," and "faker." From the Dutch came "freight," "schooner," and "landscape." From Spain and Latin America came "potato," "cargo," "tobacco," and "hurricane." And our language has continued to grow with words from dialects, different peoples, and from new developments in science, sports, and all kinds of activities.

WHAT IS THE ORIGIN OF THE DOG?

All living members of the dog family are descended from a wolflike creature called "Tomarctus." This ancient canine, called "the father of dogs," roamed the earth's forests about 15,000,000 years ago.

Tomarctus itself was descended from a small, weasel-like creature called "Miacis"; it lived some 40,000,000 years ago. This creature was also the distant ancestor of the bears and raccoons. They are the dog's closest living relatives today.

While man admires and lives with the domestic dog, he usually hates and fears such animals as wolves, coyotes, jackals, and foxes. But these are called "wild dogs." Domestic dogs are brothers under the skin to wolves, coyotes, and jackals—the typical wild dogs. All belong to the foremost branch of the dog family, the genus *anis*. All are so closely related that domestic dogs can mate with wolves, coyotes, or jackals, and produce fertile offspring. But they cannot interbreed with foxes. Foxes belong to another branch of the canine family tree.

At some time long ago early man tamed a few wild dogs. These dogs may have been wolf cubs. Or they may have been jackals or some other member of the wild dog family. Man found that these animals could be useful.

As man became more civilized he found that the dog was a good friend and a helpful guard for his home and cattle. In time, different breeds of dogs were developed for special purposes. Dogs with long noses were bred to scent game. Keen-sighted, fast dogs were bred to chase animals. Strong, heavy dogs pulled carts. Other dogs were bred for guard work. In this way the different breeds of dogs we have were developed.

WHEN WAS THE FIRST PAINTING MADE?

The earliest artists to do drawings and paintings were the caveman. Colored drawings of animals, dating from about 30,000 to 10,000 B.C., have been found on the walls of caves in southern France and Spain. Many of these drawings are amazingly well preserved, because the caves were sealed up for many centuries. Early man drew the wild animals that he saw all around him.

The cave artists filled the cave walls with drawings in rich, bright colors. Some of the most beautiful paintings are in the Cave of Lascaux in France. The pigments used by cave painters were earth ochers (iron oxides varying in color from light yellow to deep orange) and manganese (a metallic element).

These were crushed into a fine powder, mixed with grease (perhaps animal fat), and put on with some sort of brush. Sometimes the pigments were used in sticks, like crayons. The grease mixed with the powdered pigments made the paint fluid and the pigments' particles stick together. The cavemen must have made brushes out of animal hairs or plants.

As far back as 30,000 years ago, man had invented the basic tools and materials for painting. Techniques and materials were refined and improved in the centuries following, but the discoveries of the caveman remain basic to painting.

One of the first civilizations was developed in Egypt, about 5,000 years ago. The Egyptians developed their own techniques of painting. In one method watercolor paint was put on mud-plaster or limestone walls. The dry climate of the region has helped preserve some of the watercolor paintings from being destroyed.

WHEN DID MAN FIRST START TO SHAVE?

What decided whether men would let their beards grow or shave them off? All through history it was chiefly a matter of religious custom or just fashion.

We don't know exactly who the first men were who shaved their beards. But we do know that the ancient Egyptians did shave their faces for religious reasons. On the other hand, the ancient Jews were required to wear full beards, and there are many orthodox Jews who still do so for religious reasons.

The ancient Greeks wore beards, and many portraits of the great Greek philosophers show them with long flowing beards. Then Alexander the Great introduced the custom of shaving to the Greeks. He is said to have done this so that his soldiers wouldn't be grabbed by their beards in combat.

The early Romans didn't shave until about 300 B.C., when barbers were introduced. The first Roman known to have shaved every day was the great general Scipio Africanus (237-183 B.C.), and then shaving soon became a regular practice among the Romans. By the way, in time of mourning the Romans let their beards grow—and the Greeks cut their beards.

The Roman custom of shaving influenced the Roman Catholic Church to have the clergy beardless and cleanshaven. In the 16th and 17th centuries the wearing of beards was revived among popes, cardinals, and priests. Later Roman Catholic practice went back to the idea of shaving, except for members of monasteries.

The custom of shaving was introduced into England by the Saxons.

WHEN WERE THE FIRST KEYS MADE?

The ancient Egyptians were the first to use a kind of key to open a door. They had a lock that was made up of a wooden bolt that fitted into a slot. Movable wooden pins known as tumblers were fastened in the top of the slot. When the bolt slid into place, the wooden tumblers dropped into holes cut in the bolt. The bolt was held fast until the tumblers were lifted up with a key.

This first key did not look at all like a key as we know it today. It looked more like a giant-sized toothbrush with pegs instead of bristles on one end. When the key was put in the slot, the pegs went under the tumblers. By raising the key, the tumblers were forced out of the bolt, which was then easily drawn back.

The Egyptian key could only be used on that side of the door where the bolt was placed. The Greeks discovered a way to slide back the bolt from the

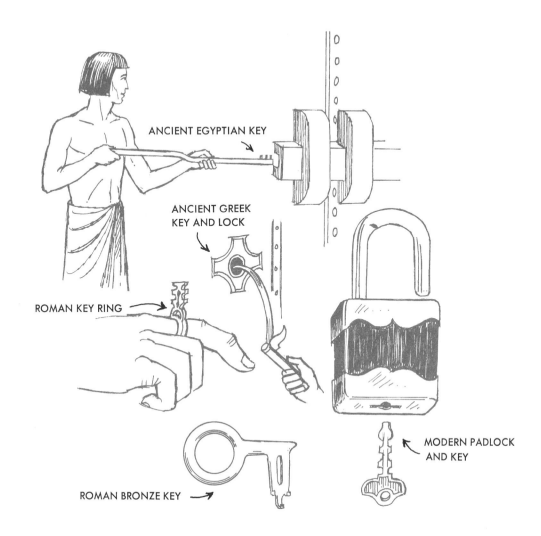

ANCIENT EGYPTIAN KEY

ANCIENT GREEK KEY AND LOCK

ROMAN KEY RING

MODERN PADLOCK AND KEY

ROMAN BRONZE KEY

other side of the door. They slid their key through a hole in the door above the bolt until its tip touched a notch in the bolt on the inside. The Greek key was a curved bar, in shape and size much like a farmer's sickle. Some of these keys were over three feet long and were carried over the shoulder.

The Romans later became the most skillful lockmakers of the ancient world. They made a great improvement in the key. The pegs on the end of the Roman keys were cut in many different shapes. Now a thief had to make a key with pins not only in the right position and of the right length but also of the right shape.

The Romans worked out a small lock that could be carried from place to place. We call such locks padlocks. The small padlock keys were often made in the shape of rings, so they could be worn on a finger.

WHY ARE THE KEYS ON A TYPEWRITER ARRANGED THAT WAY?

The modern typewriter is a complicated piece of machinery. Development to its present form took many years, and many people contributed to it.

Inventors had been thinking about a machine for writing since early in the 18th century. But it was not until 1867 that the first practical model was built, by Christopher Sholes of Milwaukee, Wisconsin.

Shole's machine was called the Type-Writer. People did not seem too interested in typewriting at first. The popularity of typewriters began to grow, however, in the early 1880's. And changes and improvements kept being introduced all the time.

But the odd arrangement of the typewriter keys has never been improved. This arrangement was the one used by the typewriter's original designer. Some typewriter designers believe that the keys could be arranged more efficiently. They have tried to make such changes in typewriters, but they have not been successful. It seems that the public is used to the keyboard the way it is and wants no change.

The arrangement of the keys is practically the same on all makes of typewriters. This common arrangement of the letters of the alphabet is known as the "universal" keyboard.

Some experts claim that this arrangement is actually a very good one. They say that the letters which occur together most often are placed so that the operator's fingers reach them successively in the most natural way.

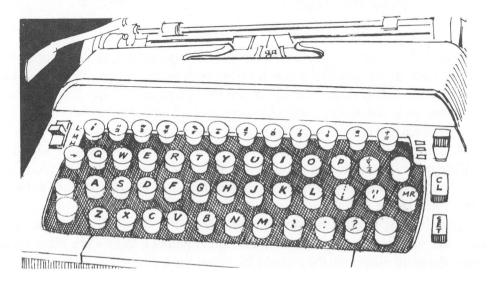

WHEN WERE GEMS DISCOVERED?

Nobody knows when man first discovered gems, but he has been fascinated by them since the earliest times. For many thousands of years gems were worn as charms, or amulets, to protect people from demons and diseases. Even today there are people who believe gems have this power.

One of the first written records about gems is found in the Bible. The 28th chapter of Exodus tells of the breastplate worn by the high priest, Aaron. The breastplate was adorned by 12 precious stones.

The ancient Egyptians used gems as ornaments and charms. They were highly skilled in the art of gem engraving, and their writings on precious stones still exist. The Egyptians wore curious amulets, known as scarabs. These were precious stones engraved with the figure of the sacred beetle of Egypt. Those who wore scarabs were believed to have charmed lives.

In ancient times, the various gems were distinguished only by their colors. The name "ruby" was given to all precious stones of a red hue. All green stones were called emeralds. All blue ones were called sapphires.

Later on it was seen that some of the gems were harder than others and endured longer. So it came about that the value of a gem depended not only on its color, brilliance, and rarity, but also on its hardness. For example, diamonds are today considered the most precious of gems because, besides their beauty, they are the hardest of all stones.

All the gems are called precious stones, but in its strict meaning the term "precious" is given only to the four most valuable stones—the diamond, the ruby, the emerald, and the sapphire.

HOW WERE THE TIME ZONES DECIDED?

Before time zones were set up, there was a great deal of confusion, especially when people had to use railroad timetables. To end this confusion the United States in 1883 began using a system of standard time zones.

In 1884 an international conference was held in Washington, D.C., to set up a system to fit the whole world. The earth was divided into 24 zones, each covering 15 degrees of longitude. This is a natural division, for the earth rotates at the rate of 15 degrees each hour.

Within each zone the time is the same, and the difference between one zone and the next is exactly one hour. Greenwich (London), England, was

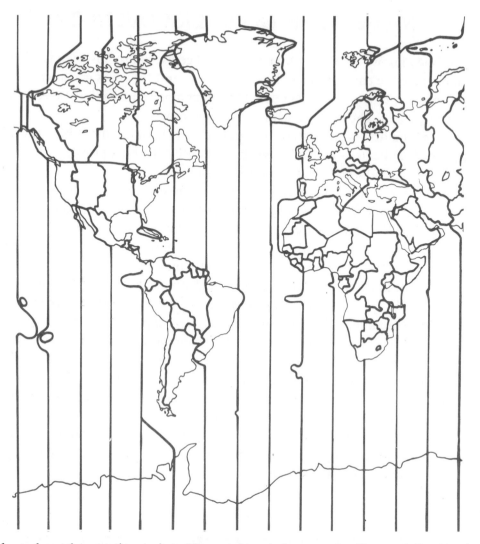

selected as the starting point. Thus, when it is noon in Greenwich, the time in the next zone eastward is 1 P.M. The time in the next zone westward is 11 A.M. In New York, five zones west of Greenwich, the time is 7 A.M.

The United States is divided into four zones based on the 75th, 90th, 105th, and 120th meridians. The times in these zones are called Eastern, Central, Mountain, and Pacific Standard Time.

On the opposite side of the world from Greenwich is another dividing line, the International Date Line. This line is approximately the 180th meridian. When it is noon at Greenwich it is midnight at the International Date Line. Crossing the line, a person gains or loses a day, depending on whether he is moving east or west.

42

WHERE WAS RICE FIRST GROWN?

Rice is one of the most important and fascinating foods in the world. Did you know that the Chinese used to greet each other not by saying "How do you do?" but by saying "Have you eaten your rice today?" This was because rice was so important to them.

Nearly half the population of the world lives partly or almost entirely on a rice diet. In some countries of Asia, each person eats from two hundred to four hundred pounds of rice a year.

It is not known for certain where rice was first grown by man, but rice probably originated in southern India. We do know that it has been grown there for many thousands of years.

Rice spread from there eastward to China more than five thousand years ago. It spread westward into Persia and Egypt soon afterward. Rice was not introduced to North America until the 17th century. Although North Americans eat some rice, most of them prefer wheat. At the present time in the United States only about five pounds of rice per person is eaten every year.

Rice with the hulls removed is called brown rice. Brown rice is covered with a brownish outer skin called the bran, in which most of the vitamins and minerals of the rice grain are stored.

Brown rice does not keep as long as white rice, however. Also, most people prefer white, well-milled, polished rice to brown rice. In some countries polished rice is enriched by adding vitamins and minerals.

Rice is used in many ways besides food. Rice flour is used for making glue, starch and in face powders. Wine is made from rice in Japan, China, and India.

WHEN WERE COWS FIRST USED FOR MILK?

Early records often mention man's use of milk and milk products, and cows were used for milk long before any records were kept.

A temple that was discovered near Babylon has a scene on one of the walls that shows a cow being milked. This temple is thought to be five thousand years old!

Instead of milking cows from the right side, as is done today, the man is milking the cows from behind. The milker sits on a milking stool. Other men

are straining the milk into a container on the ground. A third group collects the strained milk in large stone jars. So it seems that the business of getting milk from cows was pretty well organized five thousand years ago.

Today the cow and the goat are the major animals supplying milk for human use. But in various parts of the world people use milk from other animals that are native to their homelands. For example, in Asia the camel, the horse, and the yak are sources of milk. Eskimoes and Laplanders use the caribou and the reindeer. Water buffalo are used in India and central Asia. And sheep are used in Europe and Asia to provide milk for human use.

Milk contains several hundred different chemical parts, but it is best known for its calcium, phosphorus, and protein. Since milk is easily digested, the calcium, phosphorus, and other materials can be quickly and effectively used by the body. Milk sugar (lactose) and the major milk protein, casein, are found only in milk.

WHO WAS THE FIRST MAN TO EXPLORE THE NORTH POLE?

The polar regions surround the earth's two geographic poles. The geographic poles lie roughly in the centers of these two regions. They are simply called the North Pole and the South Pole. The north polar region is called the Arctic.

The Arctic has excited man's curiosity from the time of ancient Greece and perhaps even earlier. The man who is given credit for discovering the Arctic is the famous Greek explorer Pytheas. In the 4th century B.C. he sailed from the Mediterranean northward to the edge of the Arctic region. It may be that men from northern lands, such as Norway and Britain, ventured into the northern seas even earlier, but there are no written records to prove it.

In the 16th century the great search started for northwest and northeast passages from Europe to the Orient, and many explorers went to the Arctic region and learned more about it. This search continued right up to the beginning of the 20th century, when such a passage was discovered by the Norwegian explorer, Roald Amundsen, in 1903.

Now explorers were ready to try for the North Pole itself. United States Admiral Robert E. Peary led an expedition over the polar sea ice from a base at the northern end of Ellesmere Island. On April 6, 1909, he became the first man to reach the North Pole.

The first flight over the North Pole, a round trip from Spitzbergen, was made by the American explorer Richard E. Byrd on May 9, 1926.

WHEN DID PEOPLE START COOKING MEAT?

Earliest man did not cook his food. Whatever he was able to find in nature, he gathered up and ate raw. And this was simply because he had no way of cooking his food. He didn't know how to make fire.

Even when man learned how to make fire, he used it at first only for warmth and to frighten away wild animals. Cooking may have been discovered by accident. Some of the animals he killed may have been thrown near the fire. Or meat he was eating may have fallen into the glowing embers. The surface of the meat turned brown. It smelled good and tasted good—and man discovered his food would be improved by cooking.

One of the earliest means of cooking was on the hot stones around an open fire. Pits lined with stones and glowing coals formed the first oven for primitive man. Soon it was built above the ground, with an outlet for smoke, a draft, and a stone across the front opening to hold in the heat.

Man learned how to boil foods in pits lined with a large hide or skin. This was filled with water and heated to the boiling point by red-hot stones.

Primitive kettles were made by smearing clay over reed baskets and letting it harden. These kettles were placed over the fire for cooking foods, either with or without water.

So early man, many thousands of years ago, worked out the two main methods of cooking: by baking or roasting in dry heat, and by boiling or steaming in moist heat.

WHO WAS THE FIRST MAN TO STRIKE OIL?

Crude oil that seeped out from the surface was known to most ancient peoples. It was sometimes used in lamps and torches. In the United States, the Allegheny mountain region contained many rich oil fields. In places the oil lay so close to the surface that it seeped into streams.

The crude oil was used as medicine, and soon there was quite a demand for it. But no one thought of drilling for oil at first. Credit for the idea of drilling for oil is usually given to a New York lawyer named George Bissell.

Bissell had a sample of oil analyzed, and the chemist reported that petroleum could yield many useful products. So in 1857 Bissell hired a man named Edwin L. Drake to take charge of the oil properties on Oil Creek, near Titusville, Pennsylvania.

Drake decided to bore through the soft earth in search of oil. But the hole kept collapsing. Then Drake had a very important idea—why not line the hole with an iron pipe to keep the sides from falling in? This idea of a casing is used in every oil well drilled today.

On Sunday, August 28, 1859, the hole was 69 feet deep. Drake happened to come over to check the well. Down in the hole he saw a dark fluid. He let a dipper down on a string, pulled it up, and smelled the contents. It was oil!

He was the first man who had struck oil by drilling for it. The news spread quickly and the world's first oil rush began. The oil fever spread to other parts of the United States, Canada, and Europe. A new age had begun.

HOW DID FRUITS AND VEGETABLES GET THEIR NAMES?

There is no single explanation of how fruits and vegetables got their names. Some were named after their appearance, some after their place of origin, some because they resembled something else, and so on. Here are some examples of how this happened.

Strawberry was originally called "strayberry," because its runners stray from the parent plant in all directions. The blackberry owed its name to its color. The cranberry was originally called "craneberry" because its slender stalk resembles the long legs and neck of the crane.

Currants were named after Corinth, from which they first came. Cherries got their name from a city called Cerasus. Grape is the English equivalent of the Italian *grappo*, which means a bunch. Raisin is a French word which comes from the Latin *racenus*, meaning a dried grape.

Orange goes back to the Arabic word *narandj,* and lemon to the Arabic word *lamium.* Melon is the Greek word for apple. Tomato is the West Indian name for "love apple." The pineapple owes its name to its conical shape, which resembles the pine tree.

Cabbage was originally written "cabbish." It comes from the Latin *capitas,* having a head. Lettuce comes from the Latin *lactuca,* because it contains "lac," or milky juice. Rhubarb comes from the Latin *rhabarbarum.* This meant the "root of the barbarians," because the Romans considered the people who ate it barbarians!

Radish is from the Latin *radix,* a root. Bean is Anglo-Saxon from the Greek and Latin *puanos.* And potato is our way of spelling the Spanish word *patata.*

WHERE DID SUGAR ORIGINATE?

There are many different kinds of sugar, and they are found in many living things, both vegetable and animal. But when people speak of sugar, they usually mean sucrose, the sugar that comes from sugar cane or sugar beets. Today about 55 percent of the world's output of sugar is cane sugar and about 45 percent is beet sugar.

Plants whose stalks were lusciously sweet were probably growing wild in New Guinea thousands of years ago. Early man used to have wars between tribes over these stalks. Later on, as man advanced in culture, the stalks of sugar cane were bartered for other goods and their use spread. In this way traders carried sugar throughout the islands of the South Pacific and eventually to Indonesia, Asia, and the Philippines.

Sugar cane was probably known in India in prehistoric times. We do know that as long ago as 400 B.C. cane sugar was in general use in India. The first Europeans to see the sugar cane were the invaders who went to India with Alexander the Great in 325 B.C. One of them described it as a grass that produced honey without the help of bees.

From India sugar-cane culture and sugar manufacture spread to Persia between A.D. 500 and 700. When the Muslims from Persia conquered Arabia, Syria, Palestine, Egypt, and the Mediterranean areas, they introduced the use of sugar in those countries.

Sugar cane was first introduced into the United States in 1751. Jesuit missionaries brought the sugar cane from Haiti to New Orleans, Louisiana. By 1795 the commercial production of sugar had already begun.

WHY WAS THE METRIC SYSTEM INVENTED?

As science began to develop a few hundred years ago, scientists had trouble with measurements. Standards varied from nation to nation and even within one country. So during the 1700's scientists argued for a sensible system of measurement that could be accepted all over the world.

Such a system was invented in France in 1791. The French had other reasons for doing it, too. They were in the middle of a revolution at the time. The leaders of the revolution wanted to get away from all reminders of their hated past. They were therefore willing to set up a new system of measurement.

They began with length. They decided to establish the "meter" (from a Latin word meaning "measure") as a standard. Because of this, the entire system of measurement is called the metric system. Originally they tried to make the meter exactly 1/40,000,000 of the circumference of the earth. But when calculations turned out to be wrong about the earth's circumference, the meter was taken to be the distance between two marks on a platinum-iridium bar. All units of measurement in this system—length, capacity, mass—are linked in some way to the meter.

Actually, the metric system is easy to remember and easy to use. At first, though, people didn't want to change over. In 1840 the French Government had to insist that the people use the metric system or be punished.

Other nations gradually adopted the metric system, and today almost the whole world uses it. The United States is "phasing in" the system today.

HOW DID THE UNITED NATIONS GET STARTED?

The first work in planning the United Nations was done in the United States Department of State during World War II.

At the Moscow Conference of Foreign Ministers in 1943, Secretary of State Cordell Hull was able to get the Soviet Union, the United Kingdom, and the Republic of China to agree to the establishment of an international organization for keeping international peace and security, to be open to all peace-loving nations.

The following year, at the Dumbarton Oaks Conference in Washington, representatives from the Soviet Union, the United Kingdom, the Republic of China, and the United States agreed upon the outlines of a plan. But there was still a long way to go.

At Yalta, U.S.S.R., in 1945, the United States, the United Kingdom, and the Soviet Union agreed that a conference would be held in San Francisco to make plans for the new organization. The conference would be attended by all nations allied in World War II against the major Axis Powers. A charter for the proposed organization would be drafted then.

The United Nations Conference on International Organization met at San Francisco between April 25 and June 26, 1945, with 46 and later 50 nations taking part. It was here that the Charter of the United Nations was drawn up.

The United Nations is not merely an organization for keeping the peace. It has other jobs, such as bringing about cooperation in economic and social problems, furthering respect for human rights, and helping territories to develop economically and politically.

WHEN WERE THE FIRST ELECTIONS HELD?

The word "election" comes from a Latin root meaning "to choose." And the feeling people have had that they should have the right to choose their leaders goes back thousands of years.

The ancient Hebrews and Greeks fought for that right. The early kings of Israel were chosen by the people, and so were the generals of the ancient Greek armies.

The habit of freely choosing their leaders was brought to Britain by the Anglo-Saxon conquerors some 1,500 years ago. Thus, the right to vote for local officials became a part of English thinking and was brought to America by the early colonists. Even before the American Revolution, Americans had been voting in their town meetings and colonial assemblies.

But the matter of elections has always presented one big problem: who shall have the right to vote? In the early days of the American republic only about 120,000 people in a total population of more than 4,000,000 could vote. This was because each state had the right to restrict the vote.

Voting was usually limited to free white men with certain property and religious qualifications. Today we wouldn't consider that as being fair or democratic. By 1860 practically all the states allowed all white men over 21 to vote. But Negroes and women could still feel they were not being treated as equals.

After the Civil War the Constitution was amended to give the vote to Negro men. In 1920, the Nineteenth Amendment gave the vote to women. So, even though elections have been held for thousands of years, the right to vote has only recently been won by many groups of people.

WHEN WERE TOMBSTONES FIRST USED?

The first tombstones were used by Bushmen and other primitive tribes in Africa. They believed that there were evil spirits living in the bodies of dead people. By placing heavy stones on the graves they hoped to prevent these spirits from rising.

But the marking of graves in some way goes back to very ancient times. Primitive man placed stones or other markings on graves not only to keep the evil spirits from rising, but to mark the spot so he could avoid it.

The ancient Greeks used gravestones, and they were usually ornamented with sculpture. The Hebrews marked the graves of the dead with stone pillars. And, of course, the Egyptians marked the places where dead were buried with tombs and pyramids.

Different peoples used different things for this purpose. Some built vaults, others erected tall pillars of ornamented stone. Some marked their graves with simple slabs of wood or stone; others built magnificent shrines and mausoleums.

As Christianity spread, the marking of graves became common. The cross over the grave was the most popular grave mark among Christians.

Decorating graves with flowers and wreaths is a custom that goes back to ancient times, too. The Greeks used wreaths made of gold. During the early days of Christianity a custom started of making wreaths of ribbon and paper and giving them to the church as a memento of the person who died. These wreaths would be hung around the walls of the church and stay there for years and years.

53

HOW DID ADVERTISING COME ABOUT?

Advertising is a way of informing people of something. This can range from telling them of a product for sale, or a service, or urging them to do something, or even to bring one's name before the public.

So advertising came out quite naturally and took many forms from the very beginning. For example, there is a papyrus discovered at Thebes offering a reward for a runaway slave. It is three thousand years old—and it's really an advertisement! Signboards that notified people of services available were placed outside doors in Greece and Egypt around 1500 B.C.—a form of advertising.

With the invention of printing, advertising began to take on new forms. About 1477, in London, the first printed advertisement in English announced a prayerbook sale. The first newspaper advertisement appeared on the back page of a London newspaper in 1625.

It was not until 1704 that paid advertisements were printed in the United States. By 1771 there were 31 newspapers in the colonies, and all of them carried advertising.

Today, of course, we know that advertising is done not only in newspapers, but also in magazines, on the radio, and on television. The first "commercials" appeared on radio about 1920.

Commercials on television developed mostly after World War II. The idea spread very quickly and today the advertising that is done on TV is so familiar to all of us that many people can remember the commercials even better than the shows they see!

WHO INVENTED TRAFFIC SIGNALS?

Did you know that traffic was a problem long before the age of the automobile? Julius Caesar was probably the first government official on record to order a traffic control regulation. He passed a law that no woman was to drive a chariot in Rome!

After the coming of the automobile, the first traffic controllers were foot patrolmen, directing traffic by hand. Then they were given hand-operated traffic lights. It was not until the early 1920's that automatic traffic lights were first used.

But these lights left an important problem unsolved. The amount of traffic passing through an intersection changes at different times of the day.

In 1927 two men patented "traffic-actuated" controllers. These were traffic lights designed to adjust to the amount of traffic passing through an intersection at a given time. One of these lights, invented by Harry Haugh of Yale University, was first installed in New Haven, Connecticut, in April, 1928.

This device worked by means of pressure detectors in the road pavement. A car passing over a detector signaled the "call box" on the light pole, which caused the light to turn green for the approaching vehicle. This type of traffic light, with some changes, is still widely used today.

Charles Adler, also in 1928, invented a traffic light that used a microphone to activate the call box. When a motorist, facing a red light, blew his horn, the microphone transmitted the sound to the call box, which caused the light to change. Today, there are other types of traffic controllers that use sound to change the light.

WHY WERE SCHOOLS STARTED?

From the time of the cavemen, human beings have always taught what they knew to their young. If they had not, no child would have survived. He would not have known which animals were dangerous, which plants were good to eat, or how to make a fire to keep warm.

After many centuries man learned to write down what he knew. In this way he could save up more knowledge and pass it on to his children and grand-children.

Once systems of writing had been invented, schools began. The earliest schools we know about were in Mesopotamia and Egypt three thousand to four thousand years ago.

So schools were started to pass on knowledge and to help prepare young people for living in the world. But the way society was set up in most places in ancient times, it was felt that schools and a good education were not for all young people. In Egypt, for example, there were higher levels of education for young men who were going to be priests, government officials, architects, or doctors. Only a very few young men received this much education.

Another ancient people, the Hebrews, had a long tradition of education. When they were an independent nation, the father of each family taught his sons the history of their people, their laws, and their religion. Later, when the Hebrews were conquered by outsiders, they were afraid that their own customs and beliefs might be lost. They set up formal schools where everybody, rich or poor, was taught the language, the religion, and the history of the Jews. This was probably the first time in human history that formal education was given to rich and poor alike.

WHO INVENTED COMIC BOOKS?

The comic strip is usually found in daily newspapers. It is made up of three or four picture panels telling a story with one or more characters. Comic books are extensions of comic strips into magazines. Each magazine is about one set of characters and the pictures tell a complete story.

While the first newspaper comic strip appeared in 1892, it was not until 1911 that an entire publication was devoted to comics—a comic book. That year the *Chicago American* offered reprints of Bud Fisher's "Mutt and Jeff" in pamphlet form.

The pattern for present-day comics was set much later. In 1935, *New Fun* appeared. It was a 64-page collection of original material in four colors, and was sold at newsstands. In 1938, *Action Comics* appeared, and the *Superman Quarterly Magazine* came out in 1939.

Comic books are not all humorous stories. The types of comic books issued include: adventure, animal, biography, detective, fantasy-mystery, history, humor, military, religion, romance, satire, science-fiction, teen-age, and western.

Some types, such as adventure and humor, sell better, so there are more of them. The popularity of comic books, however, has led all kinds of groups to use comic books to tell a story. Many companies use comic books to tell the story behind a product or the history of their company. Comic books are also published to explain complicated subjects, to dramatize public needs, or to give the history of a particular event. So "comic books" can be as varied as the subject matter and the purpose behind them.

WHY IS SPEED AT SEA MEASURED IN KNOTS?

When ships first ventured out to sea, they had no sure way of knowing their location. Eventually, this was done by finding the latitude and longitude of the place. Latitude is distance north or south of the equator. Longitude tells how far east or west a place is. It was decided that zero degrees longitude would be the longitude line that goes through Greenwich, England.

To get an idea of their longitude, early ships first calculated how far they had traveled in a certain period of time. They used a "log" to find this out. It was a log of wood, weighted at one end, with the other end fixed to a long piece of rope. The log, thrown over the stern of the ship, floated, and the rope was let out as the ship sailed on. The speed of the ship could be calculated by seeing how much rope had been let out in a given time.

In later years, knots were tied at equal distances along the rope. A sailor counted how many knots passed through his hands in a certain time. This gave the speed of the ship. Sailors came to use the word "knots" to mean the speed of a ship.

Today, a knot has come to mean one nautical, or sea, mile per hour. A nautical mile equals 6076.1 feet, a little more than a land mile. Suppose a ship is sailing at a speed of 15 knots. This means that it is sailing at a speed of 15 nautical miles an hour.

Logs are still used to show how fast a ship is traveling. But today the logs are special metal rods with flat blades around them. As the ship sails through the water, the metal rod rotates and twists the rope round and round. The spinning rope works a device back on the ship that shows the actual speed.

WHO FIRST WROTE NURSERY RHYMES?

Hardly a child grows up without learning by heart "Hey Diddle, Diddle," "Pat-a-cake, Pat-a-cake," or "Jack and Jill." We call them nursery rhymes, and sometimes Mother Goose rhymes.

The name Mother Goose first appeared in a collection of fairy tales by a Frenchman, Charles Perrault, which was published in 1697. But it is possible that the name had been known long before that as a way of describing women who were village storytellers.

A Boston printer, Thomas Fleet, is reported to have published in 1719 a book called "Songs for the Nursery; or Mother Goose's Melodies for Children." But no copy of this book has ever been found.

Most nursery rhymes were never intended for the nursery. During the 16th century in England adults sang ballads, madrigals, and rounds, Mothers sang the songs to their infants, and so the songs were brought into the nursery.

There were also rhymes that referred to political events and were recited and sung everywhere. Children hearing them would take a catch refrain or phrase and make the musical rhymes their own.

WHEN DID PEOPLE BEGIN
TO PIERCE THEIR EARS?

Piercing the ears to wear earrings goes back to prehistoric times. The ancient East Indians, Medes, Persians, Egyptians, Arabians, and Hebrews wore earrings.

Earrings became expensive and artistic ornaments in ancient times. The Etruscans, for example, made gold earrings that took the form of flowers, fruits, vases, shields, rosettes, crescents, peacocks, swans, and so on. The Greeks made beautiful gold earrings, and even put them on statues of the goddesses. In those days, Greek men wore earrings until they reached the age of adolescence.

The ancient Romans copied the Greeks in wearing earrings, and some of the Roman women had very expensive ones made with pearls and jewels. Roman men began to pierce their ears to wear earrings, and this became so popular that in the 3rd century A.D. the Roman emperor issued an edict forbidding men from doing so.

After the Middle Ages, men began to wear earrings in the left ear only. Then the hair styles for men and women changed; and when hair was worn long and over the ears, earrings went out of style. But they came into vogue again in the 15th and 16th centuries.

Earrings for women have been popular ever since that time. Earrings for men have not been popular in recent times, but there are certain groups that still wear them. These include gypsies, sailors, and some men in Italy and Spain. At one time, doctors said that it was good for ears to be pierced, but they no longer believe that it helps the ear.

WHEN WAS COFFEE FIRST BREWED?

An interesting thing about the use of coffee is that it was first enjoyed without being brewed. East African tribes have used the fruit of the coffee tree for centuries as an article of food. They would roast the berries in an open pan or prepare them with animal fat, and then eat them. What they enjoyed was the stimulating effect the coffee berries had.

The first coffee plants probably grew in Kaffa, a province of Ethiopia. This province may have given coffee its name. In the 14th century Arabian merchants came to Kaffa and became acquainted with the coffee seeds. They then began cultivating coffee in Yemen.

There the people began to brew coffee. The followers of Mohammed were forbidden to drink wine, and coffee was a stimulating beverage that could take the place of wine for them.

About the middle of the 15th century, the use of coffee as a beverage spread from Yemen to Mecca, and from there to Baghdad, Cairo, Damascus, and other places. There were coffeehouses in Cairo as early as 1511.

Coffee was first introduced to Western Europe around 1615. It created quite a lot of excitement, and many people were against the idea of drinking coffee. They thought it was poisonous. But coffeehouses soon became a part of the social life of England.

In fact, so many people used to gather in coffeehouses that King Charles II was afraid plots against the government were being hatched there. He ordered them closed. But by this time coffee was so popular that he was forced to open them again.

WHY WAS THERE A MASON AND DIXON LINE?

Mason and Dixon's Line is a boundary line that before the Civil War separated slave states from free states and the North from the South.

This line actually goes back to colonial times. The Penn family, who were the proprietors of Pennsylvania, and the Calverts, who were the proprietors of Maryland, quarreled over the boundary line between their properties. This quarrel started in 1681.

Finally, in 1763, the families agreed to settle the argument by having their land surveyed (which means measuring it with scientific instruments). Two English astronomers, Charles Mason and Jeremiah Dixon, were hired to do the surveying.

The work was completed in 1767, and the boundary line was named Mason and Dixon's Line. Stone markers were set up to denote the line, but they were taken by souvenir hunters. They were replaced by permanent markers.

Because Mason and Dixon's Line had become famous, it was suggested the boundary be surveyed again to prove its correctness. This was done in 1849 and again between 1900 and 1907. Mason and Dixon had been so accurate that their boundary line was not changed. The line separates Pennsylvania from Maryland and a section of West Virginia.

Mason and Dixon's Line, now considered a boundary separating northern states from southern states, remains at 39° 43' 26.3" north latitude.

WHO INVENTED THE AQUALUNG?

Men have always been curious about what goes on in the water world, and history tells of many attempts to penetrate it. But the problem was how to take a supply of air beneath the surface. It was a very complicated matter.

The difficulty of movement in a liquid world and the problems of constantly increasing and decreasing pressure also had to be solved. Diving with an air supply was only being done by a few highly trained people using complicated, cumbersome deep-sea suits and helmets with high-pressure air lines to the surface.

In 1943 Captain Jacques-Yves Cousteau and Emile Gagnan invented the aqualung. This was the key that unlocked the secrets of the underwater world.

With this equipment divers are no longer tied to an air line leading to the

surface or weighed down with heavy equipment. Their air supply is carried with them in high-pressure cylinders strapped to their backs.

Breathing is as automatic and natural as breathing on the surface. A demand regulator attached to the air cylinder automatically adjusts breathing air to exactly the same pressure as that of the surrounding water. There are no valves to adjust. All the diver needs to do is breathe. The aqualung gives him air at exactly the right pressure, no matter what the depth.

After the invention of the aqualung, skin diving spread tremendously all over the world, and a great deal of other types of equipment were made to go with it.

WHO WERE THE FIRST PEOPLE
TO MAKE MUMMIES?

The ancient Egyptians believed in life after death. They thought of the soul as a bird with a human face that could fly around by day but must return to the tomb at night for fear of evil spirits. The body was therefore preserved so that the soul could recognize it and know which tomb to enter. This is where the word "mummy" comes from. It is Arabic and means a body preserved by wax or tar.

Most mummies were not made using wax or tar. The body was treated with salts. Salts, put inside the body, together with the dryness of the desert air, took out the moisture. When the body had been dried out, it was bathed, rubbed with resin from pine trees, and wrapped in hundreds of yards of linen.

Before about 3000 B.C. the Egyptians buried their dead in a curled-up position in the hot sand of the desert. The sand preserved the bodies. Later, important persons were buried in tombs cut from rock and in magnificent pyramids. But the pyramids and rock tombs were not so dry as the desert sand. This made it necessary to develop the art of mummification.

About 1500 B.C., mummies were given a plaster covering, shaped like a body and elaborately painted. Soon the coffins took the same shape and were decorated. Beards were added to some of the mummy cases. The beard in ancient Egypt was the sign of a god or king. Adding a beard showed that the dead man expected to live in very high company in the afterworld.

The Egyptians also believed that certain animals were sacred. These animals were also mummified and buried in animal cemeteries.

WHY DO WE HAVE CHRISTMAS TREES?

The Christmas tree is the symbol of the spirit of the Yuletide in many homes. The use of the Christmas tree is a custom and tradition, not a religious observance.

The custom came from Germany and dates to a time when primitive people revered trees—particularly evergreens. These trees did not die or fade in winter and seemed to be a sign of immortality. The Christians changed the custom into one honoring Christ.

The northern peoples of Denmark, Sweden, and Norway, where the forests are plentiful, adopted the custom of bringing small trees into their homes at Christmastime.

Trees were not used in English homes until a German prince, Albert of Saxe-Coburg-Gotha, married Queen Victoria. Prince Albert had the first decorated Christmas tree set up at Windsor Castle in 1841.

The first Christmas trees in the New World were introduced by Hessian soldiers in 1776, during the American Revolution. Later on, German immigrants brought the tradition into wider use in the United States.

Many other Christmas decorations used today were once pagan symbols. The Romans used flowers and leafy boughs in their rites. Records show that the Saxons used holly, ivy, and bay in their religious observances. The Druids gave the world the tradition of hanging mistletoe in the house. (Ancient Celtic priests believed the plant to be a sign of hope and peace.)

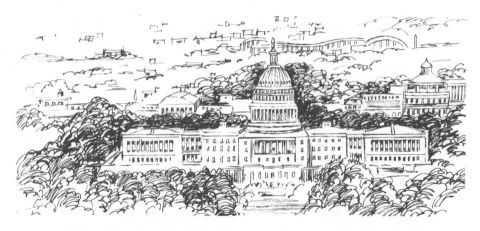

WHY WAS WASHINGTON MADE THE CAPITAL OF THE UNITED STATES?

After the American Revolution the United States needed a capital city. The selection of the site resulted from a compromise. Various cities and sections of the country wanted the honor of being the nation's capital.

It was finally decided to create a new city. Congress passed a bill in 1790 giving permission for a site to be chosen. It was to be somewhere near the Potomac River and not over ten miles square. The ten-mile square section of the land was to be called the District of Columbia, after Christopher Columbus; and the city to be built on it was to be named Washington, in honor of the country's first president.

In 1791 George Washington chose the place where the city now stands. He thought it was a good location because the Potomac River was deep enough for ships to come as far as the city.

The land was given to the federal government by the states of Maryland and Virginia. About 64 square miles were given by Maryland and about 36 square miles by Virginia. Later, in 1846, the land given by Virginia was returned to the state at her request.

President Washington chose a brilliant French engineer and architect, Major Pierre L'Enfant, to design the new city. The plan called for broad avenues lined with trees, beautiful government buildings, and monuments to honor great men.

By 1800 the president's house was nearly completed. The Capitol was built on a hill, renamed Capitol Hill, for the building in which Congress was to meet. In 1800 President John Adams and other members of the government moved to the new federal city, Washington, D.C.

WHO INVENTED ARITHMETIC?

Arithmetic is the science of numbers. It is concerned with the meanings of numbers, with their symbols, and with ways of working with them.

Nobody "invented" arithmetic. It developed to meet man's needs. At first it had to do with quantity, not with counting. Before people could count, they had a "number sense." For example, early man could tell when he had picked enough berries. A hunter could tell by looking that he had lost a spear.

But as time passed, men needed numbers and number names. Herders needed to keep track of their animals. Farmers needed to keep track of the seasons. So at some unknown time, long ago, the first numbers and number names were invented. These are counting numbers, which we also call whole numbers, or natural numbers.

Later, men needed to have numbers that were less than 1, and numbers between other numbers. So fractions were developed. Much later, still other kinds of numbers came into use. One kind was negative numbers, like -2 or -7.

The idea of negative numbers was very hard to discover. In ancient Greece it was known that if you took 5 from 7 you had 2 left. But was it possible to take 7 from 5? The Greeks decided it was not.

Not until the 1500's did people begin to see that there could be a number that was less than nothing. For example, take 7 from 5 and you have 2 less than 0, or -2.

With counting as the basic process, man learned to add, subtract, multiply, and divide—the four basic operations in arithmetic.

HOW DID THE NAME "UNCLE SAM" ORIGINATE?

"Uncle Sam," of course, stands for the United States. What is hard to believe is that this nickname arose quite by accident, and there actually was a man called "Uncle Sam"—and that most people never heard of him!

There was a man called "Uncle Sam" Wilson. He was born in Arlington, Mass., Sept. 13, 1766. His father and older brothers fought in the American Revolution. Sam himself enlisted at the age of 14 and served until the end of the war. He moved to Troy, N. Y., and began a meat-packing business.

On Oct. 2, 1812, a group of visitors came to his plant. One of them, Governor Daniel D. Tompkins of New York, asked what the initials "EA-US" on the barrels of meat stood for. A workman replied the "EA" stood for the contractor for whom Wilson worked, Elbert Anderson. And he added jokingly that the "US" (actually an abbreviation for United States) stood for "Uncle Sam" Wilson.

A story of this incident appeared in the May 12, 1830 issue of the New York *Gazette and General Advertiser.* Since Wilson was a popular man, and was an example of a hard-working and patriotic American, the idea of "Uncle Sam" as a name for this kind of man caught on quickly.

By the end of the War of 1812, "Uncle Sam" had come to symbolize the character of the nation and the government. In 1961 Congress adopted a resolution saluting "Uncle Sam" Wilson of Troy, N. Y., as the "progenitor of America's national symbol."

Today "Uncle Sam" stands for all of the United States and no one connects it with the man who originated the name.

WHEN WAS THE CROSSWORD PUZZLE INVENTED?

The crossword puzzle was both a new thing and a not-so-new thing. Since ancient times there had been what is called a word square. In a word square the letters spelled the same words horizontally and vertically.

The crossword is built on a pattern of black and white squares, with different words interlocking across and down. There are numbered definitions given as clues to the words. So the crossword puzzle added some new things.

The first crossword puzzle was put together by a man called Arthur Winn. It first appeared in a Sunday supplement of the New York *World* on December 21, 1913. It remained as a feature of this newspaper for some time, and various improvements were made in its form.

In 1924 the first book of crossword puzzles appeared. Up until that time, the crossword puzzle had not been very popular. But after this, the crossword puzzle became a nationwide and then a worldwide craze.

Other newspapers began to print crossword puzzles. In 1924, the *World* started printing one every day. Then the New York *Herald-Tribune* did the same. Pretty soon most papers began to publish crossword puzzles regularly.

The British took up crossword puzzles in 1925. At first they imported American books, but they soon developed a type of crossword puzzle that was a little different.

HOW OLD IS THE GAME OF CHECKERS?

Two of the oldest games played by man are chess and checkers. They are related in some ways, but since checkers is simpler in form it is assumed that it came first.

Checkers was played in the early history of Egypt, which means it's at least five thousand years old. Plato and Homer mentioned the game of checkers in their works, so it was known in ancient Greece. The Romans are believed to have taken the game from the Greeks.

The earliest records of the game seem to indicate that the kind of board used was similar to what we use today, and that it was played with twelve men on each side.

The first book on checkers was published in Spain in 1547. In 1620 another book of checkers was published in Spain that contained sample games and traps that would still be useful to know today. It is believed that the Spaniards may have learned about checkers from the Moors, who brought it from Arabia.

In England (where it is called "draughts"), the first book on checkers appeared in 1756. In 1800 another book by a man called Joshua Sturges became a guidebook for playing checkers that everyone followed for more than 50 years.

Today, checkers is played by millions of people all over the world. It is also recognized by educators as a good way to help people develop foresight, judgment, and concentration.

Many shut-ins and people who are recovering from illness are urged to play checkers by their doctors, who feel it has therapeutic value.

WHEN WAS COPPER FIRST USED?

Copper was used by man earlier than other metals, with the exception of gold. Long before the dawn of history, men of the Stone Age were already using it.

One of the reasons for this early use of copper was that it is found in a fairly pure state. It can be found in lumps and grains of free metal. So ancient man probably picked up lumps of copper because they were attractive. Later on, man discovered that these red stones of metal could be beaten into any shape. So they began to make knives and weapons out of copper, which was easier than making them by chipping flints.

And then, much later, man discovered that by melting the red stones he could shape the soft mass into cups and bowls. Copper became so useful that man began to mine for it and make all sorts of utensils out of it.

Copper was the only workable metal known to man for thousands of years. The problem with gold, for example, was that it was too scarce, and also too soft to be practical.

It is believed that when the Egyptians built their pyramids they used copper tools. And a piece of copper pipe used by the Egyptians more than five thousand years ago has been found. It is still in good condition!

The use of copper for many purposes dropped when iron was discovered. Today, bronze (copper and tin) and brass (copper and zinc) are two ways in which a great deal of copper is used. In fact, aside from iron and aluminum, copper is the metal most used in the world today.

WHEN WERE MUSEUMS STARTED?

Museums are places where collections of objects are preserved and displayed. The objects may be anything found in nature or made by man. There are museums devoted to art, science, history, industry, and technology.

The word "museum" comes from the Greek word *mousion,* meaning "temple of the Muses." The Muses were goddesses of the arts. One of the first institutions to be called a mouseion was founded in Alexandria, Egypt, in the 3rd century B.C.

The aim of the Museum of Alexandria, as it was known, was to collect information from everywhere that could be of interest to scholars. Scholars lived and did their research there. The museum displayed a collection of objects of art and curiosities that included statues, instruments used in astronomy and surgery, elephant tusks, and hides of unusual animals.

There were many collections that might be called museums between that time and the 19th century, but they belonged to princes and noble families and were not established for the benefit of the people. Even the British Museum, which was founded in the middle of the 18th century, admitted few people.

It took the French Revolution to open the doors of French museums to everyone. In 1793, during the Revolution, the Republican Government made the Louvre in Paris a national museum.

In the 19th century, for the first time, buildings were specially designed as museums. One of the first buildings in Europe planned as a museum was the Altes Museum in Berlin, Germany. It was constructed in 1830.

WHO INVENTED THE VIOLIN?

The violin is known as the queen of instruments. Of the more than one hundred musicians in a great orchestra, over thirty are violinists. The violin's high rank is due to the beauty of its tone and its wide range of expression.

The violin took many centuries to develop. Its history begins in India, where the use of a bow to play stringed instruments was probably invented. During the early Middle Ages in Europe various stringed instruments were played with a bow.

One of these was the vielle, which was probably introduced to Europe through the Balkan Peninsula in the 10th century. Like the violin, the vielle was held against the player's shoulder.

Later the vielle was changed through the influence of the rebec. This was an Arabic instrument that spread from Spain to the rest of Europe. By combining the sturdy body of the vielle with the clever arrangement of the pegs in the rebec, a new group of instruments was born.

The violin received its basic form between 1550 and 1600. Since that time it has changed only in small ways. The most successful violins were made in the 17th and 18th centuries.

Italy produced outstanding families of violin-makers. Probably the greatest of these was Antonio Stradivari (1644-1737). Stradivari is called the master of all masters. He developed a larger, flatter type of violin than had been made before, which gave it more tone power.

Stradivari is said to have built 1,116 instruments. Of these, 540 "Strad" violins are known to us. Most of them have nicknames, such as the Viotti or the Vieuxtemps, after the famous violinists who played them.

HOW DID THE GRAPEFRUIT GET ITS NAME?

A grapefruit is about twice the size of an orange, and certainly much larger than a grape. Yet it is named after the grape.

If you were ever to walk through a grapefruit orchard, you would probably see the reason why. This heavy fruit hangs down in clusters just as grapes do, and the clusters may be of from three to 18 fruit. So it got its name because of this resemblance.

The Spaniards, who brought the orange and the lemon, also brought the grapefruit to Florida and the West Indies. But the tree was grown only for its beauty in gardens. It has sweet-scented blossoms and dark glossy leaves.

Very few people ate the fruit in olden times. They didn't like the slightly bitter taste. So whoever owned grapefruit trees would let the ripe fruit fall to the ground and rot there.

It was actually visitors from the north who first created the demand for grapefruit. In the late 19th century they began coming down to Florida by railroad to spend the winter. They got to like the grapefruit and wanted to have it when they returned home.

The first shipments were sent to New York and Philadelphia between 1880 and 1885. For the first time, a market for grapefruit was developed. Then grapefruit orchards were set out in California, but on a smaller scale than in Florida. Today the fruit is cultivated in parts of Texas, Arizona, Cuba, and Jamaica.

The grapefruit tree is small, reaching a height of only about 25 feet. There are several varieties, but the best known are the Duncan, the Marsh seedless, and the Walters.

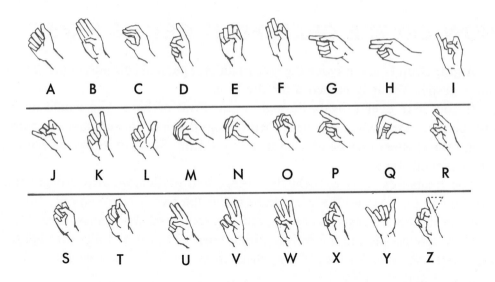

A B C D E F G H I
J K L M N O P Q R
S T U V W X Y Z

WHO INVENTED SIGN LANGUAGE
FOR THE DEAF?

Before the 16th century, people who were deaf-mute (unable to hear or speak) were treated horribly. They were regarded as idiots, incapable of intelligence, and were locked up in asylums or even killed.

Then an Italian doctor called Geronimo Cardano got the idea of teaching deaf-mutes through written characters. These would be combinations of symbols that would be associated with objects.

In the 18th century, a Frenchman, Charles de l'Epee, created a language of signs. This was a system of using conventional gestures of the hands and arms in such a way that they represented the thought that was to be conveyed. Meanwhile, in the 17th century, a finger alphabet was worked out which was similar to the one in use today.

Until about 85 years ago, this was the way deaf people were taught to communicate—signs, facial expressions, and the finger alphabet. In fact, some deaf-mutes could spell as many as 130 words a minute.

But many teachers of the deaf have begun to disapprove of the sign language and finger alphabets. They say it isolates deaf people by keeping them from communicating with persons who have normal hearing.

Nowadays the deaf and hard of hearing learn to interpret what is said by watching the lips of the speaker. They also learn to speak themselves by observing and feeling the lips and vocal organs of the teacher and then imitating the motions.

WHO INVENTED MUSICAL NOTES?

For a very long time music was not written down. It was sung or played from memory. As it was passed on from person to person, many changes crept into the tunes. A way of writing music down was needed so that it would be sung or played exactly as it had been composed. The method that man developed for writing music is called notation.

The system of musical notation generally used today in the Western world is the result of centuries of development—from about the end of the 9th century to the early 1700's. This development began in the cathedrals and monasteries of the Roman Catholic Church.

Since many of the Church's services were sung, they were sung from memory. Toward the end of the 9th century dots and dashes and little squiggles were written over the words in the service books. These signs, called neumes, showed the direction in which the melody should go. But they were still very vague.

About A.D. 900 the music was made a little easier to read. The neumes were written at certain distances above or below the horizontal red line (representing the note F) to show how high or low the note should be sung.

Then the staff was invented by a monk called Guido d'Arezzo. This was made of four lines. A method of notation that made it possible to show the length of each note was developed in the 13th and 14th centuries. Notes took new shapes and stems were added to some notes according to their length. By the 1600's the notes had become round and musical notation began to look the way it does today.

ANCIENT GREECE

JUMPING

BOXING

RUNNING

HOW DID ATHLETICS BEGIN?

If we go back far enough, athletics probably began with religion. Primitive men worshipped their gods by performing certain dances. These dances imitated the actions of fighting and hunting. Later on, these dances were performed simply for the pleasure they gave—and they were actually a form of athletics.

The Egyptians had some form of athletic sports about four thousand years ago. But athletics as we know it really began with the Greeks. The first recorded Olympic games of the Greeks took place in the year 776 B.C.

Today, we imagine that sports activities play an important part in our lives. But it cannot compare to how important athletics were to the ancient Greeks. Every boy was trained in running, jumping, and wrestling, while he was still at school. A man was supposed to be good at athletics until he was well past middle age.

The ideal of the Greeks was to have a sound mind in a healthy body. So they didn't admire men who were just athletes, nor men who were just brilliant but couldn't participate in sports. But they also had professional athletics, especially in boxing and wrestling.

The Greeks had many athletic festivals, but the oldest and most important were the Olympic games. Only young men of pure Greek descent who had undergone ten months' training could compete. At first the games were just contests in running and jumping. But later on they added wrestling, boxing, discus and javelin throwing, and chariot races.

WHO WAS THE FIRST DOCTOR?

Even before man became civilized, he "practiced medicine" in a way. That is, he did things to lessen discomfort or pain. And the earliest civilizations that we know about had physicians.

The Babylonians left such lucid medical writings describing various diseases that doctors today can recognize them. Among the ancient Egyptians it was believed that illness was caused by evil spirits. But their medical treatments also included pills and ointments containing drugs such as opium and castor oil. And surgical operations were done on the outer surfaces of the body.

So there were "doctors" in very ancient times. But about 460 B.C. a man called Hippocrates was born in Greece, and he brought a great change in medicine. In fact, he is called the Father of Medicine.

What Hippocrates did was rescue medicine from magic and superstition. While he didn't have the scientific knowledge on which medicine is based today, he had the kind of approach and attitude that might be called "scientific."

He taught that the physician should observe the patient closely and accurately. He should use gentle treatment and try to encourage the natural healing process. The physician should never risk harming the patient.

Hippocrates recognized and described many diseases. Some of the medical facts he observed are as true today as they were over two thousand years ago.

WHEN DID MEN BEGIN TO MINE FOR MINERALS?

A mineral is a chemical element or compound that occurs naturally in the earth. An ore is a deposit in the earth that is rich enough in some mineral to make mining it worthwhile.

No one knows exactly when mining began. One of the earliest mining ventures recorded in history was the Egyptian expedition into the Sinai peninsula sometime around 2600 B.C. The Egyptians went there to mine turquoise. They also found and mined a more useful mineral—copper.

The ancient Greeks mined silver in mines south of Athens as early as 1400 B.C. The Greeks worked the mines from about 600 to 350 B.C. Several of the shafts went to a depth of 400 feet. Other metals, such as lead, zinc, and iron, were later mined from these old diggings.

To supply their huge empire the Romans mined on a large scale. They had mines everywhere from Africa to Britain. Among the most valuable Roman mines were the Rio Tinto mines in Spain, which yielded large quantities of gold, silver, copper, tin, lead, and iron.

Mining became a really large-scale operation in the 18th century, when the Industrial Revolution was underway. Large amounts of coal were needed for smelting iron and stoking factory furnaces, and coal mining expanded rapidly. The development of modern mining techniques started at this time.

In the United States, "gold fever" reached its height in the 19th century. The California gold rush started in 1848. More than $500,000,000 in gold was mined in California within ten years. In 1896 a gold rush occurred in Alaska, and in 1886 the richest gold field ever discovered was found in South Africa. The world's largest diamond deposits were also found there in 1870.

WHY DO SOLDIERS SALUTE?

What is a salute? It is a gesture of respect to a person of superior rank. It is formalized, that is, it is done in a certain way every time.

Salutes of all kinds have existed in all periods of history and in all cultures. The form of salute has varied. In some cases it meant bowing, in others it meant kneeling, or lying on the ground, or various gestures of the hand and arm. The individual military salute that a soldier gives—raising the right hand to the forehead or to the hatbrim or visor—was developed quite recently in history.

Until the end of the 18th century the way junior officers saluted superiors and soldiers saluted officers was to doff the hat. In fact, civilians still do this as a gesture of respect. And this custom probably goes back to the days when a knight would raise his helmet's visor or uncover his head before a lord.

The change from taking off the hat to just raising the hand in a salute, took place for a very practical reason. When soldiers fired their muskets, black powder would settle on their hands and make them very grimy. If they then had to use their grimy hands to take off their hats in a salute, it would ruin the hats. So at the end of the 18th century the change was made to the hand salute.

An officer or soldier carrying a sword or saber at the shoulder, whether mounted or on foot, salutes by bringing the hilt to his mouth, then extending the point to the right and downward. This form of salute dates back to the Middle Ages when knights, in a religious gesture, kissed the hilts of their swords as symbolic of the cross of Christ. It was then a form of oath-taking.

HOW DID MAN LEARN TO WRITE?

Nobody knows exactly where and when writing originated. But we do have an idea of how it developed from earliest times.

Man began by making pictures to serve as records of his hunting, wars, and tribal life. Pictures could also be used for messages. A picture of the sun meant a day. Two marks next to the sun meant two days. Such signs are called pictographs.

When civilization developed, this method of writing was speeded up by simplifying the pictures. The Egyptians used a wavy line to mean a body of water. The Chinese used an ear between two doors to mean "listen." Such signs are called ideographs or ideograms.

The ancient Egyptians used a system of signs that we call hieroglyphics. At first it was entirely ideographic. But over the centuries the Egyptians developed a phonetic system as well. This is writing where the signs represent sounds rather than objects or ideas.

As civilization further developed, men needed more and more signs. So they developed a method of spelling words according to sound. For example, in English we would write the "belief" by drawing a bee and a leaf. Such signs are called phonograms, and the writing is syllabic because it uses syllables.

The next stage in the development of writing was the idea of using an alphabet of single letters. Both the ancient Egyptians and the Babylonians knew how to write in the alphabetic way. From their method came the Greek and Latin alphabets which are used today by most people outside of Asia.

WHO INVENTED INDOOR PLUMBING?

By indoor plumbing we generally mean a system that consists of two parts. There is a system of pipes and valves that brings the water from a large pipe (water main) under the street into the house and to the various rooms. There is also a drainage system of pipes through which waste liquids are taken from the house and fed into a sewer pipe in the street.

The first "plumbing" system that we know about goes back about 4,000 years. Archeologists doing excavations on Crete, an island in the Mediterranean Sea, uncovered a 4,000-year-old palace that had a water and drainage system.

The water system was formed by conduits—stone channels through which water flows. The cisterns of the conduits collected water that fell as rain or flowed down from the hills. The water was carried by the conduits into vertical shafts and from the shafts to bathrooms and toilets.

Waste water was carried away by pipes made of terra-cotta, a form of baked clay. Amazingly enough, these terra-cotta pipes were designed so that they could be installed easily. One end of each pipe was made so it would fit into the next, and the pipes were fastened together with cementing clay.

The first people to use pipes made of lead were the Romans. They called the craftsman who installed pipes a "plumbarius," meaning "worker in lead." This is the origin of the English words "plumber" and "plumbing."

While lead is still used in some kinds of pipes today, other materials used are steel, copper, brass, cast iron, concrete, and plastic.

WHO FIRST USED DRUGS?

Most of us know there are such things as "drugs," and know very little else about this whole field. A drug used as medicine to treat illness, protect against disease, or improve health is called a pharmaceutical. Pharmacology is the science of drugs and their uses as medicines.

The making of drugs is such an ancient art that we don't know when it was first started. The early drugs were made by priest-magicians because people believed it took magic to turn plants into medicine. Later, treatment of disease became a special science. The brews of herbs and minerals were fairly simple to prepare. Physicians of ancient Greece and Rome used to make drugs as well as treat patients.

The art of pharmacy came from the Arabs. By the 10th century they had compiled all the known medical knowledge. They translated the Greeks' studies of human anatomy and diseases. They borrowed the Persians' discoveries of the healing powers of plants. And the Arabs found even more drugs from plants.

In the 13th century the Arabs' skill in preparing drugs spread to Europe. But their approach to drugs was very complicated. Many of the Arabian drugs had more than 40 different ingredients. By the year 1500, some drug formulas required over 100 ingredients. Pharmacists began to study plants again to discover simpler remedies.

Pharmacy didn't really change until the 18th century. Scientists then became as interested in the composition of drugs as they were in their effects on man. They began to experiment with animals. And in the 19th century, drugs began to be manufactured by companies instead of individual pharmacists.

WHO NAMED THE CITY OF LOS ANGELES?

Los Angeles is the third most populous city in the United States and the largest in area—454.90 square miles. In its early days probably no one could have believed it would become the great city it is today.

The first white visitors to the city's site were Capt. Gaspar de Portola and a party of Spanish explorers and missionaries. On August 2, 1769 they camped along the banks of a river which he named El Rio de Nuestra Senora la Reina de Los Angeles de Porciuncula ("The River of Our Lady the Queen of the Angels of Porciuncula").

Two years later Franciscans founded San Gabriel Mission, nine miles to the northeast. Not until September 4, 1781, was Los Angeles formally founded by the Spanish governor of California, Felipe de Neve.

With the aid of priests from San Gabriel Mission, Governor de Neve established a settlement of 11 men, 11 women, and 22 children and named it El Pueblo de Nuestra Senora la Reina de Los Angeles ("The town of Our Lady the Queen of the Angels").

The town did not amount to much until California became a part of the United States in 1848 after the Mexican War. Its population then was about 1,500. Soon farms were all around the town, and oranges, grapefruit, lemons, walnuts, avocados, and grapes were being grown. The Southern Pacific Railroad reached Los Angeles in 1876, and nine years later the Sante Fe came in.

Oil was discovered shortly after 1890, and then the city really began to grow.

HOW DID UNITS OF MEASUREMENT DEVELOP?

Long before there were established units of measurement, man measured one thing in terms of another familiar thing. And one of the most familiar things was man's own body.

For example, if he wanted to measure the distance from his house to a neighbor's house, he would pace off the distance and count the number of times his right foot swung forward. The distance was so many "paces" long. To measure a room, he would put one foot before the other. The distance was so many "feet" long.

Arms, hands, and fingers were useful for measuring such things as cloth. The distance from the tip of the nose to the fingertips of one outstretched arm, the distance from fingertips to elbow, the distance from the end of the thumb to the end of the little finger when he spread his fingers, the width of his hand, the width of his thumb—all these distances were used as units of measurement.

But the problem with this was that the distances varied from person to person. One man's arm, or foot, and so on, was longer than another's. So it became necessary to establish standard units of measurement. During the Middle Ages associations of tradesmen kept watch on the measures used. Later on, governments set up standards for all sorts of measures.

Today there is international agreement about standard measures. The governments of various countries have agreed to use the same basic units. Many of them have special departments in charge of standards. In the United States the National Bureau of Standards was established in 1901 to take care of standard measures.

In 1791 the metric system of measurement was invented in France and it is used by most countries. The United States, Canada, Australia, and New Zealand are in the process of adopting this system now.

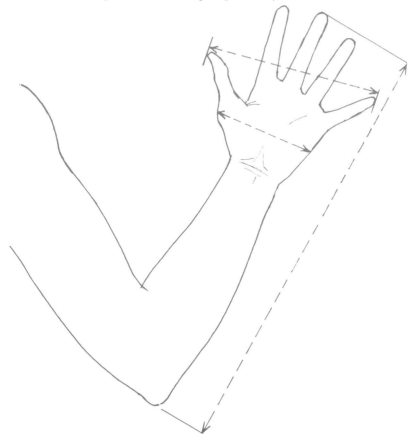

HOW DID HOROSCOPES ORIGINATE?

What is a horoscope? A horoscope is a diagram of the heavenly bodies showing the relative positions of the sun, moon, stars, and planets at a given time.

To make up an individual's horoscope, the exact time and place of his birth must be known so that the positions of those bodies will be related to that time. By establishing the relative positions of the heavenly bodies at the exact time of a person's birth, astrologers claim to be able to predict his future or advise him on decisions to make or actions to follow.

You will notice that we said "astrologers" claim this to be so, and this indicates the origin of the horoscope. It is part of astrology, which is the belief that heavenly bodies have an influence on human affairs, and that future events can be predicted by making astronomical observations.

Western astrology goes back to the Chaldeans and Babylonians of the 2000's B.C. In its beginnings, astrology was an attempt to make practical application to human affairs of what was being studied and observed in astronomy, the stars and the planets.

These and other ancient observers noticed that movements of the sun, the moon, the stars, and the planets happened with certain regularity, or in certain periods of time. The seasons, the rains, the growth cycles of plants—also had a regularity and periods of occurrence. So they linked the two together—and started the belief that the movements and positions of the heavenly bodies had an influence on the lives of human beings.

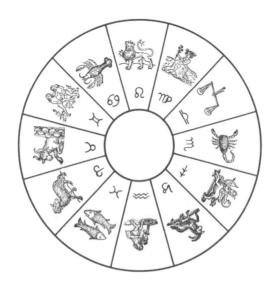

WHY DO WE SAY "GOD BLESS YOU" WHEN SOMEONE SNEEZES?

We say "God bless you" when a friend sneezes. The Germans say "*Gesundheit*," which means "good health." The Italians say "*Felicita*," which means "happiness." In the Near and Far East, people may clasp their hands and bow toward the person who has sneezed.

One explanation for this has to do with superstition. It is said that these customs began when early man believed that a person's spirit or soul was in the form of air or breath, and that it was contained in the head.

So a sneeze might accidentally expel this spirit for a short time, or even forever, unless God prevented it. "God bless you" was an appeal to God to not let it happen. The act of bowing toward the sneezer was meant to say "May your soul not escape."

But there are some experts who claim that the custom of saying "God bless you" is not based on a superstition. They believe it started during a great plague that took place in ancient Athens. A sneeze was often the first sign that a person had contracted plague.

The Romans practiced the custom of "blessing" and brought it to Britain. And when Britain had the plague, the people there said "God bless you" for the same reason that the Athenians had said it—to ask God's blessing for a person who might die.

Of course, there are many superstitions connected with sneezing, including one that says different things will happen to you, depending on the day you sneeze.

ANCIENT EGYPTIAN
RING

ANCIENT GREEK
GOLD DECORATION

GEMS

ETRUSCAN BROOCH

ANCIENT ROMAN
NECKLACE

EARRING,
MIDDLE
AGES

WHEN WAS JEWELRY FIRST WORN?

Jewelry can be made from many different kinds of materials. But we usually think of it as precious jewelry, made of the rarest and most beautiful metals and gemstones.

Gold is the oldest precious metal used in jewelry. The use of it dates back to the earliest Egyptians. In fact, more than four thousand years ago, the Egyptians were making beautiful jewelry out of gold, silver, enamel, turquoise and other gemstones. They wore rings, earrings, and brooches, just as we do now. They also wore heavy jeweled collars, breastplates, and headdresses.

To the ancient Greeks the beauty of a piece of jewelry was as important as the value of the materials used to make it. Fine threads of gold were shaped to look like butterflies or grasshoppers. The Greeks also liked cameos. Jasper, amber, and coral were among their favorite gemstones.

The most beautifully made jewelry in history was made by the Etruscans, who lived in northern Italy. They designed jewelry in intricate patterns and made it with great skill. Instead of a shiny surface, their gold jewelry had a grainy surface, as if fine gold powder has been evenly sprinkled on it.

The Romans wore very elaborate jewelry, designed to show off their wealth. Both men and women wore large gemstones. They especially liked pearls and emeralds. The Romans loaded their fingers, sometimes all their fingers, with rings.

During the Middle Ages most of the jewelry craftsmen were monks. The monks devoted their energy to making religious decorations for the churches. Guilds of jewelry makers began after the 9th century. By 1327, goldsmiths had formed their own association in London.

Chapter 2

THE WORLD WE LIVE IN

HOW DOES WATER PUT OUT A FIRE?

Let's start with what it takes to make a fire. Three things are needed for a fire. The first is a fuel, such as wood or paper or alcohol or gas.

Secondly, oxygen is needed. The fuel combines rapidly with oxygen. When wood burns in bonfires or gas burns in stoves, the fuel combines rapidly with oxygen in the air.

The third thing needed is heat. Paper or wood that is simply exposed to air does not catch fire. Usually a burning match is applied to paper to make it catch fire. When the paper becomes hot enough, oxygen can begin to combine freely with it. The paper then bursts into flames.

There are three main ways in which a fire can be put out. In each, one of the three things needed for burning is removed. The first way is to remove some of the fuel. A second way of putting out a fire is to keep oxygen from getting to it. If there is no oxygen supply, the fire goes out. For example, a fire cannot burn in carbon dioxide. Some fire extinguishers blanket a fire with carbon dioxide. The oxygen is thus blocked from the fire.

A third way to put fires out is to remove heat from the fire. That is why water is sprayed on fires. The water absorbs heat from the burning materials and lowers their temperature. Once the temperature drops below the kindling temperature, the fuels stop burning.

Some fires cannot be put out with water. For example: oil and grease float on water. If you try to put out an oil fire—such as a burning pan of cooking oil—with water, the flaming oil will come to the top of the water and continue to burn.

WHY DO PLANTS TURN TOWARD THE SUN-LIGHT?

If plants didn't do this, they wouldn't be able to live. They would have no food.

Leaves produce food, in the form of sugar, for the entire plant. The leaves contain a special green substance that enables them to do this. This substance is chlorophyll. Chlorophyll can produce sugar only in the presence of light. This food-producing process is called photosynthesis, which means "putting together with light."

So we can see why plants have to turn their leaves toward the sunlight. But how can plants do this? Botanists say that the plant is "phototropic," that is, it turns toward the light, and it does it this way:

Plant cells contain growth substances known as auxins. These substances move away from the light. When the plant is not in the light, the auxins gather in the cells on the side of the stem away from the light. The auxins make the cells on that side grow faster than the cells on the lighted side. This makes the plant bend toward the light.

We do not usually think of plants as moving at all. This is because the movements of plants are usually too slow to be seen. But if you could see certain plants on a fast-motion film, you could see that the leaves, flowers, and stems are almost constantly moving—even when no wind is blowing.

Some plants move quickly. A pumpkin, squash, or cucumber vine may form a complete coil around a string support in ten minutes.

WHY IS THERE NO LIFE
ON THE OTHER PLANETS?

We are not sure yet that there is no form of life on any of the other planets, and that is one of the things that space exploration is trying to find out. But we do know that for life to exist, certain conditions must be present.

There must be the right temperature. All living things must remain with certain limits of temperature. Living material must not be "cooked" by heat or frozen. Another condition is water. All living things require water. Light is essential for green plants, and so are certain minerals. Animals need a source of food. They cannot exist in places where they cannot obtain food.

Do all these conditions necessary for life exist on any other planet? It doesn't seem that way, judging by what we know so far about conditions on the other planets. Let's examine what they are on some of the planets.

Venus is more like the earth than any other planet. Some astronomers even think a form of plant life may exist there, because they have detected water vapor in the air above the clouds of Venus. But it is possible that the surface of Venus may be as hot as eight hundred degrees, and if this is true, life could not exist there.

Planets like Jupiter and Saturn are covered by very thick layers of clouds made up of gases that are poisonous to us. And both these planets may be very hot beneath the layers of clouds. So it goes for the other planets. Each seems to have some conditions that either make life impossible, or don't have the conditions necessary for life.

WHY DO COMETS DISAPPEAR?

A comet, like a planet or a moon, is a member of the sun's family, the solar system. A comet travels on a path or orbit around the sun on a regular schedule.

But most comets travel very elongated orbits. That is, the path they take resembles the shape of a long, fat cigar. Their orbits may carry them as far as halfway to the nearest stars. A comet following such an orbit takes thousands of years to complete one trip. So we may feel that it has "disappeared."

Comets are strongly influenced by the gravitational pull of the planets. A few comets have been pulled out of their regular orbits and forced into shorter ones. Jupiter, for example, has collected a number of comets, each of which takes about six years to orbit the sun. Comets which appear at fairly regular intervals are known as periodic comets.

But do any comets "disappear" forever? Some do. In 1826, the astronomer Wilhelm von Biela saw one of these "lost comets." It returned several times and was observed each time by a number of astronomers. Then in 1846 it split in two, making a pair of comets. Finally, both parts of Biela's comet broke up into bits too small to be seen.

These pieces are thought to form the shower of meteors that appear in the heavens in the latter part of November. The history of Biela's comet shows that comets eventually die; that is, they break up and are scattered along their orbits in the form of meteoric dust. So comets *do* disappear eventually.

WHO DISCOVERED AUSTRALIA?

Australia is the world's largest island and its smallest continent. Its total area of 3,000,000 square miles is about the same as that of the continental United States (excluding Alaska).

Even in medieval times there were stories about a large continent in the Southern Hemisphere. But no one had ever seen it. People wondered what it was like and whether it was inhabited. They called this land "terra australis incognita," or "the unknown southern land."

The Dutch were the first Europeans to visit Australia. They discovered it while making their journeys between the Netherlands and the island of Java, a Dutch colony in Southeast Asia.

Ships sailing from the Netherlands to Java used to go around the southern tip of Africa (the Cape of Good Hope) and then sail across the Indian Ocean with the westerly winds. Many navigators sailed too far east before turning north toward Java and found themselves on the west coast of Australia. They later gave the name New Holland to this western part of the continent.

In 1642 Captain Abel Tasman was sent by the Dutch to discover what lay in the east of the continent. He discovered the island now named Tasmania, and also discovered New Zealand. Later he explored Australia's north coast.

In 1770 the English captain James Cook discovered the east coast of Australia and named it New South Wales. He visited Botany Bay, near what is now modern Sydney. In 1788, the first English colony was established in what later became the city of Sydney.

WHY IS SNOW WHITE?

Snow is actually frozen water, and as we know, ice has no color. Why then, is snow white?

The reason is that each snowflake is made up of a large number of ice crystals. These crystals have many surfaces. And it is the reflection of light from all these surfaces that makes snow look white.

Snow forms when water vapor in the atmosphere freezes. As the vapor freezes, clear transparent crystals are formed. The currents that are in the air make these crystals go up and down in the atmosphere.

As the crystals do this, they begin to gather around tiny particles that are in the clouds. When a group of ice crystals is big enough, it floats down to earth as a snowflake.

The crystals that make up a snowflake always arrange themselves in a special way. They either form six-pointed stars or thin plates shaped like a hexagon. Each branch of the six-pointed star is exactly like the others.

While all the branches of a snowflake are identical, no two snowflakes have ever been found to be exactly alike.

We can only think of snow as being white. But there have actually been cases where colored snow has fallen. One famous case of this was reported by Charles Darwin. During one of his expeditions, he noticed that the hoofs of the mules were becoming stained red as they walked through the snow.

The red snow was caused by the presence of certain tiny plants, called algae, which had been in the atmosphere when the snow formed.

WHAT ARE THE ROMANCE LANGUAGES?

There is a group of languages that is descended from the form of Latin spoken by the ordinary people of ancient Rome. They are known as the Romance languages, and they are: French, Provencal (including Catalan), Spanish, Portuguese, Italian, Romanian, and the Rhaeto-Romantic dialects.

These languages developed in the region of the Roman Empire in Europe. When the Roman soldiers, traders, and colonists came to these areas, they made the natives use their language.

In ancient Rome there was classical Latin, the speech of literature, oratory, and formal conversation. But at the same time there was the everyday speech of the common people, the vulgar Latin.

This grew in Rome and then was carried to the provinces by those who went to settle there. But there were local differences, and new nations began to grow, so this form of Latin then developed into separate languages.

As time went on, the various Romance languages began to change even more in pronunciation. Words from outside sources were used and changed to fit the language. For example, French picked up about four hundred Teutonic words. During the Crusades, French took over some Greek and Arabic words. Spanish has many words that were taken from the Arabic.

At the same time the Romance languages were developing dialects. People in one part of the country began to talk a language slightly different from that in other parts. In Paris, for example, they still speak a slightly different French than in other parts of France.

HOW ARE AMENDMENTS ADDED
TO THE CONSTITUTION?

The Constitution of the United States has grown with the needs of the American people. One of the ways this has happened is through amendments. An amendment means that the words that make up the Constitution can be changed.

When two-thirds of the members of Congress agree on an amendment, the amendment may then be given to the states for their approval. The states may consider the matter either through their legislatures or through special conventions. Congress decides which. And when three-quarters of the states have ratified an amendment, the amendment is in force and the Secretary of State announces the fact.

The first ten amendments, the Bill of Rights, were really unfinished business of the Constitutional Convention. In other words, they were part of the creation of the Constitution. Amendments Eleven and Twelve were also added in that way.

After a long period with no amendments, Thirteen abolished slavery. Fourteen further protected the rights of citizens, and Fifteen granted equal voting rights regardless of race or color. Sixteen permitted Congress to levy an income tax. Seventeen called for the election of senators by the people instead of by state legislatures.

Eighteen outlawed alcoholic drinks—and was repealed by amendment Twenty-one in 1933. The Nineteenth amendment gave women the right to vote. Twenty changed the terms of office of the president, vice-president, and Congress. Twenty-two limits presidents to two terms. Twenty-three gives the presidential vote to the District of Columbia. Twenty-four bars the poll tax as a requirement for voters in federal elections. And Twenty-five covers presidential disability.

HOW TALL IS THE LEANING TOWER OF PISA?

Even if the tower in the city of Pisa, Italy, didn't "lean," it would be quite a marvel. It is built entirely of white marble. The walls are 13 feet thick at its base. It has eight stories and is 179 feet high, which in our country would be about the height of a 15-story building.

There is a stairway built into the walls consisting of three hundred steps, which leads to the top. And by the way, those people who climb these stairs to the top get a magnificent view of the city and of the sea, which is six miles away.

At the top, the tower is 16½ feet out of the perpendicular. In other words, it "leans" over by 16½ feet. If you were to stand at the top and drop a stone to the ground, it would hit 16½ feet away from the wall at the bottom of the tower!

What makes it lean? Nobody really knows the answer. Of course, it wasn't supposed to lean when it was built; it was supposed to stand straight. It was intended as a bell-tower for the cathedral which is nearby and was begun in 1174 and finished in 1350.

The foundations of the tower were laid in sand, and this may explain why it leans. But it didn't suddenly begin to lean—this began to happen when only three of its stories, or "galleries" had been built. So the plans were changed slightly and construction went right on. In the last hundred years, the tower has leaned another foot. According to some engineers, it should be called "the falling tower," because they believe it will eventually topple over.

HOW DO SEEDS GROW?

Each seed is like a tiny package of plant life. It contains a tiny new plant and food to nourish it. You can see the plant and its food if you split a large seed, like a bean, in half.

You will see that it is made of two pale, thick leaves, called cotyledons. These are filled with starch for the developing plant. If you look carefully, you will see a tiny white sprout at one end between the cotyledons. This is the future bean plant. Some plants have only one cotyledon.

Some seeds germinate, or sprout, as soon as they fall from the plant, but most need a resting period of several months. The root appears first. Then a leafy shoot pushes upward.

Seeds enclosed in fleshy fruits, such as apples and tomatoes, do not sprout until they have been removed from the fruit. This is because the fruit contains substances that prevent sprouting.

The tiny new plant in the seed, called the embryo, has an upper part called the plumule. This grows into stems and leaves. The rest of the embryo is the hypocotyl, a very short stem that produces a root at its lower end.

Seeds sprout into new plants when conditions are favorable. The conditions that make seeds sprout are warmth, abundant moisture, and an adequate oxygen supply. Given these conditions, the food stored in the cotyledons passes to the growing regions of the embryo. The embryo bursts through the seed coat and emerges as a young plant that gradually comes to look like the parent plant.

WHAT IS HUMOR?

You laugh at something, your friend doesn't. Your father laughs at something, you don't. Why? Is humor simply anything that makes somebody laugh? Writers, doctors, psychologists, comedians have written books on the subject of humor—and there is still no single, accepted explanation of it.

But we do know that certain things make some people laugh, so we can at least describe certain types of humor. For example, wit can make us laugh. If a person says: "A bird in the hand is an awful mess" (instead of "is worth two in the bush"), we consider that humorous. So surprise can make us laugh.

Slapstick and farce make us laugh. Being hit in the face with a pie, or being stuffed into a laundry basket, makes a man seem funny and we laugh. All kinds of things that are done with words can be funny, such as puns and plays upon words.

We all know limericks that we have considered amusing. A person who is good at mimicking someone else makes us laugh. Or when we hear a dialect being imitated it can be funny. Or there can even be a whole show, or play, that is a "burlesque" of certain people and things we recognize, and we laugh at it.

Satire is an old form of humor that has been used by many authors to ridicule ways of life. We all use understatement and hyperbole (overstatement) to be funny. An example of the first would be: "Willie Mays? He's a fairly good ballplayer." An example of hyperbole is to come home after a hard day and say: "I'm dead." There is also irony and sarcasm, which we all use—or have used against us. So you can see that humor takes many forms, and we can enjoy it in many different ways and for many different reasons.

HOW FAR DOES OUTER SPACE GO?

Most astronomers think that the universe we can observe is only part of the whole universe. They picture the whole universe as extending much farther into space. But how far does it extend? Does it go on forever? Or is there perhaps an end to it somewhere? And if there is an end, what lies beyond it?

Astronomers think the answers may lie in the nature of space itself. According to the present theory, space curves around on itself. This means that you can never get "outside" space, for your path will always curve around and lead you back again.

Here is an example to help understand this: Imagine a plane flying from New York to San Francisco. If it flew in a straight line, by the time it was over San Francisco it would be a couple of thousand miles up in the air. The reason is that the earth is curved. A plane flying in a straight line is flying away from the earth into space.

To fly from New York to San Francisco, the plane actually follows a curved path. And if the plane continued in that same curved path, it eventually would come back to the earth.

Astronomers believe that space curves around in a special way. The curving is not as simple as the earth's. A picture of it cannot be drawn on paper, nor can a model of it be made. (The curvature of space, however, can be figured out by using complicated mathematics.)

So, just as it is possible to fly around the earth indefinitely without leaving it, so you could travel out in space for as long as you wished—but never outside it.

WHAT WAS THE ICE AGE?

Ice ages are times when thick sheets of ice have spread over large parts of the continents. The ice sheets form when glaciers of high mountains and polar regions grow to great size. Slowly, over hundreds and hundreds of years, the glaciers reach out. They cover the land with sheets of ice that may be several thousand feet thick.

During the earth's long history, there have been several ice ages. The last one, which is often called the Ice Age, began about 2,500,000 years ago. Four times during the Ice Age great sheets of ice advanced over the land. Four times they melted and drew back.

The last advance ended about 18,000 years ago. At that time a large part of North America was covered by ice. The ice reached as far south as the site of New York City today. Other continents in the Northern Hemisphere were also partly covered by ice, but none so much as North America. Then the ice began to disappear. Some of it evaporated directly into the air, and some melted. About six thousand years ago the continents of the Northern Hemisphere were once more almost free of ice.

Great changes affected the earth during the advances of ice. Air and ocean temperatures fell. Places that are now deserts were well-watered and covered with plant life. Sea levels fell hundreds of feet because great quantities of water were trapped in glaciers on land. Is another Ice Age coming? Scientists cannot answer this question because they still must discover what causes ice ages.

WHAT IS BOTULISM?

Botulism is a form of food poisoning. It comes from the eating of food that contains certain toxins developed by bacteria. In the case of botulism, the toxins are produced by bacteria called *Clostridium botulinum.*

The condition is usually the result of eating improperly prepared home-canned foods. The term "botulism" came from the Latin *botulus,* meaning "sausage," because most of the cases used to come from eating improperly cooked sausage.

When a person has a case of botulism, there is nausea, vomiting, and there may be paralysis of the muscles, so that it becomes difficult to see, speak, or swallow. The diaphragm may be paralyzed, so that an iron lung is necessary to maintain life.

The bacteria that cause botulism may or may not produce any detectable odor or taste in food. This means one cannot tell from the absence of odor in home-canned food that those bacteria are not present.

No home-canned food should be tasted until it has been thoroughly cooked. Fruit and vegetables should be washed as soon as possible after picking, before they are canned. Meat, fish, and poultry should be cooked in a pressure cooker before canning. And any canned food that has not been treated in this way, should be boiled before eating. If any can of food that is opened has a bad odor, it should not be tasted.

WHEN WAS THE GREAT SPHINX BUILT?

One of the greatest "wonders" that still survives from an ancient civilization is the Great Sphinx at Giza, in Egypt. A sphinx is a mythical animal that has the head of a human and the body of a lion.

The sphinx became part of Egyptian religion and many sphinxes were made, but the most famous and the oldest is the Great Sphinx. This sphinx was built in the 26th century B.C. The face had the features of the king at that time, King Khafre, so that his people could worship him in this special form.

It is carved from a natural bluff of rock that lies in the center of a large quarry. The body and the head are carved right from the rock, while the outstretched paws are added in masonry. The figure was originally covered with painted plaster, and there are still some traces of this.

While we can still see and admire the Great Sphinx, it is quite different now than it was originally because of all the damage it has suffered. Drifting sand has caused a great deal of erosion and created a kind of ripple effect on the body.

It has also been injured by humans. In 1380 a ruler of Egypt did great damage to the face. At one time the monument was used as a target for guns.

The Great Sphinx is 66 feet high, its length is 240 feet. The nose is 5 feet 7 inches and the mouth 7 feet 7 inches in length. The face is 13 feet 8 inches wide.

WHAT WAS CRO-MAGNON MAN?

In the development of man over thousands of years, there was a time when he lived in caves. Probably the most interesting of the cave dwellers was Cro-Magnon man. He lived in Europe at the end of the Ice Age.

He is called Cro-Magnon man simply because the first remains of these cave dwellers was found at a spot called Cro-Magnon in southern France. And he is interesting to know about because experts who have examined the skeleton of the first Cro-Magnon man that was found say he was very intelligent. If he had lived today he might have been a scientist, or statesman, or business leader.

Cro-Magnon man lived in very rough times, surrounded by wild beasts and other dangers. But despite this, they found time to draw excellent pictures on the walls of their caves. These pictures can still be seen and they are admired for their skill and beauty.

These people also had a well-developed social life. They lived in families, and since they hunted in groups, they must also have lived in tribes. They believed in a spirit world—that the dead would arise and live in another world again.

Gradually they developed better stone tools and new weapons. They learned to carve spearheads and harpoons from horn or bone. They also invented throwing sticks for weapons. The women learned to cure skins and sew them into garments with needles made of bone. So Cro-Magnon man, as we can see, was very intelligent and reached quite a high stage of development.

ARE THE CONTINENTS MOVING?

The theory that the continents have moved or drifted about ("continental drift") was first advanced by a German scientist, Alfred Wegener, in 1912.

He pointed out that coal was present all over the northern hemisphere, yet coal forms from plants growing in tropical forests. And among other things, he said the west coast of Africa and the east coast of South America matched so well that they looked as if they had been torn apart.

Wegener thought all the continents had at first been together in one great land mass. Then they had drifted apart to their present location. Most geologists didn't agree with him because no one could think of any way by which continents would move about.

Then scientists began to suggest ways in which this could happen. One was that heat from the interior of the earth creates convection currents that make the continents move. Other scientists now think that the ocean floor is being pulled apart by currents in the mantle of the earth's crust.

So there is no agreement on the subject. Earth scientists tend not to accept the idea; those who study under-ocean geology are more ready to accept it. If all geologists were to accept the theory that the continents have drifted, and may still be moving, a great revolution in our ideas on earth science will have to take place.

Science would have to come up with new answers about our climate, about how plants and animals evolved, about how mountains were built, and many more areas.

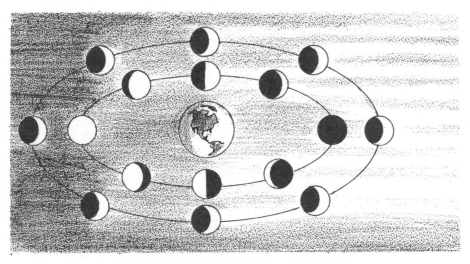

WHY DOES THE MOON
HAVE DIFFERENT SHAPES?

The moon circles the earth in an orbit that takes about one month to complete. It also spins, or rotates, on its axis, and it takes 27 days, 7 hours, and 43 minutes to make one rotation. Because the orbit and the rotation take about the same amount of time, the moon always keeps the same side facing the earth.

The moon does not shine with its own light the way the sun does. It only seems to shine, because it reflects the sun's light. As the moon travels around the earth different parts of it are lighted up by the sun.

Sometimes you see the whole visible face of the moon lighted up, and at other times you see only a part of the moon's face lighted up. This is what makes the moon look as though it were changing shape in the sky. These changes are called phases of the moon—and it only means we are seeing different parts of the moon.

The cycle of phases begins with a new moon. This is when the moon is between the earth and the sun. A new moon is not visible. Then the side of the moon facing the earth begins to be lighted up by the sun. The lighted part looks like a thin curved slice of a circle. This is called a crescent moon.

The sunlit part of the moon grows larger until it becomes a half-circle. This is called the first quarter. When the whole face of the moon is lighted by the sun we call it a full moon. Then the moon's face becomes less and less lit, and we reach the last quarter. The cycle ends with a crescent moon that changes to the next new moon. The whole cycle, from one new moon to the next new moon, lasts just over 29½ days.

WHY IS LAVA HOT?

The center of the earth is a very hot place. If we could dig down thirty miles into the earth, the temperature would be about 2,200 degrees Fahrenheit. At the core or center of the earth the temperature may be about 10,000 degrees Fahrenheit. At such temperatures, rock exists in a molten form.

Lava is the molten rock, mixed with steam and gas, that is forced out of the interior of the earth. It comes from the center of the earth through cracks in the solid surface.

Sometimes the crack may be a rounded hole. When the lava comes out, it spreads out into a kind of round puddle and cools into rock. If more lava is forced out later, it flows over the first deposit and makes it a little higher. As this continues to happen, layer after layer is built up and there is finally a mountain of rock which we call a volcano.

When a flow of lava occurs and spreads over the land, it destroys everything in its path. This is because it is a heavy stream of molten rock with a temperature of 2,000 to 3,000 degrees Fahrenheit.

Cities that are close to volcanoes are always in danger of being destroyed by such a flow of lava. Sometimes a very long period goes by without this happening, and people assume they are now safe forever. Then suddenly the flow of lava begins again.

This happened two thousand years ago to a Roman city in Italy, called Pompeii. It was buried completely under the flow of lava from the famous volcano, Mount Vesuvius.

HOW IS HUMIDITY MEASURED?

Water in the atmosphere is the only reason we have clouds, fog, rain, snow—and warm, sticky days. The atmosphere carries water in three different forms: water vapor, liquid water, and solid water.

A hot humid day is different from a hot dry day only because of water vapor. The amount of water vapor in the atmosphere is called humidity. When we say "relative humidity" is 80 percent, we mean that the air is holding 80 percent of the water vapor it could hold. When air is at 100 percent relative humidity, it is holding all the water vapor it possibly can, and we call it saturated air. Warm air can hold more water vapor than cold air.

The instrument used to measure the amount of water vapor in the air is a hygrometer. The most accurate kind is called the wet and dry bulb hygrometer. Two thermometers are mounted side by side on a base. The bulb of one is covered with muslin or some other coarse material which is kept wet. The bulb of the other is left bare and dry.

Evaporation of water on an object cools it. If the air contains much water vapor, the moisture on the wet bulb evaporates slowly, and the wet bulb thermometer doesn't show much lowering in temperature. If the air is dry, the moisture on the wet bulb evaporates rapidly, and the wet-bulb thermometer shows a much lower temperature than the dry-bulb thermometer.

By consulting a prepared table, the relative humidity can be learned by comparing the two temperatures. There are other types of hygrometers that use currents of air, or chemicals, or a hair, to measure the increase or loss of moisture in the air.

WHAT IS CARBON DIOXIDE?

Carbon dioxide is a compound, usually in the form of a gas. It can become a solid if it is cooled enough.

There is a very small amount of carbon dioxide present in the air, about one gallon in 2,500 gallons of air. Most of this carbon dioxide gets into the air when plant and animal tissues, which are carbon, decay. Fuels that are made up of carbon, such as wood and coal, give off large amounts of carbon dioxide when they are burned.

The human body needs a small amount of carbon dioxide in order to live. It controls the rate at which the heart beats and also other functions in the body. But inhaling too much carbon dioxide can do harm and even cause a person to suffocate.

Human beings take oxygen from the air they breathe. This oxygen is taken into the bloodstream. There it combines with food and is changed to carbon dioxide. Then the carbon dioxide returns to the lungs and is breathed out.

Plants, on the other hand, take in carbon dioxide to live. Green plants draw carbon dioxide from the air through the pores in their leaves. This combines with water, and with the help of sunlight the carbon dioxide and water change to starch and other food for the plant. The plant then gives off oxygen as a waste product.

So plants give off oxygen and take in carbon dioxide. People and animals take in oxygen and give off carbon dioxide. This keeps the supply of oxygen and carbon dioxide in the air fairly stable.

Carbon dioxide also has many commercial uses, the best known of which is for "carbonating" soft drinks.

WHY DID ROME FALL?

For over four hundred years the Roman Empire governed all the lands around the Mediterranean Sea and most of the rest of Europe.

Much of what is now England and France, Belgium and the Netherlands, Spain and Portugal, Switzerland, Austria, Hungary, part of Germany, Romania, Bulgaria, Greece, Turkey, Israel, Syria, Arabia, the United Arab Republic, Tunisia, Algeria, and Morocco—all this was ruled by the Romans from their base in Italy.

The decline of this great Roman Empire in the west came very gradually. Contrary to the well-known expression, Rome did not "fall." Between A.D. 400 and 430 several large groups of people from the outside forced their way into the empire and settled down in France, Spain, and North Africa.

Little by little they asserted their independence from the Romans. By about 500 all the western parts of the empire—Italy, North Africa, France, and Spain—were ruled by Germanic kings who were independent of Rome.

The emperor Diocletian (A.D. 245-313) had divided the empire into two parts in 286. Long after the western part of the empire "fell," the eastern part remained strong. Its center was the old city of Byzantium, renamed Constantinople, and now called Istanbul.

For almost a thousand years this city was the chief city of the world and capital of the Roman Empire in the east. At last this empire fell when the Turks captured Constantinople in the year 1453.

The Roman Empire kept peace for two hundred years and did another valuable thing for civilization—it helped to preserve the literature and science of Greece and pass them on to the modern Western world.

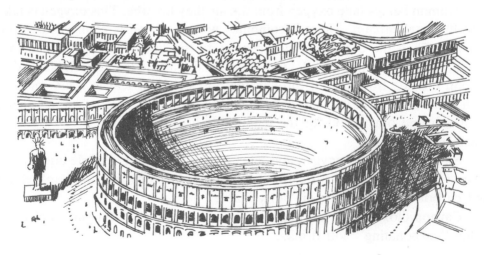

WHY IS THE WHITE HOUSE WHITE?

The White House wasn't always white, nor was it always called the White House. But it has always been the official residence of the president of the United States.

It is the oldest federal structure standing, its cornerstone having been laid on October 13, 1792. It was designed by an Irish-born architect James Hoban, who won an architectural competition to select a design for the president's house.

Originally it was called President's House, President's Mansion, and even President's Palace. How did it come to be called the White House? The house was originally built of gray sandstone. During the War of 1812, British troops invaded Washington and burned the structure (August 24, 1814). Only a shell was left standing.

Under Hoban's direction the building was restored, and this was completed in 1817. To cover up the smoke stains, the gray sandstone walls were painted white. So the building came to be called the White House, but this didn't become its official name until 1902, when Theodore Roosevelt adopted it.

It is interesting how many rooms in the White House are known by their colors. The Blue Room, which is oval in shape, is the reception room for the president and his wife. The Red Room is furnished with objects of the Empire period. The Green Room is furnished with objects going back to the days of John Adams and Thomas Jefferson. There is a Rose Guest Room upstairs where the president and his family live.

WHAT IS A FOLK SONG?

Since the beginning of the human race, people have been singing folk songs. There are so many different kinds of folk songs that it is hard to define a folk song. Basically, folk songs tell us how people feel about life.

Since life consists of so many things, folk songs deal with many subjects. One type is work songs, sung by workers on plantations and the railroads, songs for building roads, and so on. There are songs about occupations, which are sung at any time. They may be about shepherds, shoemakers, blacksmiths, tailors. They can be about mills and mines—and about cowboys.

Another type of folk song has to do with love and marriage. Songs such as "I know where I'm going," and "Frankie and Johnny," and "Matilda," are examples of this type. Children's songs and games can also be folk songs.

Some folk songs combine fact and fancy and are sung just for fun. They might be nonsense songs or tall tales. A type of folk song—the play-party song —developed from children's games, such as "London Bridge" and "All Around the Mulberry Bush." There are also folk songs that have to do with animals.

Still another type is the religious folk song. The "spiritual" is one of the most beautiful of this kind. There are also folk songs that have to do with the seasons.

And there are still more: wedding songs, lullabies, songs of mourning, songs of war and military life. So you see, folk songs can be about anything in life that people want to sing about.

WHAT IS OZONE?

Ozone is a form of oxygen. Oxygen is a chemical element, the most abundant element on earth. Oxygen is all around you. It makes up about one-fifth of the air. (Most of the rest of the air is nitrogen.)

Ordinary oxygen exists in the form of molecules made up of two oxygen atoms. There is also a second form of oxygen, called ozone, made up of three oxygen atoms.

Most ozone is formed in the upper atmosphere by ultraviolet radiations. These radiations break apart oxygen molecules into separate oxygen atoms. When these atoms become attached to some other oxygen molecules, ozone is formed.

Ozone collects in a layer from 12 to 22 miles above the earth. This layer, called the ozone layer, tends to protect life on earth by filtering some of the sun's powerful radiations. Ozone is also formed close to earth during lightning storms and by X-ray and electrical equipment. You may have seen blue sparks shooting off when metal is cut with an oxygen torch. These sparks are an indication that ozone is being formed.

Ozone combines with other substances much more rapidly than oxygen does. Ozone destroys germs very quickly and for this reason is used to purify water and to clean public places. It is also used as a bleach for many common substances, such as flour, wax, and cloth.

Ozone has a strong ''electric'' smell and may harm lung tissues if too much is breathed in.

WHAT DESTROYED THE EMPIRE OF THE INCAS?

In 1531 Francisco Pizarro first landed on the coast of what is now Ecuador. He entered an empire that extended nearly three thousand miles along the western coast of South America. This was the great Inca Empire.

With perhaps 16,000,000 people, it was larger than any kingdom in Europe at the time. It was well-governed. Every citizen was employed. The royal storehouses contained grain, so that no one went hungry even if the crops failed in some province. There were good roads to all parts of the kingdom. Messengers carried news and delivered orders to every village.

Life was so completely controlled in the Inca Empire, all the people were so obedient, that this may have helped lead to the downfall of the empire. When

Pizarro entered the empire with 180 soldiers, a contest was going on between Huascar and his half-brother Atahualpa over who would be the Inca (ruler). Atahualpa was winning the war.

Pizarro captured him by treachery. In the meantime Huascar had been captured and killed. Pizarro then killed Atahualpa. Now the Inca Empire had no leader, and it could not resist the brutal Spanish adventurers.

The average Indian was used to doing what he was told. Now the Spanish conquerors gave the orders. The Spaniards were interested in what the Inca mines produced, so they ordered the people to work in the mines. Farming was neglected. Many Indians died from overwork and lack of food. The Inca Empire was destroyed.

Many Indians survived this period, and their descendants still form the majority of the population in the Andes of Ecuador, Peru, and Bolivia.

WHAT IS INFLATION?

Basically, inflation is a rise in prices. Families, businesses, and government groups are all buyers. The things they buy are called goods and services. During an inflation people spend money faster than goods are being made. It is a period when too many dollars are chasing too few goods. During an inflation a dollar buys less.

Even if we knew all the causes of inflations, we might not be able to keep them from happening. Sometimes government spending is blamed for starting an inflation. Sometimes businesses and labor unions are blamed. Even family spending is blamed. Often inflations are caused by wars.

In an inflation, a steady rise in prices cuts back the amount that a dollar will buy. Then people hurry to buy before costs get any higher. Then businessmen think that there is a growing demand for their products. So they put money into new products, machinery, and factories.

This creates a greater demand for workers. People get bigger incomes and they spend their extra money. Businessmen see that their goods are selling well and borrow money to expand their businesses.

The people who suffer during an inflation are the savers, creditors (the people who have loaned money), people on pensions, and those who earn a fixed salary.

Before a government tries to control an inflation, it tries to understand what is causing it. If the wrong controls are used, they may not solve the problem.

WHAT'S THE DIFFERENCE BETWEEN MUSHROOMS AND TOADSTOOLS?

The answer is, there is no difference! In fact, scientifically speaking, there is no such thing as a "toadstool." Many people call poisonous mushrooms "toadstools." But a botanist never uses that term at all, and there is no difference between a mushroom and what is called a toadstool.

There are a great many other ideas about mushrooms that people have which are completely wrong. The kinds of mushrooms which are poisonous are quite few. But these few are deadly. So no one should ever eat or even taste a mushroom unless he is certain that it is wholesome.

But the "tests" that some people believe in for detecting poisonous mushrooms are worthless. For example, it is not correct that all mushrooms with umbrella-shaped caps are poisonous. It is not true that poisonous mushrooms when cooling will blacken a silver spoon if they are stirred with it.

The poisonous mushrooms contain a poison so powerful that to eat them is almost certain death. There is a story that the Emperor Nero once killed off a whole party of guests by feeding them poisonous mushrooms. The best thing to do is to eat only the mushrooms you buy in stores—and not pick your own.

Mushrooms are fungi. Like other fungi, they lack the green coloring matter called chlorophyll without which a plant cannot manufacture food for itself. They must grow near, and depend for food on, plants that have this green coloring matter. Mushrooms are very delicate plants. They consist chiefly of water, which is why most of them cannot bear hot dry winds or the summer sun.

WHY DOES A COMET HAVE A TAIL?

As seen through a telescope, a comet has a "head" and a "tail." The head is a large cloud of glowing gases called the "coma" of the comet. The coma may be more than 1,000,000 miles in diameter. Its gases are so light that the "wind" from the sun blows them. The tail of a comet forms when gases are blown back by the solar wind.

As a comet approaches the sun, its tail grows larger and larger because the pressure of the solar wind is increasing. As the comet moves away from the sun into the coldness of space, the pressure of the solar wind continues to blow against the gases. For this reason the tail of a comet always points away from the sun.

A small, shining point of light can sometimes be seen in the center of the coma. The point of light is called the "nucleus" of the comet. Astronomers think that the nucleus is like an enormous, dirty snowball—a mixture of ice and dust particles forming a ball about one-half mile in diameter.

In their trip around the sun, most comets travel very elongated orbits. That is, the path they take resembles the shape of a long, fat cigar. A comet may take thousands of years to complete one trip.

About three or four times a century, a comet passes so close to the sun that its bright, glowing tail can easily be seen. We see a comet only when one happens to pass close to the sun. Then the heat of the sun changes the ice in the nucleus into gas. Radiation from the sun passing through these gases ionizes them and causes the gases to glow with light.

HOW WAS PETROLEUM FORMED IN THE EARTH?

Petroleum is believed to have been formed from the remains of ancient living things. Millions of years ago many land areas of today were underwater. The sun shone on these waters and the living things in them.

Marine plants and animals stored the sun's energy in their bodies. As they died, their remains sank to the bottom and were covered by sediments (tiny particles of rock and soil).

While organic remains of these animals and plants settled under layers of sand and mud, chemicals and bacteria were at work. How these agents actually formed gas and oil from the fats and oils of sea life is uncertain. But over long periods of time tiny oil droplets were formed. . .or what we call petroleum.

Later on, the layers of muds and clays became rocks of sandstone and limestone. These rocks are called sedimentary because they were formed from sediments. In time, tiny droplets of oil seeped into layers of these porous rocks and were held there the way a sponge holds water.

Over millions of years the earth's crust was shifting. Old sea floors, and the oil they held, were in some cases changed to land areas. Others were pushed deeper into the sea. The earth shifted and continents changed in appearance.

This is why oil-bearing rock layers are today sometimes found far inland, and also why some of the most productive oil fields are located in desert regions. Millions of years ago they may have been areas under water.

WHAT IS ECOLOGY?

Today we read and hear a great deal about "ecology," and there is a good reason why this is so. Though ecology is one of the youngest of the sciences, it is one of the most important for the future of mankind.

Every living thing has its own way of life. The way of life depends partly on its own form and activities and partly on its environment (surroundings). Every organism (living thing) is affected by all that surrounds it—whether living or nonliving. And in turn each organism has some effect on its surroundings. Each organism is part of a complex web of life.

At the same time, every organism lives as part of a community, or group, of other organisms. These organisms, too, make up part of the surroundings.

Therefore, when we study an animal or plant in its natural surroundings, we are really studying a web of life. A scientist who studies these webs of life is called an ecologist. His subject is ecology, which comes from two Greek words meaning "study of the home, or surroundings."

Ecology studies the relations of living things to the world in which they live and tells us, among other things, how we can most effectively use and conserve our resources. It deals with such things as: How can we make the best use of our land? How can we save our soil, our forests, our wild life? How can we reduce the great losses caused by harmful insects? These are examples of the practical questions the ecologist asks and tries to answer.

WHAT IS AN EARTHQUAKE BELT?

Earthquakes are tremblings or vibrations of the earth's surface. The real cause of earthquakes is usually a "fault" in the rocks of the earth's crust—a break along which one rock mass has rubbed on another with very great force and friction.

Because of this, earthquakes do not occur in all parts of the world. They are confined to certain definite areas, which are called "belts." The most important belt is the rim of the Pacific Ocean, where most of the world's earthquakes have occurred.

This belt begins at the southern tip of Chile, reaches up the Pacific coast of South America to Central America (branching into the Caribbean), runs along the Mexican coast to California, and on to Alaska.

But that isn't the end of it. The belt continues from Alaska to Kamchatka. Passing through the Kurile Islands and the Aleutian Islands, it stretches on to Japan, the Philippines, Indonesia, New Guinea, and through various South Pacific islands.

Most of the big earthquakes in history have taken place within the Pacific belt. However, another earthquake belt branches off from Japan. It runs through China, India, Iran, Turkey, Greece, and the Mediterranean.

In some regions, such as Japan, earthquakes occur almost every day. Fortunately, most of these earthquakes are not severe and cause no damage. On the other hand, in the New England states there have been no destructive earthquakes since the last Ice Age, many thousands of years ago.

WHAT MAKES THE EARTH
TRAVEL AROUND THE SUN?

Let's start with what made the earth, and all the planets, begin to move in the first place. According to one theory about the origin of the solar system, about 5 billion years ago a huge dust cloud was formed and began to spin. It flattened into a disk, and the hot central mass became the sun. The outer parts of the dust cloud broke away in swirling masses, and they condensed as planets.

So now we have the planets, of which the earth is one, in motion. Why didn't the earth and the planets just fly off into space? Gravitation, the pull of the sun, is the answer.

According to Newton's law of motion, an object in motion tends to remain in motion in a straight line unless acted upon by some outside force. Thus, a planet in motion would tend to fly away from the sun in a straight line. The outside force keeping it from doing so, and keeping it in orbit, is the sun's gravitation.

A planet moves in its orbit at a speed that depends on its distance from the sun. The planet moves faster when it is closer to the sun than when it is farther away. The earth moves at a speed of 18.8 miles per second when it is closest to the sun, and 18.2 miles per second when its orbit takes it farthest from the sun.

A planet in an orbit that is closer to the sun is attracted to the sun with more force than one that is farther away. The greater force also causes that planet to move faster than the one that is farther away. For example, Mercury moves at an average speed of 29.8 miles a second, Pluto at an average rate of 2.9 miles a second.

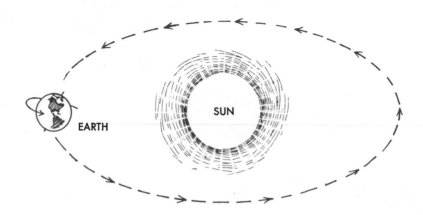

WHAT'S THE DIFFERENCE BETWEEN A COLLEGE AND A UNIVERSITY?

A university is an institution of higher learning that generally includes many kinds of schools and colleges.

In addition to an undergraduate college of liberal arts and sciences, the university has graduate schools. These are for students preparing for professions in law, medicine, engineering, or other special fields. A graduate student is one who has already earned a degree.

The typical college offers a four-year course that generally leads to a bachelor's degree in science or art. A college may be part of a university or, as in the United States and Canada, a separate institution. There are also schools called institutes, which stress scientific and technological studies.

The junior college is a 20th-century American development in education. It offers a two-year course of study in liberal arts or vocational training. With the credits earned in a junior college, a student may be able to transfer to the junior, or third, year of a four-year college or university.

Modern universities and colleges had their beginnings in the institutions started by the Christian Church in Europe during the Middle Ages. European universities were not the first in the world, however.

The University of Al-Azhar, founded in Cairo in the 10th century, is the oldest that is still in operation. One of the earliest in Europe was the University of Bologna, which was begun in Italy in the 11th century.

WHERE DOES THE MONEY FOR TAXES GO?

Nobody enjoys paying taxes. And today, there are so many taxes and some of them are so high, people wonder: where does all that money go?

Taxation is the process by which governments get the money to pay for the things that the people want governments to do. In the United States, city and state governments and the national government collect taxes to pay for the many services which the people have decided the government should provide. It is much cheaper and more efficient to have schools and streets, fire and police departments, and the armed forces run by the government than to have each family try to provide its own education, highways, and protection.

The expenses of all kinds of governments have increased greatly over the years. The main reason for the increase in the cost of running the national government is national defense. In the states, cities, and towns the need for government spending has also increased.

It is necessary to have better streets and highways to take care of the large number of automobiles. More and better schools are needed, and larger universities are necessary. People want to have better hospitals, parks, and other facilities that may be provided by cities and towns.

The federal income tax is the most important source of funds for operation of the United States Government. Cities and towns get most of their money from property taxes. States get their money more and more from income taxes and sales taxes. Without these taxes, none of the services, help, and protection that people want would be possible.

WHAT IS SAND MADE OF?

When a solid rock is exposed to the action of the wind, rain, and frost, and broken up into smaller particles, if the particles are small enough (between one five-hundredth of an inch in diameter and one-tenth of an inch in diameter), these particles are called "sand."

Since sand is formed of small grains of the minerals making up the rocks, any of these minerals may be found in sand. The principal mineral found in sand is quartz, because it is very hard and is quite abundant. Some sands have as much as 99 per cent pure quartz. Other minerals sometimes found in sand are feldspar, calcite, mica, iron ores, and small amounts of garnet, tourmaline, and topaz.

Sand is found wherever rocks have been exposed to the weather. One of the principal sand-forming regions is the beach of a sea. There the action of the tide upon the rocks, the action of windblown sand rubbing against the rocks, and the dissolving of some of the minerals in the rocks by the salt water, all combine to make sand.

What about the sand often found in deserts? Most of the loose sand there has been brought to this place by wind. In some cases, the desert sands may have been formed by the decay of rocks. In still other cases, the desert was once really a sea bottom and the water retreated thousands of years ago, leaving the sand.

Sand is a very useful substance. It is used in making concrete, in making glass, in sandpaper, and as a filter in helping keep water pure.

WHAT IN THE SOIL MAKES PLANTS GROW?

There are many things in the soil, and many things about the condition of the soil, that make it possible for plants to grow in it.

Soil is a mixture of organic and inorganic materials. The organic part consists of living things and the remains of once-living things. The inorganic part is made up of particles of rocks and minerals.

The decaying organic matter in soil is called humus. Humus separates otherwise tightly packed rock particles, thus allowing more air and water to enter the soil. Humus also provides food for bacteria and other micro-organisms in soil. These micro-organisms decay, or break down, dead organic matter, forming substances that plants can use. So humus is very important to the fertility of the soil, or helping plants grow.

Many kinds of animals live in the soil. The body wastes of these animals enrich the soil. Earthworms are important, too They turn over the soil, and improve it in many ways. Micro-organisms present in the soil feed on particles of organic matter. This breaks the organic material into minerals, gases, and liquids. These decay products are broken down still further and result in new combinations of the basic elements. Plants can then use the substances for growth.

There are ten elements that all plants need to grow. Three of these, oxygen, hydrogen, and carbon, are present in either air or water or in both. The others are obtained from the soil by the plants. They are: nitrogen, phosphorus, potassium, calcium, magnesium, iron, and sulfur.

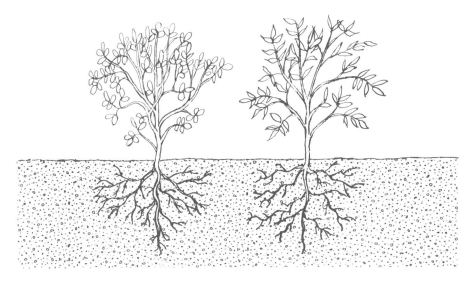

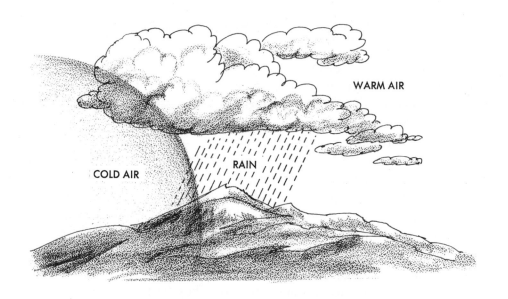

WARM AIR

COLD AIR

RAIN

WHAT IS A CLOUD?

Here is how clouds are formed. Warm air, laden with moisture, rises into the sky. When it gets to a certain height, the warm air cools. At the cooler temperatures it can no longer hold all its moisture in the form of water vapor. So the extra moisture changes into small drops of water, or bits of ice, and this forms clouds.

No two clouds are exactly alike, and they are always changing their shape. The reason we have different types of clouds is that cloud formation takes place at different heights and temperatures. And clouds will be composed of different particles, depending on their height and temperature.

As the water vapor in the air changes back into a liquid (this is called condensation), it comes into contact with dust and other particles in the air. A droplet of liquid water forms around each tiny particle.

It takes about 100,000,000 droplets to form one large raindrop. And so it would take about a million million million droplets to make up a cloud a mile wide, a mile long, and a mile deep. Such a cloud may have about 1,400 tons of water in droplet (liquid) form and nearly 14,000 tons of water in water-vapor (gas) form.

The water vapor condenses into droplets to form clouds around many kinds of particles. There are dust particles blown from deserts, dry topsoil, and volcanoes. There are tiny crystals of salt from the oceans, solid particles from the burning of coal, and many other kinds.

WHAT IS THE EYE OF A HURRICANE?

In a hurricane, there are spiraling winds going around and around at great speed. When the winds are blowing at about 75 miles an hour, the pressure falls very rapidly in a small region of the center of the air column. The very low pressure region in the center is called the eye of the storm.

The eye may be from 10 to 20 miles across. The low pressure in the eye of the hurricane causes sea water to rise slightly within the eye. The water sometimes rises to about three feet.

Very heavy rains come down in the low-pressure area. The heaviest rains come from clouds surrounding the eye of the storm. The eye can be thought of as the hole in a doughnut. The winds rage around the eye, but within it all is calm. The sky overhead may be clear or have scattered clouds. The winds are light, usually less than 15 miles an hour.

If a hurricane passed directly over you so that you stood in the path of the eye, you would first be gripped by the winds and drenched by the rain of the front edge of the storm. Next, there would be a period of calm and of clear sky as the eye of the hurricane passed by. Then there would be another period of rain and strong winds, this time blowing from the opposite direction.

Why does the pressure fall very rapidly in a small region of the center of the air column that is a hurricane? Why does the eye of the hurricane form? Meteorologists, who have been studying this, are still not sure why it happens.

HOW CAN SCIENTISTS KNOW WHAT THE SUN IS MADE OF?

We know that the sun is a great ball of hot gases, made up of many layers of hot gases. But how do we know this, or any of the other things that make up the sun?

Astronomers have obtained many of their facts about the sun by using special instruments. Some of these instruments are the spectroscope, spectrograph, spectroheliograph, coronagraph, radio telescope, and space probe.

The spectroscope is used to study the glowing gases of the sun. It enables them to tell what chemicals produced the colors in the light from the sun. The spectrograph enables scientists to keep a permanent record of the colors.

The spectrohelioscope enables astronomers to see how different substances are distributed on the sun. And when this instrument has photographic equipment attached, it is called a spectroheliograph.

A coronagraph is a special kind of telescope. With a coronagraph astronomers can photograph the sun's corona without having to wait for an eclipse of the sun. A radio telescope enables scientists to study radio waves that are emitted by the sun.

Because the earth's atmosphere stops many of the sun's radiations from reaching the earth, scientists send instruments high up into the atmosphere. Such space probes help them learn more about the sun. While the technical ways in which all these instruments work have not been explained here, you can see that scientists do have instruments that enable them to learn a great deal about the sun.

WHAT ARE CAVERNS?

Although no two caves look alike, all of the really big caves in the world were formed in the same way. They were hollowed out of limestone (or related rocks like gypsum and marble) by acid water. They are called solution caves. Most people call them "caverns."

Some big caverns ha d their beginnings some 60,000,000 years ago. As rains poured down and rivers flowed, the solid rock of the cave-tò-be was slowly eaten away.

The special kind of rock in such places is limestone. It is a fairly soft rock that can be dissolved by a weak acid. The acid that dissolves away limestone comes from rainwater. Falling drops of rain pick up carbon dioxide from the air and from the soil. This carbon dioxide changes the rainwater into carbonic acid.

So millions of years ago the acid rainwater fell on a bed of limestone. It nibbled away at the rock until thin cracks began to appear. More rain fell. The water trickled down, enlarging the cracks. It found new paths between the layers of stone. The paths widened into tunnels. The tunnels crisscrossed and grew into rooms. Over millions of years, the caverns took shape. As long as water filled its tunnels and flowed through its rock-walled rooms, the cavern grew bigger and bigger.

Caverns are not the only kind of cave. For example, there are sea caves, which are formed by the steady pounding of waves on the rocky cliffs along the shore. The waves don't dissolve the rock; they dig it out by grinding away at it year after year with pebbles and fine sand.

WHAT IS SATIRE?

When certain things in society—the way people live and act, their attitudes and ideas—are criticized in a literary form, that is satire. It may be a poem, a book, a play, a film, a joke.

For example, the American humorist Ambrose Bierce wrote many lines that scoffed at things. Examples: "A bird in the hand is worth what it will bring." "Think twice before you speak to a friend in need."

Aesop, who wrote the famous ancient fables, and James Thurber, who wrote *Fables for Our Time*, both gave human stupidities and vices to birds and foxes and other animals. This kind of wit that ridicules man's vices and follies is called satire. Satirists are usually more cynical, or distrustful of human behavior, than other writers.

Perhaps the two greatest satires in all literature are Voltaire's *Candide* and Jonathan Swift's *Gulliver's Travels.* The first makes fun of the idea that "All is for the best in this best of all possible worlds." The second attacks man's vices in general. The satire is hidden beneath Gulliver's adventures and humorous incidents.

Another classic satire is Miguel de Cervantes' *Don Quixote.* Don Quixote is an idealistic knight. He and Sancho Panza, his squire, try to correct the injustices of the world. But they "tilt against windmills"—that is, they fight senseless battles. Many dramatists, especially of the 17th century, wrote plays that were satires. One of the greatest of these was Molière.

WHY DOES CORN HAVE SILK?

The silk on a corn plant is needed by the plant to produce seeds. Here is how it works:

The corn plant has a woody stalk that grows from 6 to 20 feet high. At the top there is a spiked tassel. This part grows the male flowers of the plant. Farther down, the stalk grows one or more spikes which develop into ears. The spikes have threadlike filaments (silk). These are the female flowers.

Each filament grows from a germ on the spike called an ovule. The ovules are arranged in rows along the spikes. Each one will produce a seed, called a kernel, if the filament of silk is fertilized by a grain of pollen. To catch pollen, the tender tips of silk stick out from the top of the leafy wrapping around the spike.

When the flower parts develop, the tassles produce yellowish dustlike grains of pollen. Each grain of pollen contains two sperms. Summer breezes shake the pollen-laden tassles and the pollen grains are jarred loose. The wind carries them to the silk of nearby plants.

Tiny receivers, called stigmas, at the ends of the silk, catch the pollen. The pollen grains quickly send tubes growing down through the silks to the ovules. Then the sperm cells pass down the tubes and fertilize the ovules.

The spike now grows into a large, pithy structure called a cob, while the ovules grow and ripen into seeds (kernels). The growing seeds are made up of a soft yellow hull filled with a milky liquid. When field corn is ripe, the kernel is hard, firm, and starchy.

WHAT IS MAGMA?

Inside the earth it is very hot. This great heat melts some rock material that is there and makes it liquid rock. Liquid rock lies in huge underground pockets. This liquid underground rock is called magma.

Magma is lighter in weight than the colder, hard rocks around it. So it is slowly pushed upward by the pressure of the rock around it. In many places the magma never does reach the surface but slowly cools and hardens underground.

It takes many thousands of years for magma to harden into rock. In other places the cold, hard rocks near the surface cannot withstand the pressure of the magma beneath them. They crack a little bit and the magma rises up along the cracks.

Magma often remains hot enough to stay in liquid form until it reaches the surface of the earth. It then flows through the cracks and spreads out on the ground. Magma that reaches the surface of the earth is called lava.

Magma usually starts cooling while it is still being pushed upward. As the magma slowly rises, certain minerals in it grow into big crystals sooner than the other minerals do. The crystals float in the magma. When this magma reaches the surface of the earth, the liquid rock turns to a solid in a short time. The big crystals carried in the liquid are "frozen" into the fine-grained lava rock. The whole rock is then made of many large crystals embedded in a very fine-grained rock, such as basalt. Such a rock is called porphyry. It is very attractive when polished and is often used as a building stone.

HOW FAST DOES THE EARTH MOVE?

The earth, as most people know today, has two motions. It spins around on its axis, and it moves in an orbit around the sun.

The first motion of the earth that was discovered by man was its rotation about an axis. This rotation causes the apparent rising and setting of the sun, moon, and stars, and the changes of day and night. The period of rotation through 360 degrees (one complete turn of the earth) takes 23 hours, 56 minutes, and 4.091 seconds.

It was believed that the rate of the rotation of the earth never changed, or was constant within a thousandth of a second over centuries of time. But there are tiny variations. And because of the friction of ocean tides and changes in the earth's crust, our day may be getting longer at the rate of about one-thousandth of a second per century. (Scientists are interested in such tiny details and measure them.)

The earth also moves around the sun. At some points in its orbit it is closer to the sun than at other points. When it is nearest the sun it is at "perihelion"; when it is farthest away, it is at "aphelion." The earth, and all planets, move in their orbit at a speed that depends on the distance from the sun. A planet moves faster when it is closer to the sun than when it is farther away. So it moves fastest at perihelion and slowest at aphelion. Since the earth's distance from the sun does not stay the same at all times, the orbital speed is constantly changing.

At perihelion the earth moves in its orbit at a speed of 18.8 miles per second. At aphelion it travels at the rate of 18.2 miles per second.

HOW WERE STARS FORMED?

First, what are stars? A star is a huge ball of bright, hot gases. Stars contain a great deal of hydrogen, which is their main source of energy. Stars also contain many different chemical elements, such as helium, nitrogen, oxygen, iron, nickel, and zinc. All the elements in a star are in a gaseous state.

Stars come into existence in the vast clouds of dust and gas that move through space. A star begins to form when a large number of gas particles whirl together within such a cloud. The whirling particles attract more particles, and as the group of particles slowly gets larger and larger, its gravitational pull gets stronger. The particles form a giant ball of gas.

As the ball grows larger, the particles press down on those below them and pressure builds up inside the ball. Finally the pressure becomes strong enough to raise the temperature of the gases, and the gases begin to glow. When the pressure and temperature inside the ball get very high, nuclear reactions begin to take place. The gases have become a star. How long does all this take? Probably a few million years.

If a large amount of matter comes together in forming a star, the star will be large, bright, and hot. Because it is hot, the star will burn up its nuclear fuel in about 100,000,000 years. If a much smaller amount of matter comes together in forming a star, the star will be small, dim, and cool. It will burn up its fuel slowly and may shine for thousands of millions of years.

Our sun is a star, and it is about an average-size star. It is 1,300,000 times larger than the earth.

WHY IS BREAD SO IMPORTANT?

Bread in some form is eaten practically everywhere in the world. It has been called the staff of life. In many countries, bread furnishes 50 per cent or more of the daily intake of calories for large segments of the population.

Where there are a great many people with low incomes, bread, which is one of the most economical foods, is an important part of the diet. In the United States, which has a higher level of income than most countries, large quantities of more expensive foods are eaten. Only about 14 per cent of the calories in the average diet are furnished by bread.

But even this quantity of bread furnishes the following percentages of the nutrients that are considered necessary: 20 per cent of the protein; 26 per cent of the thiamine; 24 per cent of the niacin; 14 per cent of the riboflavin; 34 per cent of the iron; and 17 per cent of the calcium. So you can see why bread is important.

Because white bread is eaten by most people, and because people of low income eat such great quantities of it, it was realized that this was a good way to provide the population with extra amounts of nutrients that might otherwise be missing from their diet. So the baking industry was asked to "enrich" white bread, that is, add the extra nutrients to the bread.

Later on, laws were passed by many states requiring the enrichment of white flour, bread, and rolls. This has helped eliminate nutrition deficiencies in large groups of the population. Bakers in several other countries have followed the lead of the United States, and are enriching their bread.

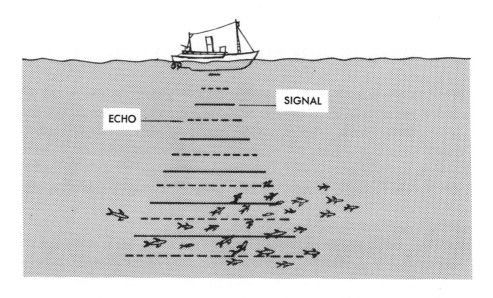

CAN SOUND TRAVEL THROUGH WATER?

All sounds are produced by very fast, back-and-forth motions called vibrations. Vibrations are the source of all sounds.

Sound travels from a vibrating object to your ear by means of a medium, or sound carrier. The medium may be a solid, a liquid, or a gas.

Sound travels from a vibrating object to your ear by means of compression waves in the air. The vibrating object pushes against the tiny particles of air next to it and the particles are compressed, or squeezed, together. As it moves back, it leaves a space with fewer particles in it. The thinned-out air is called an expansion. Sound waves are made up of such compressions and expansions of air.

Not only does sound travel through water in this way, but it travels about four times as fast in water as it does in air. Sound travels through air at a speed of about 1,100 feet a second. Sound travels in sea water at about 4,800 feet a second.

The fact that sound travels through water is very useful to man. Ships and submarines are equipped with sonic devices for finding depth or for discovering the direction and distance of other vessels or of rocks.

By sending out a sudden pulse of sound from an underwater loudspeaker and finding the time it takes for the sound to return as an echo from the bottom of the sea, one can know the depth of the water beneath a vessel.

By sending out sound pulses horizontally and listening for echoes, one can detect other vessels or submerged rocks. The direction in which they lie and the distance can also be determined.

130

WHY IS MONEY BACKED BY GOLD?

Money is not a metal coin or a piece of printed paper. These are only symbols. But they do represent something real.

Money is backed by large stores of precious metal that is held by the government that issues the money. The standard of measurement for the value of money that is widely used throughout the civilized world is gold and silver. They are scarce enough to retain their value, yet plentiful enough to meet the demands of the marketplace.

In other words, the paper and coins that a government issued as "money" was accepted as having a certain value because there were supplies of gold and silver backing up that money.

In 1821, Great Britain made monometalism (one metal) the basis of its monetary system. Gold was adopted as its official currency. By 1914 gold was the measuring stick for almost all the currencies of the world. By having one standard of value, countries were able to trade more easily with each other. Dollars from the United States, francs from France, and marks from Germany all had a set value in gold. This is known as the gold standard.

By 1933 most countries had gone off the gold standard. But many currencies, including that of the United States, are still based on a set price of gold. And gold is still very important in international trade. Governments buy and sell gold bars known as bullion. Part of the gold is used to pay off international debts, and part of it is stored. The stored gold is called a "reserve."

WHAT IS A STOCK?

Stocks and bonds are certificates that business companies sell to the public to raise money. To start a new company, or to buy new equipment for an existing company, usually requires a very large amount of money. To raise the money, the company sells thousands, sometimes millions, of shares of stock.

When a person buys stock in a company, he becomes one of the company's owners. As an owner, a shareholder hopes to receive a dividend, or a share in the company's profits. The amount of the dividend may change from year to year, depending on the kind of business the company has done during the year.

There are two types of stock: common stock and preferred stock. The owner of the common stock has the right to attend the yearly stockholders' meeting and vote for the directors of the company.

Preferred stock is so named because its owners have certain rights that owners of common stock do not have. When dividends are paid, first preference goes to the holders of preferred stocks. The dividends paid on preferred stocks have a set rate, while dividends on common stocks depend on how well the company is doing. If the company goes out of business, holders of preferred stock are paid off before the holders of common stock.

When a person buys stocks or bonds, he buys from another investor. When he sells, he sells to another investor. The marketplace for this selling and buying of stocks is the Stock Exchange.

Stocks are bought and sold through a broker. His business is to buy and sell stocks for investors. The price of stocks may go up or down for a variety of reasons relating to the company concerned, business conditions in general, and so on.

WHY DOES A CACTUS HAVE SPINES?

The cactus is a remarkable example of how, if plants and animals are to survive, they must be fitted for the climates and places in which they live.

Cacti are plants that live in hot, dry regions, so going without water for long periods is a problem. As the climate became drier, the roots of cacti gradually spread out, closer to the surface of the ground. That's why cacti can absorb water quickly from the earth when there is a rainfall.

The water has to be stored. This is done in the spongy or hollow stem of a cactus plant. What's more, the outer layer of the plant is thick and waxy, to prevent the escape of water.

Other plants have leaves which give off water in sunlight. Cactus plants have spines—and these prevent the loss of water. But the spines help save the life of the cactus in another way, too. Suppose there are thirsty animals roaming about in search of water. There is water in the cactus plant—but can you imagine any animal taking a bite at a cactus?

Except for their special structures that enable them to store water, cacti are regular flowering plants with blossoms that develop into seed-bearing fruits. In fact, the flowers of most cacti are very beautiful. When a desert is in full bloom, you can see bright yellow, red, and purple blooms springing from the polished stems of the cacti.

True cacti are native only to the Western Hemisphere. They grow mainly in the dry lands of South America, Central America, and the southwestern United States.

WHAT ARE GASES?

Matter can exist in a variety of forms. When the form resembles that of the air about us, it is a gas.

A gas is made up of tiny particles, which move about freely. They tend to spread out as widely as possible. So a sample of gas does not have any particular shape. If a gas is placed in a container, it spreads out and fills the entire container.

When a gas is inside a container, the moving particles strike the walls and bounce off. Trillions upon trillions of particles are constantly bouncing off all the walls. Each particle gives a little push as it does so. All these pushes make up the pressure of the gas.

If the container is made smaller—and has less volume—the gas particles are pushed closer together. The particles have less room to move about in. More of them hit the walls each second. So, as the volume goes down, the pressure goes up.

If a gas is heated, its particles move more quickly and the pressure increases. If the temperature is lowered, the particles move less rapidly. If the temperature is lowered enough, the attraction of the particles for each other causes them to come together and stay together. The gas is no longer a gas. It has liquefied and become a liquid.

There are many different gases. Air is the most common gas. It is actually a mixture of different gases, but mostly oxygen and nitrogen. Other common gases are ammonia, carbon dioxide (present in the air we breathe out), carbon monoxide (produced in automobile exhaust), helium, hydrogen, and methane.

WHAT WAS THE FAVORITE FOOD
OF THE INDIANS?

Most people refer to "the Indians" as if they were people who had one set of customs and way of life. But the Indians had many different tribes, who lived in different parts of North America, and had many different ways of life.

Some were hunters, some were gatherers, fishermen, and farmers. So naturally the food they ate varied quite a bit. We'll just consider a few.

In what is called the Bison Area (from Saskatchewan to Texas and from the central Missouri River to the Rocky Mountains), Indians hunted bison. Bison meat and fat, and berries were pounded into a pulp. The result was pemmican, the chief food of all the tribes in the Bison Area. It could be stored in rawhide bags for many months.

In the Caribou Area, Indians hunted caribou (their favorite food), as well as moose, elk, bear, beaver and porcupines. They also caught trout and whitefish in the lakes, as well as waterfowl.

There were many Algonkin tribes. In New England they were farmers; in other areas they were fishermen and hunters. In Algonkin country there were berries, fruits, roots, and nuts growing wild. In the summer they killed ducks, geese, herons, and cranes. Women and children gathered wild strawberries and blueberries, hazelnuts, wild apples, grapes, and roots.

Among some Indians the seeds of the mesquite tree was the chief food; among others it was wild rice they gathered. So we can see that there was no single type of food that the Indians ate. It depended on where they lived, and whether they were chiefly fishermen, farmers, or hunters.

HOW WERE THE GREAT LAKES FORMED?

The five Great Lakes together form the greatest connected area of fresh water on earth. In fact, one of them, Lake Superior, is bigger than any other fresh-water lake in the world. The only saltwater lake that is bigger is the Caspian Sea.

The basins of the Great Lakes were probably scooped out by glaciers during the Ice Age. As the glaciers pushed down from the north, the great moving weight of the ice made these valleys deeper and wider.

Then, when the ice melted, it left huge beds of sand, gravel, and rock where the rim of the glaciers had been. These beds blocked what used to be the outlets of the valleys.

At the same time, as the weight of the ice was removed, the land began to rise, beginning in the southwest. This caused the surface of the region to be tilted, so that water flowed from the southwest to northeast. By the time the ice had retreated, all the lakes were draining down this tilt into the St. Lawrence River and the Atlantic Ocean.

What keeps the Great Lakes filled with fresh water? Some streams do drain into them, but most of the rivers in the area flow away from the Great Lakes basin. The main source of supply for the lakes is the ground water that lies close to the surface of this whole region.

The lake beds are like basins that dip below the level of this ground water, and so they are kept filled by seepage and by the flow of many small springs. So the Great Lakes are really like huge drainage ponds or rain pools—and in this way have a constant supply of fresh water.

The combined area of the Great Lakes and their channels is 94.710 square miles.

IS ALL RICE WHITE?

Nearly half the population of the world lives partly or almost entirely on a rice diet. In some countries of Asia each person eats from two hundred to four hundred pounds of rice a year!

Threshed grains of rice are called rough rice. Rice in this state is still covered with coarse hulls. The hulls must be removed before the rice is cooked.

Rice with the hulls removed is called brown rice. Brown rice is covered with a brownish outer skin called the bran, in which most of the vitamins and minerals of the rice grain are stored.

However, brown rice does not keep as long as white rice. Also, most people prefer white, well-milled, polished rice to brown rice. When rice is milled, the bran and germ are removed by sending the kernels through a hulling machine that gently grinds the surface of each grain. When the milling is complete, the kernels are white and have a polished surface.

Converted rice is a slightly darker milled rice that has more B vitamins and minerals than ordinary polished rice. Before converted rice is milled, it is prepared by soaking it in water having a temperature just below the boiling point and then steaming it under pressure.

This process is called parboiling. Vitamins from the bran soak through into the middle of the grain when this is done.

Rice probably originated in southern India, where it has been grown for many thousands of years. From there it spread eastward into China more than five thousand years ago. Rice was not introduced to North America until the 17th century.

HOW IS A BANANA TREE GROWN?

The banana "tree" is actually not a real tree. This is because there is no wood in the stem rising above the ground. The stem is made up of leaves growing very close together, one inside the other. The leaves spread out at the top of the stem and rise in the air, making the plant look like a palm tree.

To grow bananas, pieces of rootstock (bits cut from the base of growing plants) are planted in holes about 1 foot deep and 11 to 18 feet apart. Each piece of rootstock must have one or more sprouts, or "eyes," like the eyes of a potato. Green shoots appear above the ground three or four weeks later. Only the strongest shoot is allowed to become a plant. This plant forms its own rootstock, from which other plants later grow up beside the first one.

Banana plants need a lot of care and attention. They must be provided with water by irrigation if the normal rainfall doesn't supply enough. The area around the plants must be kept free of weeds and grass.

About nine or ten months after planting, a flower appears on the banana plant. This flower is at the end of a long stalk, which grows from the base up through the center of the stem and turns downward when it emerges from the top. Small bananas form on this flower stalk as it grows downward. Bananas really grow upside down. As the small bananas form on the stalk, they point downward, but as they grow they turn and point upward.

Bananas are harvested while they are still green. Even when they are to be eaten where they are grown, they are not allowed to ripen on the plant. A banana that turns yellow on the plant loses its flavor.

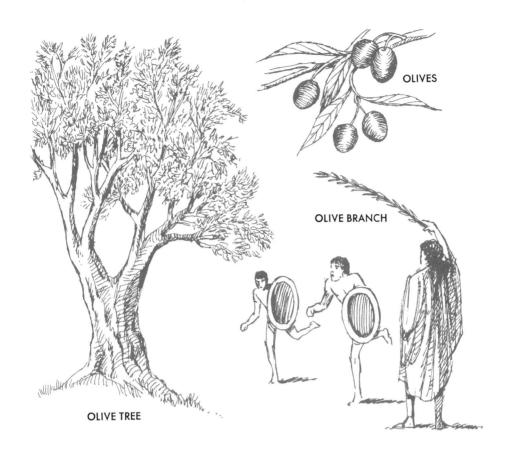

OLIVES

OLIVE BRANCH

OLIVE TREE

WHAT IS OLIVE OIL?

Olive oil comes from olives, which grow on the olive tree—which tree has one of the most interesting histories of any plant in the world!

The ancient Greeks had a legend that the olive tree was a gift to them from the goddess Athena, which was why they named the city of Athens after her. The boundaries of estates in Greece were marked by olive trees. The tree was to ancient Greeks a symbol of freedom, hope, mercy, prayer, purity, and order. A crown of olive leaves was the reward given to winners at the Olympic games in ancient Greece.

Olive oil has been obtained from the olive and used for many purposes since very ancient times. Before soap was discovered, wealthy Greeks and Romans had the custom of anointing the body with olive oil. In the Mediterranean countries it has been used as we use butter and other fats for cooking.

In ancient times the oil was extracted from olives by crushing the fruit with large stone rollers. After crushing, the mashed olives were put between cloth mats and squeezed.

Today the process has been refined and mechanized. Modern grinders crush the olives. Hydraulic presses squeeze out the oil. The oil is then carefully filtered to clarify it, that is, make it clear and pure. The oil is about 15 to 30 per cent of the total weight of a fresh, ripe olive.

At one time, in certain parts of the world, kings judged their wealth by the number of jars filled with olive oil in their storerooms.

DO THE OTHER PLANETS MOVE LIKE THE EARTH?

The earth moves in two ways. It travels around the sun in a fixed path called an orbit. The time it takes to do this is called a year. The earth also rotates on its axis. The time it takes to do this is called a day. The other planets also orbit the sun and also rotate, but at speeds different from the earth's.

The earth travels around the sun at an average distance of about 93,000,000 miles and takes slightly more than 365 days to make one orbit. It takes a little less than 24 hours to rotate once on its axis. Now let's consider the other planets. Mercury's average distance from the sun is about 36,000,000 miles and it takes 88 earth days to complete one trip around the sun. It is believed that Mercury rotates once every 58 or 59 days.

Venus, about 67,200,000 miles from the sun, takes about 225 days to make one trip around the sun. It is believed that Venus takes 243 days to rotate just once—and this planet rotates backward! In other words, on Venus you would find the planet turning from east to west.

Mars, an average distance of 141,600,000 miles from the sun, takes about 687 days for one orbit, but rotates nearly as fast as the earth. Jupiter, 483,300,000 miles from the sun, takes about 11.9 earth years to complete one orbit, but takes less than ten hours to rotate once. Saturn, 886,200,000 miles from the sun, takes nearly 29½ earth years for one orbit, but only about ten hours to turn once on its axis.

Uranus, 1,783,000,000 miles from the sun, completes an orbit in 84 years. And Neptune, 2,794,000,000 miles from the sun, takes almost 165 earth years to complete one orbit.

WHAT IS RADIO ASTRONOMY?

We are able to see the stars in the sky because they send out light which reaches us. Light is a form of radiation.

Besides light, stars send out other forms of radiation, and one of these is radio waves. Some of these waves can be detected by special radio receivers here on earth. The radio receivers collect and magnify the radio waves, just as ordinary telescopes collect and magnify the picture the light waves give. That's why these radio receivers are called radio telescopes, and their use to study the stars is called radio astronomy.

The length of radio waves from outer space is very short compared with the wavelengths used in radio broadcasting and television. So radio astronomers must build special radio sets and antennae to be able to receive them.

Radio telescopes consist of two parts—an antenna and a radio receiver. The antenna is often a huge metal dish, mounted so it can be pointed to any part of the sky. The radio waves collected by the antenna are often very weak, so the signals have to be amplified.

Usually radio astronomers make a record of the radio waves on paper. A pen recorder writes down the signals in the form of a wavy line on a strip of paper, so the astronomers have a permanent record of their observations.

Radio telescopes can operate in all kinds of weather, unlike ordinary telescopes. Radio telescopes can also be built almost any place that is convenient, and need be put on high ground or on mountains.

WHY DO WORDS HAVE CERTAIN MEANINGS?

Words are really "codes," or symbols that stand for something. They are produced by sounds that human beings make. When two or more human beings decide that a certain sound or set of sounds have the same meaning for them, they have a language.

So words have certain meanings only because certain groups of human beings have decided that they should have this meaning. When the sounds of D, O, and G are lined up, they produce the word "dog," English-speaking people agree that the word "dog" represents a particular animal. If one English-speaker says "dog," another English-speaker will automatically see the image of a "dog."

But what about a Russian? It will be meaningless to him. A Russian uses the word *sobaka* for the dog image. And an Italian uses the word *cane* when he means to indicate a dog.

Even the rules for using words are not the same in every language. It all depends on what has been agreed upon for that language. In English, if you want to speak about more than one dog, you add the letter "s" and get "dogs." In Italian you change the last letter of *cane* to "i" and get *cani*.

People learn the use and meanings of words of a certain language from childhood. As a baby, you began to imitate the sounds produced by your parents and other people around you. You connected the sounds, with certain objects, actions, or ideas. You learned to string your words along in a certain way and to make changes in them when necessary for their meaning. You learned a language.

WHERE DO GRASS SEEDS COME FROM?

The grasses make up the most widespread plant family in the world. There are about 7,000 different kinds. Great "seas" of grass cover natural fields, sometimes for thousands of square miles. These are called prairies, or plains, or ranges. The pampas of South America, the Russian steppes, the South African veld, are all "seas" of grass.

Most grasses reproduce by means of seeds. The seeds are scattered in many ways. Some grass seeds are covered with long hairs, and they are carried by the wind. Others are blown along the ground. Birds spread seeds by picking up the seeds in their beaks for food. As they fly away, they may drop some of them.

Some grass seeds have sharp spines. These seeds are spread by animals or by people who pass by the plant and carry away the seeds that stick to their fur or clothing.

Many kinds of grass seeds have been carried, sometimes by accident, along trade routes to distant parts of the world. For instance, ships brought seeds of molasses grass to the New World from Africa. The stalks of the plant were used as bedding for slaves. When the bedding was thrown away on the ground, the seeds took root. In this way the grass spread from Africa to North America.

Some of the grasses live for a season and then die. They must be planted again each year. Other grasses come up each year. The roots of pasture grasses, and the grasses you see growing on lawns, live through the winter. New blades come up in the spring. Such grasses are called perennial grasses.

WHO CARVED THE FACES
ON MOUNT RUSHMORE?

In the Black Hills of South Dakota, about 25 miles southwest of Rapid City, is one of the most impressive sights to be seen anywhere. It is Mount Rushmore National Memorial.

It honors four American presidents: George Washington, Thomas Jefferson, Abraham Lincoln, and Theodore Roosevelt. Giant likenesses of the four are sculptured into the granite of Mount Rushmore, which is 5,725 feet high. Each face is about 60 feet from chin to forehead, which, by the way, is twice as high as the great Sphinx.

The work was designed by the American sculptor Gutzon Borglum. Borglum was a man who was interested in producing American art, art that related to this country and its history. Well-known works done by him include the colossal head of Lincoln in Washington, D.C., the statue of General Sheridan, and the figures of the twelve apostles for the Cathedral of St. John the Divine, New York City.

Borglum began his work on Mount Rushmore in August, 1927. The first figure, that of Washington, was dedicated on July 4, 1930. After Borglum died on March 6, 1941, work on the memorial continued until October under the direction of his son, Lincoln. But the last sculpture, of Roosevelt, was never quite completed.

Fourteen years passed between the beginning of the project and its termination. But only about six and one-half of these were spent in actual work. The lapses of time without any work being done were due to bad weather and a lack of funds.

The total cost was just under $1 million. The federal government gave 84 percent of this; the rest came from private donations.

HOW DID THE CAVE MEN
MAKE THEIR TOOLS?

According to scientists, Peking man, a type of man living about 300,000 years ago, was the first cave dweller. Early man lived mainly by hunting.

Each man was his own toolmaker. With a hammerstone he broke large pebbles until they were a proper size for grasping. The resulting tool was a crude chopper, with one end slightly sharpened to make a rough cutting edge. Choppers could be used for digging, scraping, hacking, or cutting.

Other common early tools were crude hand axes. One end formed a heavy butt for grasping. The other end was chipped on both sides to a rounded or pointed tip. Hand axes were probably all-purpose tools, useful for digging up roots, cracking nuts, or cutting up dead animals.

Neanderthal man, who lived from about 150,000 to 30,000 years ago, was a real cave dweller. In addition to hand axes, Neanderthal man had flake tools. These were skillfully made of broad thin flakes of flint having a good sharp edge. Some of the flake tools were points in the shape of rough triangles. They probably served as knives for skinning and cutting up game animals. Other flake tools were side-scrapers having one curved edge.

During the next period, called the Upper Paleolithic (about 50,000 to 10,000 years ago), blade tools appeared. These were long, sharp flakes struck from specially prepared cores of flint. The blades were shaped into scrapers, chisel-like burins, and drills. Other tools were designed to do one particular job—for example, bone needles with eyes were used in sewing animals skins together.

WHEN DID PLANTS APPEAR ON EARTH?

Scientists believe that when life first began on earth more than two billion years ago, the only plant life was in the sea. The land was bare and lifeless.

Then, about 425,000,000 years ago, a few small green plants appeared on land. They probably developed from certain kinds of green sea weeds (algae). The first land plants looked very much like the mosses, liverworts, and hornworts you can see growing in damp, shady places.

About 400,000,000 years ago more complicated plants existed. These resembled modern ferns, horsetails, and club mosses. Ferns were the first plants to have roots, stems, and leaves.

By the time the first dinosaurs walked the earth, vast forests of seed ferns, ginkgoes, cycads, and cordaitales stretched across the land. These were the first trees to reproduce by means of seeds.

Pines and other conifers (cone-bearing trees) developed somewhat later, 300,000,000 years ago. This group includes many familiar trees, such as pines, firs, spruces, cedars, hemlocks, and redwoods. All of these trees bear their seeds on cones.

The first flowering plants developed about 150,000,000 years ago. Their well-protected seeds gave them a great advantage over plants with more exposed seeds, and they increased in numbers and kinds. Today flowering plants are found almost everywhere.

ARE MEXICANS OF SPANISH ORIGIN?

Three major groups make up Mexico's population. Between 20 and 25 percent are Indians, descendants of the country's original inhabitants. About 10 percent are of Spanish or other foreign descent. The remaining 65 or 70 percent are mestizo, people of mixed Indian and Spanish blood.

Who were the first inhabitants of Mexico? Anthropologists say they were mostly of Asiatic origin. It is believed that they came to Mexico, as they came to North America, by way of the Bering Strait. This may have happened anywhere from 10,000 to 25,000 years ago.

There were many great Indian empires in Mexico more than a thousand years before Hernando Cortés landed there. First, there were the Olmec, then the Maya, followed by the Toltec, Zapotec, Mixtec, and Maya once again. At the time of the Spanish conquest, the Aztecs, ruled by Montezuma, were the most powerful of Mexico's Indians.

From 1522 to 1821, Mexico, called New Spain, was a Spanish colony. At the beginning of the 19th century the blending of Spanish and Indian civilization began that make up the pattern of Mexican life today.

But during the time of Spanish control the ruling group was a minority, made up of Spaniards born in Spain. Next came the Spaniards born in Mexico. After them, in power, were the mestizos, persons of mixed Indian and Spanish descent, who held no government positions at all. The largest group were the Indians, who lived under conditions of virtual slavery. One can see why a movement began to gain independence for Mexico and to win rights and equality for its people.

WHY WASN'T AMERICA NAMED
AFTER COLUMBUS?

There are two things involved in this: one is why America wasn't named after Columbus, and the other is why it was named after someone else.

Columbus, as you know, set out to find a westward route to Asia. And he thought that he had done so. But actually, he had only discovered San Salvador, Cuba, and Hispaniola. This is not to take anything away from the importance of his discoveries and his great courage—but it created certain problems.

Since he had not found the riches of India, doubts began to arise about his voyages. The rulers of Spain and Portugal began to ask just what lands Columbus had found. There was also a question as to which of those lands belonged to Spain and which to Portugal.

A man called Amerigo Vespucci was sent to find out. In his letters Vespucci described two voyages he had made along the coast of what is now known as South America. In his description of the land he said "which we observed to be a continent."

In other words, Amerigo Vespucci knew this land was not part of Asia and was a new continent. In 1507, a geographer called Martin Waldseemuller issued a map showing the new continent. Along with it was a pamphlet in which he proposed naming it "after its discoverer, Americus, and let it be named America."

The public instantly adopted the name, and liked it so well that it was used for North America as well. Waldseemuller, we must remember, proposed the name "America" after Amerigo Vespucci only because he felt Vespucci had proven that a new continent existed.

HOW FAR AWAY ARE THE STARS?

There are stars in the universe so far away from us that we have no way of knowing the distance, or how many of them there are. But how far away from the earth is the nearest star?

The distance from the sun to the earth is about 93,000,000 miles. Since light travels at the rate of 186,000 miles a second, it takes eight minutes for light from the sun to reach us.

The nearest stars to the earth are Proxima Centauri and Alpha Centauri. Their distance from the earth is 270,000 times greater than the distance from the sun to the earth. So their distance from us is 270,000 times 93,000,000 miles! It takes their light four and half years to reach the earth.

Distances to the stars are so great that a unit for measuring this distance was worked out. It is called the light-year, and it is the distance that light travels in one year. This is about six million million miles (6,000,000,000,000). Four and a half times that amount is the distance to the nearest stars.

Of all the stars in the sky, only about 6,000 can be seen without a telescope. One-fourth of these stars are too far south to be visible in North America.

Actually, at any one time, looking up and counting the stars, the most one would be able to count would be a little over one thousand stars. Yet with a powerful telescope it would be possible to photograph more than one *billion*!

WHO DISCOVERED ATOMS?

The idea of the atom as the smallest possible particle of any substance goes back to the ancient Greeks. Today we know the atom is not the smallest particle—there are other particles within the atom itself. And we also know that we still don't know a great deal about the atom.

The first man to develop a scientific atomic theory was John Dalton, an English chemist who lived at the beginning of the 19th century. He found that gases, as well as solids and liquids, were made up of unbelievably tiny particles which he (like the ancient Greeks) called atoms. He figured out relative weights for the atoms of those elements with which he was familiar.

At the end of the 19th century, Ernest Rutherford developed the idea of a "solar-system" atom. In an atom there was supposed to be a center, a heavy nucleus carrying a positive charge of electricity, which was surrounded by negatively charged electrons. The electrons traveled around the nucleus like planets around the sun.

Later on, Niels Bohr developed a new theory about the atom. He showed that the electrons could revolve only in certain orbits or energy levels. When electrons moved from one level to another they gave off energy.

But what man knows about the structure of the atom is constantly changing as new experiments give us new information.

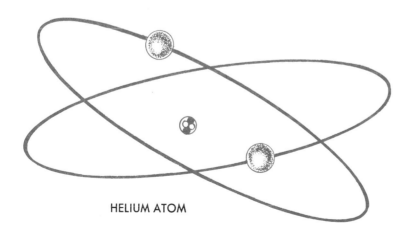

HELIUM ATOM

WHY IS THERE NO LIFE ON THE MOON?

Now that man has actually explored the surface of the moon, he has learned many new things about it. But one thing man knew before he ever reached the moon was that there was no life on it.

There is no atmosphere on the moon. Astronomers knew this because there is no twilight on the moon. On earth darkness comes gradually because the air reflects the sun's light even after the sun sets. On the moon, one moment there is sunlight, the next moment night has arrived.

The lack of air means that the moon is not protected from any of the sun's rays. The sun sends out heat and light radiation. Life on earth depends on heat and light.

But the sun also sends out dangerous kinds of radiation. The earth's atmosphere protects us from most of them. On the moon, however, there is no atmosphere to stop the radiations. All the sun's rays beat down on the surface of the moon.

Because there is no atmosphere, the moon's surface is either extremely hot or extremely cold. As the moon rotates, the side of it that is lighted up by the sun becomes very hot. The temperature there reaches more than 300 degrees Fahrenheit. This is hotter than boiling water. The hot lunar day lasts two weeks.

It is followed by a night that is also two weeks long. At night the temperature drops to 260 degrees below zero. This is more than twice as cold as temperatures reached at the earth's South Pole.

Under these conditions, no form of life that we know of here on earth could exist on the moon.

WHAT IS THE HIGHEST MOUNTAIN IN THE WORLD?

First, what is a mountain? A mountain is a part of the earth's surface that stands high above its surroundings. Mountains differ greatly in size and ruggedness. Some are huge, steep masses several miles high. Others are low and gentle. A mountain rises at least 1,000 feet above the surrounding land.

Some mountains are isolated peaks. But more often they are grouped together in a mountain range. Some mountain ranges have hundreds or even thousands of peaks.

Mountains rise not only from land areas but also from the bottom of the sea. In fact, the deep ocean basins hold some of the mightiest mountains on earth. If we would consider the total height of a mountain to include what is below the sea and what is above the sea, the tallest mountain of all would be Mauna Kea on the island of Hawaii. It is 13,796 feet above sea level and 16,000 feet or so below the sea. So its total height of about 30,000 to 32,000 feet would make it the tallest in the world.

The highest mountain above ground is Mount Everest, on the Nepal-China border. It is 29,028 feet high. The second highest is K2 or Mount Godwin Austen in Kashmir. It is 28,250 feet high.

The highest mountain in North America is McKinley, 20,320 feet. The highest in Europe is Mount Elbrus, in the Soviet Union. It is 18,481 feet high. The highest in Africa is Kilimanjaro, 19,565 feet. The highest mountain in South America is Aconcagua, on the Argentine-Chile border, 22,835 feet high. The highest in Australia is Kosciusko, which is only 7,305 feet high.

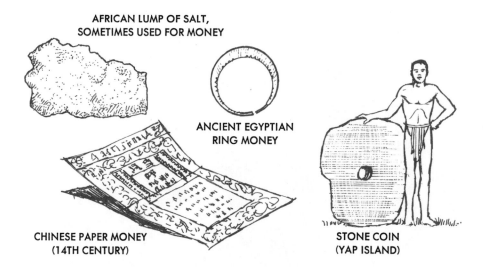

AFRICAN LUMP OF SALT,
SOMETIMES USED FOR MONEY

ANCIENT EGYPTIAN
RING MONEY

CHINESE PAPER MONEY
(14TH CENTURY)

STONE COIN
(YAP ISLAND)

WHY DON'T ALL NATIONS
HAVE A COMMON MONEY?

To begin with, money is very difficult to define. A London banker and the chief of a remote African tribe have widely different ideas of what money is.

Money is not a metal coin or a piece of printed paper. It is not a nickel or dollar bill, a French franc, an Italian lira, a Spanish peseta, or a Russian ruble. Why? Because, while these things are used as money, so is a pile of stones on a certain Pacific island.

In other words, all of these things are only symbols. They represent something real. The simplest way to define money is to say that it is a convenient means of exchange and a measure of the value of goods and labor. When a person wants something, he can exchange his form of money for the desired object. He can also exchange his services for money.

Down through history, money has gone through many changes. Cattle was an early form of money. Grain and salt later came into use as money. In early societies around the world, different objects and products were used as money. Later on, coins came to be used, and then—about three hundred years ago—paper money came into general use.

As these more modern forms of money developed, local governments began to control the form of money and its value. Each country had its own form of money—and this is still true today. We simply haven't reached the stage of civilization in the world where all the people, wherever they live, use the same money.

WHAT IS WITCHCRAFT?

At one time a great many people believed in witches and in witchcraft. A witch was a person of great power and authority, whose goal was to do harm, and who worked with the help of the devil. The mischief that such a person was able to commit was witchcraft.

Witchcraft could be directed against a personal enemy, or even against a community. Even hurricanes and epidemics were thought to be the result of witchcraft. Because people then lived in fear, ignorance, and superstition, witchcraft was an easy way of explaining unforeseen disasters.

Early societies and religions forbade witchcraft on pain of death. The Old Testament says: "Thou shalt not suffer a witch to live." In later times, the Christian churches fought against witchcraft. In 1484, the Pope issued a papal bull formally condemning witchcraft. One reason was that the plagues in Europe were being blamed on witchcraft.

Witch hunts took place in the American colonies. Between 1647 and 1663 hundreds of people in Massachusetts and Connecticut were accused of witchcraft, and 14 were hanged. But with the beginning of the 18th century, belief in witches faded. For the first time people began to understand the real causes of the things they had feared—drought, thunder and lightning, mental and physical illness.

Today, doctors believe that the dreams and visions once thought to be the results of witchcraft, were really the products of hysteria or mental illness.

HOW DO MUSHROOMS GROW?

Mushrooms are remarkable plants. They have no roots, no stems, and no leaves. They grow so fast that you almost feel you can see them grow. They are fungi, which means they have no chlorophyll to manufacture their own food. And some of them are delicious to eat while others are so poisonous that it is almost certain death to eat them.

The part of the mushroom plant that rises above the ground is only the fruiting part of the fungus. The rest of the plant lies under the ground in the form of a mass of dense white tangled threads. These threads are called the mycelium or spawn.

The mycelium threads grow from little spores, which are tiny dustlike particles shed from the full-grown mushroom. On these threads small whitish knobs of tissue bud out, and they push upward, expand, and finally break out in an umbrella shape or in the form which is characteristic of each kind of mushroom.

On most mushrooms, underneath the umbrella, there are little radiating gills, set very close together. It is on these gills that the tiny spores are developed. The spores then drop out and are carried away by the wind. When the spores fall on surfaces favorable for growth, they develop into new plants.

Most mushrooms grow in moist shady woodlands, or in the bottoms of ravines where there is a lot of shade and plenty of warmth and dampness. The common field mushroom and a few other types are different. They grow best in open grassy meadows where they are fully exposed to the sun. But since mushrooms consist chiefly of water, most of them cannot live where there are dry hot winds or the hot summer sun.

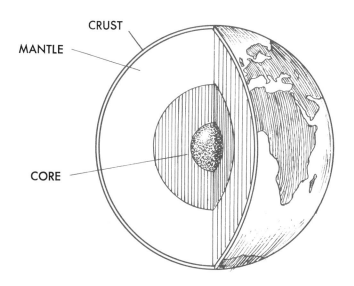

CRUST

MANTLE

CORE

WHY IS THE CENTER
OF THE EARTH HOT?

The earth is made up of three main layers—the crust, the mantle, and the core. The topmost layer is the crust. It is made of solid rock, and under the continents it is about 20 to 30 miles thick.

The next layer, the mantle, goes down to a depth of about 1,800 miles. It is also made of solid rock. The innermost part of the earth is the core, which is about 2,100 miles in radius. Because of the great heat, the material of the core is liquid. Some scientists have suggested that there is an inner core of solid metal about 1,600 miles in diameter.

One theory about the origin of the earth is that it was originally a swirling eddy of gas and dust. Some of the gas flowed away into space. The dust collected together because of gravity and became the solid earth.

Trapped in the solid dust were radioactive elements. A radioactive element continuously breaks down, producing heat. The radioactive heat gradually raised the temperature of the earth. Eventually the dust inside the earth began to melt.

The molten material came to the surface and lost heat to the surrounding space. The surface then solidified to make the beginnings of the earth's crust.

About three billion years ago the crust was already well developed. But beneath this crust the earth remained very hot. The heat produced by radioactive elements never escaped.

WHY DID INDIANS TAKE SCALPS?

Most of us think that only the Indians took scalps, and that the white man would have nothing to do with this practice. But there are some interesting facts concerning scalping.

Scalping means partly cutting and partly tearing off the skin of the head, with the hair attached. The victim could be living or dead. Scalping goes back to very ancient times. It was done by savage and barbarous peoples of Asia and Europe long before it was done by the American Indians.

And among the Indians it was not done by many tribes. For example, the Indians in the Canadian Northwest and along the whole Pacific Coast never practiced scalping.

A scalp was regarded, by those who did this, as a trophy of victory. It was a sign that the scalper had courage and skill in fighting. Among some tribes the scalps were used in religious ceremonies.

When the American colonies were fighting the Indians, many of the colonies offered rewards of money for Indian scalps. In 1724, Massachusetts offered about $500 for each Indian scalp. In 1755, the same colony offered about $200 for the scalps of male Indians over 12 years of age, and about $100 for the scalps of women and children. So this is something in our history not to be proud of.

Because of this official encouragement to scalping, many Indian tribes that had never practiced it began to do it. To them it had no importance at all in their ceremonies.

WHO OWNS THE STATUE OF LIBERTY?

The Statue of Liberty in New York harbor is the property of the United States government. It became a national monument in 1924. It is maintained by the National Park Service of the U. S. Department of the Interior.

But the strange thing is that this statue, of which we are all so proud and which symbolizes the freedom we cherish, has a history of money problems associated with it.

The idea of the statue was suggested in 1865 by a French historian, Edouard de Laboulaye. It was to be a gift from the French people as a memorial to American independence and as a symbol of friendship between the two countries.

To raise money for the statue, the Franco-American Union was formed in 1875. By 1882, Frenchmen had contributed $250,000 for the statue. The statue was built in France in sections and in 1885 it was shipped in 214 cases to the United States.

An American fund-raising committee was formed so that the pedestal for the statue could be built. But work on the pedestal had to stop in 1884 because enough money hadn't been raised. Two months after the statue arrived in New York, the required amount of money, $250,000, was finally raised and the work was completed. The statue was dedicated by President Grover Cleveland on October 28, 1886.

The Statue of Liberty, which is on an island now called Liberty Island in New York harbor, is reached by ferry from Manhattan. About 800,000 people come to see it every year.

WHAT ARE ANTIQUES?

It is very hard to define an antique. Antiques are usually old objects made by skilled craftsmen. The nearest thing we have to the definition of an antique is based on certain government regulations.

Most governments allow antiques to be imported into the country without payment of import duties. But to qualify as an antique, the object must have been made a certain number of years ago. In the United States, it's before 1830. In Canada, before 1847. In Britain, the object must be 100 years old. In most countries, the object must be 60 years old to be considered an antique.

Of course, people can call any old object an antique. And there is no limit to the type of object. Furniture is one of the most common antique items, and certain pieces of furniture made in the 18th century bring very high prices.

Old glass objects, such as flasks, tumblers, goblets, vases, and pitchers, are also valuable antiques. Pottery of all kinds, from porcelain to stoneware, is a favorite of antique collectors.

Objects made of silver, such as spoons, cups, tankards, and mugs, are a familiar kind of antique. Early ironwork made by hand, such as latches and hinges for doors, andirons for fireplaces, pots and pans for cooking, are valued as antiques.

Many objects that were made of pewter, such as plates and tea and coffee pots, are collected by antique lovers. So are old objects made of brass, copper, and tinware.

People who collect antiques sometimes don't even care if they are rare or beautiful. They like them because they give a picture of the people and customs of other times.

WHAT IS ETYMOLOGY?

The word "etymology," comes from the Greek words *etymon* ("true") and *logos* ("word"). So etymology is concerned with the first, true meanings of words. Etymologists study words to uncover the changes that have occurred in them.

There is a wide variety of ways in which the words we use originated and developed. Greek and Latin supplied most of the words used in English today. For example, from the Latin word *manus* ("hand") we got the words manufacture, manicure, emancipate, and manipulate.

A Greek word, *graphein* ("to write"), gave us telegraph, "to write far away"; phonograph, "writing sound"; geography, "writing about the earth," and so on.

Latin and Greek prefixes gave us many words. Anti ("against") is used to make antiknock, antiseptic, etc. Astro ("star") gave us astronaut. There are over one hundred common prefixes that were used in creating words.

English includes words borrowed from many other languages of the world. From the Vikings we got: leg, gate, freckle, seat, dirt, bull, birth, ugly, and many other words. The Normans introduced such words as prayer, ministry, parliament, poverty.

Later, as explorers ranged throughout the world, English obtained words from everywhere. From India we got bungalow, punch, faker, and coolies. From the Dutch came freight, schooner, scour, and landscape. From Spain and Latin America came armada, potato, cargo, tobacco, and hurricane.

It is impossible in a short article to give even an idea of all the sources of words that today make up the English language. An etymologist, who makes this his study, has certainly a big and interesting field of work!

HOW DO TREES GROW?

A tree has three main parts. The roots anchor it in the ground and absorb water and minerals from the soil. The trunk and branches carry sap and lift the leaves into the sunlight. The leaves are the food factories of the tree.

A tree grows higher and wider by lengthening its twigs and branches at the tips. At the ends of the twigs, the terminal buds are continually adding new cells. Meanwhile, the branches, twigs, and trunk grow thicker.

Most trees have a section called the cambium, which is a layer of cells where growth in diameter occurs. Every year the layer of cambium between the sapwood and the inner bark adds a layer of new cells to the older wood. Each layer forms a ring—and by counting the rings one can tell the age of a tree.

Water and dissolved minerals travel up from the roots to the leaves in the new layers of wood inside the cambium. This part of the trunk is called the sapwood. Other sap carries plant food down from the leaves through a layer inside the bark.

As the tree grows, the older sapwood stiffens and loses connection with the leaves. Then it just stores water, and finally it becomes solid heartwood.

While the cambium makes the tree trunk and its branches grow in size, the leaves produce the food which builds the tissues of the tree. Using the energy from sunlight, the green coloring matter in the leaves (chlorophyll) takes carbon dioxide out of the air. It combines the carbon dioxide with water and dissolved minerals from the roots to form sugars and starches.

WHY DO PEOPLE KILL WHALES?

The killing of whales as an industry goes back quite a long time. The Basques were doing it in the Bay of Biscay as early as the 11th century. Whaling was being carried on in North America in the 17th century.

The chief reason for killing whales was to obtain whale oil. This was the oil from the large baleen whale, and the blue, fin, humpback, and sei whales. The oil obtained from sperm whales is called sperm oil.

Until the middle of the 19th century, whale and sperm oil was used for nearly every purpose where oil is required. It was used for lighting, for lubrication, steel tempering, leather finishing, and many other processes. Whale oil has been used a great deal in the soapmaking industry and in the manufacture of margarine. Sperm oil is now used for a variety of purposes in the chemical industry.

The oil yield is highest from whales taken in Antarctic and Arctic waters in the spring and summer, when the whales are feeding heavily. A blue whale provides about 120 barrels of oil, and a sperm whale about 50 barrels.

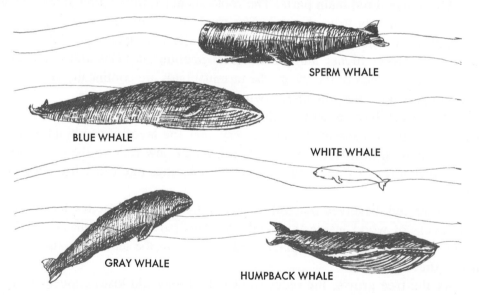

SPERM WHALE

BLUE WHALE

WHITE WHALE

GRAY WHALE

HUMPBACK WHALE

As a result of this hunting of whales, certain ones—the blue whales, white whales, and gray whales—are almost extinct. An International Whaling Commission was established in 1946 to control the number of whales taken. But it wasn't very effective. The blue and humpback whales became more rare, and the fin whale became scarce, too.

More efforts are being made now to protect whales from becoming extinct.

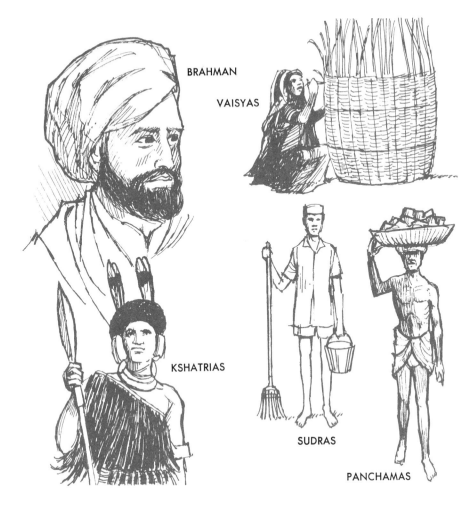

BRAHMAN

VAISYAS

KSHATRIAS

SUDRAS

PANCHAMAS

WHAT IS THE CASTE SYSTEM?

In India there is a system that divides people into different social classes, or castes. The particular caste a person belongs to is the one he is born into.

The major castes, starting from the top, are: the Brahmans, the priestly caste; the Kshatriyas, the warriors and earthly rulers; the Vaisyas, the merchants and artisans; the Sudras, the servants; and the Panchamas, or outcasts. The Panchamas really belong to no caste and are known as "untouchables."

An Indian born in a low-caste family cannot change his caste to a higher group by education or wealth. There are many rules about the kind of contact people of one caste can have with members of another caste. The caste system controls Indian society very strictly.

How did the caste system start? One theory is that when the Aryans came to India about 1500 B.C., they established it. The Aryans were tall, fair of skin, with thin noses and straight black hair. Their life was well organized into social groups, and the caste system enabled them to guard their standing as a ruling minority.

The new Indian constitution prohibits discrimination on account of caste. But the caste system continues to flourish—and it is believed probable that it will continue there for a long time.

The reason is that the caste system has existed in India for thousands of years, and it is also a kind of religious institution.

HOW ARE CALORIES MEASURED?

A calorie is a measurement of energy or heat. One calorie is the amount of heat it takes to raise the temperature of one gram of water one degree Centigrade.

What does this have to do with food? Well, we eat food to supply us with energy, and so energy in foods is measured in calories. When foods are metabolized—that is, utilized—by being combined with oxygen in the body cells, they give off calories (energy). In measuring the energy value of food, we use the "large" or kilogram calorie, which equals one thousand regular calories.

Each type of food, as it "burns up," furnishes a certain number of calories. For instance, one gram of protein furnishes four calories, but one gram of fat furnishes nine calories.

The amount of calories the body needs depends on the work the body is doing. A man who weighs about 150 pounds needs only 1,680 calories per day—if he does nothing at all. If he does a little work, he may need about 3,360 calories per day. And if he does heavy work, he may need as much as 6,720 calories a day to keep the body functioning properly.

There are other factors that decide how many calories a person needs, such as age, sex, size, physical condition, and even climate. Suppose you take in more calories than you need? The body uses up what it needs and stores some of it away for future use. The body can store away about one-third of the amount it needs each day. The rest becomes fat! And that's why it's important to "watch your calories."

WHAT HAPPENED TO THE ANCIENT AZTECS?

One of the most remarkable peoples of ancient America were the Aztecs. They lived in the valley which now contains Mexico City.

These American Indians developed a way of life that was the equal in many ways of European civilization. They built temples and towers and homes of solid masonry. They were skilled in astronomy and in law and government. They were expert in many arts and crafts. They were fond of music, dancing, plays, and literature.

That isn't all. They had botanical gardens, or nurseries, which the Europeans didn't have. They had a system of canals for irrigation. They had a textile industry. They had hospitals, doctors, surgeons as good as those in Europe. They had quite a wonderful civilization!

In 1519, a Spanish captain, Hernando Cortes, with a small army, attacked the Aztecs. After much hard fighting he was able to destroy the Aztec power.

The Spaniards then made Mexico into a part of the Spanish empire.

But even today there are many Indians living in Mexico who still speak the language of the Aztecs. Modern Mexico and Mexicans are proud of their Aztec ancestry. They have preserved much of the way of living, eating, and dressing that the Aztecs had before the Spanish conquest. Some of the Aztec words are still used not only in Mexico, but are part of the English language. They include chocolate, tomato, ocelot, coyote, avocado, among others.

So, while the power and the empire of the ancient Aztecs was destroyed more than four hundred years ago, their influence still lives on.

HOW IS COPPER OBTAINED?

Copper is one of our most common and most useful metals. It is found in nature in two forms—as "native copper" (the metal itself) and in mineral ores (combined with other elements). There are more than 160 known mineral ores that contain copper.

About half of the world's copper supply is found in a bright-yellow mineral called chalcopyrite. This ore is a compound of copper, iron, and sulfur. It contains 34.5 per cent copper. One of the richest copper ores is dark-gray chalcocite. It contains about 80 per cent copper.

The first step in refining copper ore is to crush it into a fine powder. The finely crushed ore is then washed in flotation tanks. The tanks are filled with water with a layer of some oily substance on top. Compressed air is blown in through the bottom of the tank.

The air and the oil form a thick froth on top of the water, and the metallic ore particles cling to the froth. The next step is to roast the ore to burn out the sulfur.

After the sulfur is removed, the remaining ore is melted and treated chemically to help separate the iron that the ore contains. Finally the ore is transferred to a converter where the air blown through the molten metal burns away most of the remaining impurities.

The metal emerges as blister copper, which is about 98 per cent pure. Blister copper must be refined still further before it can be used by industry. This is usually done electrically. The final product is about 99.9 per cent pure.

Copper was probably one of the first metals ever used by man because it could be found as a pure metal, not mixed with minerals.

DO ANY CANNIBALS EXIST TODAY?

Cannibalism, the eating of human flesh, is not a pleasant subject to discuss. But there is a great deal of curiosity about it, and it is part of the history of man, so it's a good idea to get the facts straight.

It is possible that the earliest humans fed on human flesh, as on any other. There is some evidence that cannibalism existed in central Europe in the late ice age, and possibly among the most ancient Egyptians.

At one time cannibalism was customary in most of Polynesia, in New Zealand, and in Fiji. It also occurred in Australia and New Guinea. Most of equatorial Africa had cannibalism at one time. It was also widespread in northern South America and the West Indies.

But cannibalism was seldom practiced only to obtain food. It had to do with warfare, or with the idea that one could acquire the enemy's strength by eating him, or that certain magical things happened when this was done.

As civilization spread throughout the world, cannibalism ended or was prohibited by police and government. During the last few hundred years it has existed only in certain tropical and subtropical areas.

It is probable that cannibalism today occurs only in the most remote districts of New Guinea, perhaps in the northeast Congo, and in certain inaccessible parts of South America.

HAS THE ICE AGE REALLY ENDED?

Ice ages are times when thick sheets of ice have spread over large parts of the continents. The ice sheets form when glaciers of high mountains and polar regions grow to great size.

There have been several ice ages. The last one, often called the Ice Age, began about 2,500,000 years ago. Four times during the Ice Age great sheets of ice advanced over the land and four times they melted and drew back. The last advance ended about 18,000 years ago. About 6,000 years ago the continents of the Northern Hemisphere were once more almost free of ice.

But Antarctica and Greenland did not lose their ice. They are still covered by ice sheets between one and two miles thick. This raises the question: Has the Ice Age really ended, or will glaciers advance again?

Scientists don't have the answer, because it really depends on what causes ice ages. And this is one of the great mysteries of science. There are many theories about what makes the earth's climate become colder and warmer. One is that there are actual changes in the amount of energy given off by the sun from time to time. Another is that dust from volcanic eruptions could cut off large amounts of sunlight from the earth.

Another theory is that changes in the amount of carbon dioxide in the air would cause great climate changes. Or climate changes could be related to changes in the distance between the earth and the sun and in the tilt of the earth's axis. And there are still other theories. So until we know exactly what causes sheets of ice to advance over the land and then melt and draw back, we won't know whether the last Ice Age has really ended.

HOW MUCH DOES THE ATMOSPHERE WEIGH?

The earth is surrounded by a thick blanket of air. This is its atmosphere. The earth's atmosphere is made up of about 20 gases. The two main ones are oxygen and nitrogen. It also contains water vapor and dust particles.

Air is matter, and like all matter it has weight. Weight is the measure of the pull of gravity on matter. If a scale registers ten pounds when a stone is placed on it, this means that gravity is pulling the stone with a force of ten pounds.

Similarly, earth's gravity pulls on each particle of gas and dust in the atmosphere. Because our atmosphere is a vast ocean of air, it has considerable weight. If it could somehow be compressed and put on a set of scales, it would weigh about 5,700,000,000,000,000 (quadrillion) tons!

The air presses down on us and against us from all sides. Something like a ton of air is pressing against you at this moment. Yet you are not aware of this because your body is made to live with this pressure.

Air pressure is greatest at sea level, where it amounts to 14.7 pounds a square inch. It is greatest there because that is the bottom of the atmosphere. At higher altitudes the pressure is less. That is why space suits and the cabins of high-flying planes are pressurized—designed to maintain the air pressure our bodies must have.

Earth's atmosphere is one of the things that make it a planet of life. It is the air we breathe, it shields us from certain rays of the sun, it protects the earth from extremes of heat and cold, and serves us in many other ways.

WHY DO PINE TREES STAY GREEN ALL YEAR?

The leaves on a tree have several functions. One of them is to make food for the tree. Leaves take in carbon dioxide from the air and water and minerals from the soil. The chlorophyll in the leaves absorbs energy from the sun. Powered by the sunshine, the chlorophyll changes the carbon dioxide and water into sugar. The sugar made in the leaves is the tree's basic food.

But leaves also give off enormous quantities of water. Only a small fraction of the water that flows up through the sapwood pipes is used in making food. Most of the rest evaporates through millions of tiny holes on the surface of the leaves.

In much of North America a tree's water supply is cut off in winter. After the ground freezes, trees can't release gallons of water into the air. They would need more water than they could get from the frozen ground. So the trees "lock up" by shedding their leaves so that they won't lose water by evaporation through the leaves.

But certain trees have different kinds of leaves. Pines and firs and hemlocks have narrow, needlelike leaves with a thick, waxy outer covering. This prevents evaporation of water. And so the leaves on such trees remain for several years. When the leaves fall, new ones grow at the same time, and the branches never look bare. That's why these trees are called evergreens.

There are also trees with broad leaves that stay green all year round. The live oak and the California laurel have leathery leaves that help the trees keep their moisture during the cold months.

DID THE VIKINGS VISIT AMERICA?

The homeland of the Vikings was Denmark, Norway, and Sweden. Starting in A.D. 787, and for about 250 years, they explored, discovered, plundered countries all over Europe. They built cities in Ireland, penetrated all of England, gained a province in France, raided Spain, Italy, and North Africa, established a kingdom in Russia, settled Iceland, and founded a colony in Greenland.

Did they also discover America? There is now evidence that they did. About the year 1000 Leif Ericson sailed west from Greenland with 35 men. They made two landfalls, and finally reached a pleasant place where game, grass, and salmon abounded. They called this Vinland (Wineland).

The site of Vinland was long sought and never found by modern explorers. Many scholars refused to take seriously the old Scandinavian sagas that told of Viking expeditions to the New World—because there was nothing to confirm them. There were no ruins, no buried arms, no stones with inscriptions.

Then, in 1963, a Norwegian explorer, Dr. Helge Ingstad, unearthed on the tip of Newfoundland the remains of nine buildings and a smithy, which were unquestionably Viking in origin.

By modern methods these relics can be dated at about the year 1000, almost five hundred years before the voyage of Columbus. They may have been Leif Ericson's Vinland or they may have been built by other Viking voyagers to the New World. But they are proof that the Vikings did visit America.

WHAT IS A WEED?

When we call something a "weed," we are not using a scientific plant classification. It is just a way people have of designating certain plants. Weeds are usually defined as plants that grow where they are not wanted.

A dandelion in the middle of a lawn is a weed; dandelions cultivated for fresh greens are not weeds. Clover sown in a pasture is not a weed; clover in a flower bed is a weed.

Sometimes one man's weed is another man's wildflower. City people gather daisies, buttercups, goldenrod, and black-eyed Susans. But the farmer who sees these flowers in his hayfield says, "Weeds!" and sets out to get rid of them.

Weeds, then, are plants that are out of place. And they are plants with a special ability for rapid and vigorous growth. In one way or another, weeds are better fitted to survive than most cultivated plants.

Some weeds are tall. Wild lettuce may be seven feet high, and great ragweed grows as high as 15 feet above the ground. Some weeds are small. Chickweed, carpetweed, creeping spurge are weeds that trail along the ground. They are among the shortest of flowering plants.

Many weeds work underground. Wild carrot and dandelion, for example, have long, thick taproots. These help them get water even during dry spells. Some weeds have creeping roots that grow sideways just below the surface and send up whole colonies of new plants.

Chemical weed killers in the form of sprays have been developed to control the growth of weeds.

WHY IS GRAVITY IN SPACE
NOT THE SAME AS ON EARTH?

Every object in the universe pulls on every other object. This is called gravitation, or gravity. But the strength of that pull—of gravity—depends on two things.

First, it depends on how much matter a body contains. A body (object) that has a lot of matter has a lot of gravitation. A body that has very little matter has very little gravitation. For example, the earth has more matter than the moon, so the earth's pull of gravitation is stronger than the moon's.

Secondly, the strength of gravitation depends on the distance beween the bodies. It is strong between bodies close together. It is weak between bodies far apart.

Now let's take a human being on earth. The earth has more matter than the human being, so its gravitation pulls him to the earth. But the earth behaves as if all its matter were at its center. The strength of gravity at any place, therefore, depends on the distance from the earth's center.

The strength of gravity at the seashore is greater than at the top of a mountain. Now, suppose a human being goes some distance up into the air, away from the earth. The pull of the earth's gravity will be even weaker.

When man goes out into space, he is away from the earth's gravitational field. There is no pull on him. He is in a condition of weightlessness. And this is why, in rockets and space capsules, weightless astronauts and objects float about in the air.

WHAT IS SPANISH MOSS?

Many people have seen Spanish moss without knowing what it really is. In the South, it can be seen on oak trees, pine, and cypress trees, in the form of long gray streamers.

The strange thing is that is is neither "Spanish" nor a moss! It is actually a flowering plant of the pineapple family. It grows in tropical and subtropical climates that have a moist atmosphere.

Nobody knows exactly how it came to be called "Spanish moss." In fact, it has other names as well, such as old man's beard, or southern moss, or Florida moss.

The seeds of this plant are carried by the wind to the rough bark of tree branches, where they stay and germinate. The plant gets its food from the air and dust and uses the tree on which it grows only for support.

Its long narrow leaves are covered with tiny hairs which absorb moisture. Its flowers are small. When Spanish moss is dried and cured, it is called vegetable hair. It is used for stuffing mattresses, pillows, cushions, harnesses, and dolls.

To obtain this stuffing material, the gray outer covering is soaked off or beaten off. Then the tough remaining fibers are dried in the sun until they are nearly black.

One problem in connection with Spanish moss is that in the South it provides a winter home for the cotton boll weevil.

WHAT MAKES A BEAUTIFUL SUNSET?

The sun itself has nothing to do with creating a beautiful sunset. And strangely enough, one of the things that helps create that effect is the dust in the air. In fact, dust particles help make the sky blue and give us those red sunsets.

The sun's white light is actually made up of all the colors of the rainbow. Each color has its own wavelength. Violet has the shortest wavelength, red has the longest.

At sunset the sun is near the horizon. We see it then through a much thicker layer of dust and air. All these particles change the direction of more and more short-wave light from the sun. Only the longer wavelengths—red and orange—come through directly.

Violets, blues, and greens are scattered out of the direct beam; they mix and make a gray twilight glow all around the sky. The disk of the sun itself looks red. Sometimes there are clouds in the part of the sky where we see the sun. They reflect this red light and we see a blazing sunset.

Violet and blue light waves are scattered more than the longer red ones. The scattered violet and blue light bounces from particle to particle in the atmosphere, thus spreading light through the whole sky. Since our eyes see blue light more easily than violet, the sky looks blue to us. This, of course, is what happens during the day.

By the way, the redness of a sunset depends on the kind of particles in the air that will be scattering the sun's light. Tiny water droplets are especially effective at this, which is why certain cloud formations appear so red at sunset.

WHY IS IT COOLER ON TOP OF A MOUNTAIN?

Our atmosphere is divided into layers, each different from the others. The main layers are called the troposphere, the stratosphere, and the ionosphere. Together, they form a blanket several hundred miles thick.

The troposphere is the bottom layer of the atmosphere. This is where we live. Above the United States and southern Canada, the troposphere is about 40,000 feet (nearly eight miles) thick.

Instruments carried aloft in balloons have proved that the temperature drops steadily in the troposphere. The higher one goes into the troposphere the lower the temperature becomes. For each one thousand feet, the temperature drops about 3.5 degrees Fahrenheit.

So when we go up a mountain to the top, we are going up into the troposphere. A mountain that is about a mile high can thus be about 15 degrees cooler in temperature at the top. And there are mountain peaks that are more than five miles (more than 26,000 feet) high! No wonder it's always cold up there. At the top of the troposphere, the temperature is nearly 70 degrees below zero.

The air is always warmest near the earth's surface. The reason is that the sun heats the earth and the earth gives off heat that warms the air. The sun does not warm the atmosphere directly.

In the very top layer, the ionosphere, the air is very thin and the atoms and molecules are bombarded by radiations from the sun. At 150 miles above the earth temperatures are as high as 3,000 degrees Fahrenheit during the day!

WHAT IS A MIRACLE?

When we deal with the whole question of "miracles," we enter the field of religious belief. For example, we can simply say that a miracle is an event that is supernatural.

But what does that mean? We have to define a miracle further by saying it is an event that seems to go against the established laws of nature—as a direct result of divine intervention. Or it happened because certain laws are operating which we, as humans, cannot understand. But since for God all law is natural, nothing is accidental or against God's will or permission.

So, from the religious point of view, a miracle is an event which makes us aware of the power, the presence, or the purpose of God. Many such miracles are described in both the Old Testament and the New. Miracles have also been reported from all ages and all parts of the world.

Did the miracles really happen? That is, did something supernatural take place? Religious authorities say that to understand the miracle stories, as they were understood by those who believed in them, we must forget about looking at things scientifically.

In other words, while a scientist may say: "Miracles do not happen"—and be right from the scientific point of view—it has nothing to do with the religious point of view. From the religious point, miracles are believed in not just on the basis of evidence but because of the meaning they have for those who accept them. To believe that certain "miracles" happened becomes an act of faith.

WHY IS THE GREAT SALT LAKE SALTY?

Everybody knows the ocean is salty. But why should an inland lake like the Great Salt Lake be salty? To understand this, we have to know how lakes are formed and what happens to them.

Lakes result from the flow of water into low areas. Lake water comes largely from rainfall and melting snow. The water enters a lake basin through brooks, streams, rivers, underground springs, and groundwater. Dissolved mineral matter is in the fresh water entering the lake. This dissolved mineral matter is obtained from the ground and from rocks in the area.

In places where the climate is dry, lakes lose water rapidly by evaporation. When the amount of water that flows into a lake is matched by evaporation, salty minerals are left behind in the lake. Such lakes become salty, and the saltiness increases with time.

Great Salt Lake is such a lake. The mineral matter there has been accumulating over the ages and it now contains over 20 percent mineral matter, most of which is common salt. Because of the high salt content, only shrimp live in the lake. Great Salt Lake is more than 4,000 feet above sea level and is located in northwestern Utah.

The Dead Sea, which lies on the border between Israel and Jordan, is really another example of a salt lake. It is 1,292 feet below sea level. The lake is fed by the Jordan River, but it has no outlet. This fact, plus little rainfall and high evaporation, cause the mineral matter to accumulate in the lake. It contains more than 24 percent mineral matter, one third of which is common salt.

WHAT IS A RECESSION?

We might say that when business goes into a decline, a really bad decline, we have a depression. When the decline is not so great, we have a recession. A recession is a sort of minor depression.

What is a depression? It is a period of time in a country's history when most business is bad. It affects all kinds of people, from bankers to laborers to storekeepers. Workers lose their jobs in factories. Sales of things go down as a result. Stores order less goods, borrow less money. So banks are hurt, also. The entire economy suffers. It's a depression. And if all this happens—but on a smaller scale—it's a recession.

In the past 150 years, people have come to realize that business activity moves through a series of good times and bad times. These movements are known as business cycles. For a while there are good times. Business flourishes, people are fairly well off. Then, once in a while, something goes wrong, and business goes into a decline. After a while, business gets better, and the cycle starts all over again.

No one is sure exactly what causes recessions or depressions. There is no single explanation that is accepted by all economists. And while governments and businesses take various steps to end recessions and depressions, there is still no one sure way of doing it.

WHAT MAKES A SEED?

We all love to smell and look at beautiful flowers. So it's a little hard to realize that the only function a flower has is the production of seeds.

Inside the petals of a flower are the reproductive organs necessary for producing seeds. In the very center of the flower there are one or more pistils. Around the pistils is a ring of stamens.

The pistil is the female part of the flower. The bottom of it is enlarged and is called the ovary. If you cut through the ovary, you will find little white round ovules. These later become seeds. But they become seeds only if they are fertilized—joined by the contents of a pollen grain.

Pollen grains are produced in the male organs of the flower, the stamens. Every stamen has an anther, containing two little sacs of pollen grains on the top of a stalk. If seeds are to be formed, the pollen grains must somehow reach the ovules hidden inside the ovary at the bottom of the pistil. The only way they can do so is through the top of the pistil, which is called the stigma.

Pollen grains fall on the stigma, swell and grow there, and the contents of the grain push out and become a tube. The tube keeps growing right down through the stalk of the pistil, through the wall of the ovary, and into an ovule. There the contents of the tube empty into an ovule and fertilize it—and it becomes a seed. Only pollen from the same kind of plant will grow tubes and reach the ovules.

WHERE DO METALS COME FROM?

Pure metals are chemical elements. This means that they cannot be broken down into other substances. There are over a hundred chemical elements known, and about 80 of these are metals.

A few metals, such as gold, platinum, silver, and sometimes copper, are found in the earth in their pure state. Most metals, however, are not found free in nature. They are found only in chemical combinations with other elements.

Chemical compounds that are found in nature are called minerals. Minerals that are valuable for the metals they contain are called ores.

The value of an ore depends on how much metal is in the ore and how costly it is to remove the metal from the ore. It also depends on the demand for the metal.

Many processes are used to obtain pure metal from ore. Some ores need to go through only a few steps, while other ores must go through many steps.

When ore comes from the mine, it usually contains large amounts of unwanted material, such as clay and stone. This worthless material is usually removed before the valuable part of the ore is processed further.

Copper and gold were probably the first metals man learned to use. They occur in nature in a free state as well as in ores. Copper was used as long ago as 5000 B.C. Gold was first used some time before 4000 B.C.

SUMERIAN SCULPTURE
(ABOUT 3050 B.C.)

GOLD BOWL—
ANCIENT EGYPT

177

WHY DOES WATER EVAPORATE?

Everybody knows that if you hang out wet clothes on a wash line, they will become dry. Or that the wet pavement after a rain will gradually become dry.

Evaporation is the process by which a liquid exposed to the air gradually becomes a vapor or gas. Not all liquids evaporate at the same rate. Alcohol, ammonia, and gasoline, for example, evaporate more quickly than water.

There are two forces that act on the molecules that make up every substance. One is cohesion, which draws them together. The other is the heat motion of the molecules, which makes them fly apart. When the two forces are fairly evenly balanced, we have a liquid.

At the surface of a liquid, there are molecules of the liquid moving about. Those molecules which are moving outward more quickly than the neighboring molecules may fly off into space and thus escape the force of cohesion. Evaporation is this escape of molecules.

When a liquid is warmed, evaporation takes place quicker. This is because in a warmer liquid more molecules will have the speed to escape. In a closed container, evaporation stops quickly.

This is because when the number of molecules in the vapor reaches a certain point, the number of molecules that fall back into the liquid equal the number that are escaping from the liquid. When this happens, we say that the vapor has reached its saturation point.

When air is in motion above a liquid, it speeds up evaporation. Also, the greater the surface of the liquid exposed to the air, the faster the evaporation. Water in a shallow pan evaporates faster than in a tall pitcher.

WHAT ARE DIATOMS?

Diatoms are tiny one-celled plants. They are found by the billions and billions in all the waters all over the earth.

The largest diatoms are barely visible to the naked eye and the smallest are less than a thousandth of an inch long. Yet even though they are so tiny, each of them builds for itself a stone shelter hard as granite. There are more than 10,000 species of diatoms, and they have many shapes.

A diatom shelter consists of two shells or valves, one fitting over the other like the top and bottom of a box, and held together along the edges by a girdle. Inside lies the living plant.

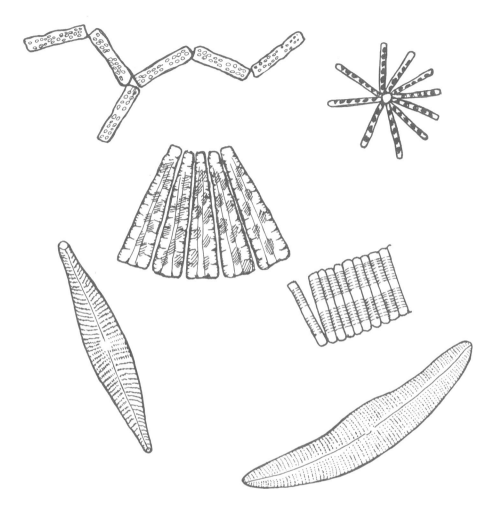

Most diatoms float about in the water or fasten themselves with a sort of jelly to stones or larger water plants. A few are able to swim slowly from place to place, but how they propel themselves is not clearly understood.

Diatoms usually reproduce by splitting in two. The interior living cell divides, the valves separate, and each half grows a new valve on its exposed surface.

Diatoms are very important to us. Together with certain other tiny forms, they are the main plant life of the oceans. While alive, they change nutrient materials that are dissolved in the water into organic substance, and so they are a source of food for all kinds of creatures in the sea, even including fish and whales. The oil which they produce is rich in vitamins and is accumulated in fish livers, from which commercial vitamins are produced.

179

WHAT ARE GEMSTONES?

In order to be considered a "gem," stones must have certain qualities. They must have beauty, they must be hard and tough enough to take considerable wear, and they must be rare enough for people to prize. Diamonds, rubies, and emeralds have all these qualities to a great degree and are the most prized gems.

Gemstones, with only four exceptions, are minerals. Minerals are inorganic (not formed from living things) combinations of chemical elements that are found naturally in the earth. There are four gemstones that are made of organic materials formed by plants or animals. These four exceptions are pearl, amber, coral, and jet.

The beauty of a gemstone depends on one or more of four things: its color, its brilliancy, its "fire," or its special optical features. Brilliancy means the stone's shininess, or ability to reflect light. Fire is the rainbow effect caused by the breaking up of white light. The glittering colors seen in a diamond when it is turned are an example of fire.

Gemstones can be found in almost any color. Rubies are intensely red, and emeralds are intensely green. Brilliancy is the amount of light that is reflected from a gemstone.

Each gemstone has a characteristic hardness and toughness. Hardness is the gem's resistance to scratching or wearing away. Toughness is its resistance to breakage.

Gemstones are formed by the same natural processes that form all minerals. But they are formed under unusually good conditions that yield transparent stones without faults.

WHAT IS THE OZONE LAYER?

Man is becoming more and more aware that things he does in his daily life can have an effect on the climate, the water and food he takes in, the air he breathes, and so on. There is now some concern that things we release into the air can have a harmful effect on "the ozone layer."

What is the ozone layer and why is it important? The earth is surrounded by a thick blanket of air, the "atmosphere." Earth's atmosphere is one of the things that make it a planet of life. It is the air we breathe. It shields us from certain dangerous rays sent out by the sun. It protects the earth from extremes of heat and cold. And it serves us in many other ways.

Our atmosphere is divided into layers, each different from the others. The bottom layer, about ten miles high, is the troposphere. Most of our weather takes shape in the troposphere. The second layer of air, going from a height of ten miles to a height of 30 miles, is the stratosphere.

Somewhere between 12 and 22 miles up, in the middle of the stratosphere, is the "ozone layer." It is a layer of ozone, which is a form of oxygen. Here the winds have died away and the air is warm. It is the ozone that makes the air warm.

This gas absorbs most of the ultraviolet rays sent out by the sun. One result is the band of warm air. But more importantly, the ozone stops most of the ultraviolet rays from reaching the earth. A few of them are good for us, but a large dose would actually broil us alive. So you can see why it is important not to let anything we send into the air have an effect on the ozone layer.

WHAT ARE ABORIGINES?

The earliest known inhabitants of a region are the aborigines. They are the people who were there before any new settlers arrived from another part of the world.

The word comes from the Latin *aborigine*, meaning "from the beginning." It was first used by Roman writers to describe the tribes who originally lived in the territory on which Rome developed.

Bushmen are described as the aborigines of South Africa because they occupied the land before Bantu-speaking Negro tribes. The primitive tribal people who occupied Australia before the coming of the Europeans are called the Australian aborigines.

They are probably the best-known aborigines in the world today. The Australian aborigines live mainly inland and in the remote northern coastal areas. They total about 50,000 people. Their ancestors led a nomadic life and wandered about in tribes. Today, fewer than a third of these aborigines live that way.

The Australian aborigines belong to a separate family of man, and are known as Australoids. It is not known how long they have been in Australia. Before they were influenced by the Europeans, they wore no clothes, built no permanent dwellings, cultivated no crops, and lived as nomadic hunters.

Now many of them have organized together to fight for their rights in Australia. They have the right to vote at federal elections and are entitled to all the social benefits available to other Australians.

WHAT IS THE QUANTUM THEORY?

Light is still one of the great mysteries to man. We know that light travels in waves, and that light waves are made up of electrical and magnetic forces traveling along together. They are one kind of electromagnetic wave.

In 1900, a German physicist named Max Planck found that waves do not tell the whole story about light. He was trying to explain how a hot object gives off radiation. His theory was that radiation is sent out in little bundles, or packets, instead of in a steady stream. Each little flash of energy is called a quantum (plural: quanta), and the idea suggested by Planck is now known as the quantum theory.

A single quantum of radiation energy is so small that the energy stream really seems to be steady. For example, even from such a weak source as starlight, about 60,000,000 quanta enter your eyes each second, and the light looks perfectly steady.

Today physicists think of light as waves for some purposes and as quanta for other purposes. Neither idea by itself is able to explain everything that is observed. Waves explain fully what happens when radiation passes through space or through a material. But the quantum idea must be used to describe how radiation originates and what happens to it when it is absorbed in matter.

Light and other kinds of electromagnetic radiation involve some of the most complicated events in nature. So it is no wonder that neither waves nor quanta alone can describe everything that is observed.

WHY DIDN'T SCHUBERT FINISH THE "UNFINISHED SYMPHONY"?

It is sometimes hard for people to understand that a creative genius, like a writer, composer, or artist, doesn't always lead a well-regulated life. He doesn't "produce" his work like someone in a factory.

Franz Schubert was one of the most productive composers. He lived to be only 31 years of age, yet he wrote over 600 songs, many beautiful symphonies and sonatas, and much choral and chamber music. And he had a hard time doing it.

Creating the music was not his problem. He couldn't get a permanent position to support himself. He was underpaid by the publishers of his music. He was usually short of money. So there could be all kinds of reasons why he could start a work and not finish it.

The exact date when he composed the Eighth Symphony in B Minor (Unfinished) is not known. It was dedicated to a music society in Austria, and Schubert delivered the first two movements to the society in 1824.

The manuscript gathered dust for more than 40 years until it was discovered in 1865 by a Viennese conductor and given its first performance.

Schubert's reasons for not finishing the Eighth Symphony remain a mystery. It is assumed that he intended to complete the work, for the first nine bars of a scherzo movement were fully written and the rest of the movement sketched out. But something must have happened to prevent him finishing it—and it remains unfinished. But it is still a masterpiece.

WHAT CAUSES NIAGARA FALLS?

Niagara Falls is located on the Niagara River, about 16 miles northwest of Buffalo, New York. The Niagara River flows out of Lake Erie, draining four of the Great Lakes into Lake Ontario. About midway on its 36-mile course, the swift water surges forward and plunges over the edge of a high cliff—Niagara Falls!

Actually, Niagara Falls consists of two cataracts—the Horseshoe, or Canadian, Falls and the American Falls. About 94 percent of Niagara's waters, or some 84,000,000 gallons, flows over the deeply curved Horseshoe Falls every minute.

Niagara Falls is considered by geologists to be quite young—perhaps no more than 10,000 to 15,000 years old. In the Ice Age, glaciers covered all of what became known as the Niagara region. As the glacial ice melted, Lake Erie was formed. The overflow from the lake found an outlet to the north and became a river.

As the river flowed northward, it spilled over an escarpment (cliff). The escarpment, topped by a hard layer of limestone rock, created the original Niagara Falls. Since then, the falls have been cut back by the powerful force of the water. They are now some seven miles upstream from their original location!

By the way, the first account of Niagara Falls appeared in 1697. It was written by a French missionary and explorer, Father Louis Hennepin. Father Hennepin had seen the falls in 1678 while on an expedition to the New World with Sieur de la Salle.

Chapter 3

THE HUMAN BODY

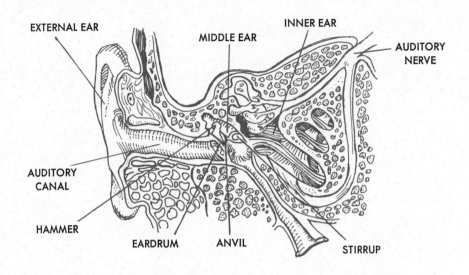

EXTERNAL EAR

MIDDLE EAR

INNER EAR

AUDITORY NERVE

AUDITORY CANAL

HAMMER

EARDRUM

ANVIL

STIRRUP

WHAT CAUSES AN EARACHE?

There are many different conditions that cause an earache, and even the form of the earache varies a great deal. Aside from mechanical injuries, most earaches arise from some type of bacterial infection.

In many cases an earache is caused by a foreign body that has become trapped in the ear. Children sometimes deliberately put something into their ear or another child's ear.

Sometimes earache is caused by hardened wax in the ear. This, and the removal of any object in the ear, should be done by a physician, because he knows how to avoid injury to the delicate parts of the ear.

Infection of the outer ear may be the result of using unclean hairpins, matches, or other objects to relieve itching of the ear caused by wax. These objects may break the skin and introduce infection. This causes a boil to form, the ear swells up, and there will be painful earaches.

A fungus infection of the outer ear and canal can produce a swelling of the canal which causes pain. Sometimes shooting pains are felt in the ear after a cold or other respiratory infection. The eardrum, which divides the outer ear from the middle ear, may become inflamed.

The middle ear may become infected simply because the person has blown the nose incorrectly. Both nostrils should be blown at the same time, because blowing only one side at a time may force infectious material into the sinuses. And there are many other causes of earaches, too. So it is advisable to see a doctor when one has frequent earaches.

WHAT IS YELLOW FEVER?

Did you know that when the French tried to build a Panama canal, they had to give up chiefly because the construction crews were struck down by yellow fever?

In 1900, Walter Reed discovered the cause of yellow fever and how it was transmitted. As a result, work on the canal was able to be done and the canal was completed in 1914.

Yellow fever is an acute disease in which the patient has fever, jaundice, and vomiting. If it is an isolated case, the attack may be mild and the patient is fairly certain to recover. But if there is an epidemic of yellow fever, as many as 50 per cent of the patients may die.

Yellow fever is caused by a virus which attacks the liver chiefly. The liver cells are extensively damaged, which results in jaundice. In fact, it is the yellow-to-brown color of the skin which gives the disease its name.

The virus is transmitted by mosquitoes. The female mosquito of a certain species sucks the blood of a person with yellow fever during the first three days after that person became infected. After about twelve days, the virus in the mosquito becomes infective. Then, when it bites a person who is not immune to yellow fever, that person will develop the disease.

There is no drug that can cure yellow fever, so prevention is what is important. There is a vaccine that makes people immune to yellow fever. Also, once a person has it, he is immune. And, of course, mosquito control in those areas where yellow fever is found is also a way to prevent it.

WHY HAVEN'T THEY FOUND
A CURE FOR CANCER?

First, what is cancer? Basically, it is when the process of cell division in the body gets out of hand. As the new "wild" cells continue to divide, they form a larger and larger mass of tissue. So cancer is an uncontrolled growth (and spread) of body cells.

Cancer can occur in any kind of cell. Since there are many different kinds of cells, there are many different kinds of cancer. In man alone there are hundreds of different kinds of cancer—so cancer is not one disease but a large family of diseases. This is one of the problems in finding a cure for cancer.

One approach in dealing with the problem of cancer is to learn what agents cause cancer. Scientists also need to know exactly how such agents cause normal cells to produce cancerous cells. In this way they hope to be able to prevent the disease. Other lines of research involve the search for agents to destroy the cancer cells in the body, just as modern antibiotics destroy bacterial cells.

Scientists have found many cancer-causing agents that are chemicals. Steps have been taken by governments to keep such chemicals out of food and to prevent other forms of contact with them. Such actions do help prevent cancer.

Because of the close links between cancer and viruses in certain animals, more and more scientists are coming to believe that many types of cancer are caused by viruses. But exactly how a virus can produce cancer in the human body is still not known.

So the search for the causes of cancer is a difficult one, but much progress is being made. Eventually, it may be discovered that the different kinds of cancer have little in common. Or it may be that all the different agents work in the same way. But at present we still don't know.

WHAT IS CEREBRAL PALSY?

Cerebral palsy is a condition in which the patient has little or no control over the movements of his muscles. It happens when one of the three main areas of the brain that control muscular activity is damaged.

One such area of the brain is called the motor cortex. This is where all movements that are planned and controllable start. When it is damaged, there is stiffness of the muscles.

A group of nerve cells in the brain, called basal ganglia, hold back or restrain certain types of muscle activity. When there is damage in this area, unplanned movements of the muscles occur. It might be slow, squirming, and twisting movements of the arms. Or it may be slight shaking or violent jerking.

The third area of the brain, called the cerebellar area, controls muscle coordination and balance. If this area is injured, there is a lack of balance and clumsiness.

There are many causes of cerebral palsy. The brain may not develop as it should before birth. The mother may be sick or injured during pregnancy. The brain may be injured during birth. Difficulty in breathing at the time of birth may prevent oxygen from getting into the blood and injure nerve cells.

Treatment is a long, slow, and continuous process. The aim of it, which must be realized, is not to restore the child to a normal condition. It is to make the child useful to himself and the world, so that he will be happier. Muscle training is the most valuable way of treating children with cerebral palsy.

It is also important to make the child feel accepted by others.

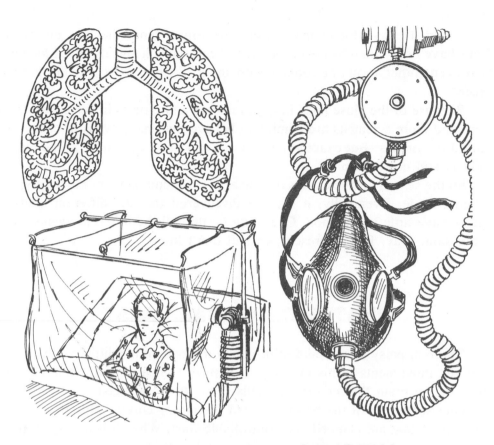

WHY DO WE NEED OXYGEN?

Animals can go for weeks without food, and for days without water. But without oxygen they die in a few minutes.

Oxygen is a chemical element. It is the most abundant element on earth and it is all around you. It makes up about one-fifth of the air (most of the rest of the air is nitrogen).

Oxygen combines with almost all other elements. In living creatures, oxygen is combined with hydrogen, carbon, and other substances. In a human being it accounts for two-thirds of body weight.

At normal temperatures oxygen combines with other elements very slowly. When oxygen combines with other elements, new substances, called oxides, are formed. The combining process is called oxidation.

Oxidation goes on all the time in living creatures. Food is the fuel of living cells. As food is oxidized, energy is released. This energy is used for moving the body and for building new body substances. The slow oxidation in living creatures is often called internal respiration.

In man, oxygen is breathed in through the lungs. From the lungs, oxygen passes into the bloodstream and is carried to all parts of the body. The breathing process supplies the cells with oxygen for respiration. So we need oxygen for the energy to keep the body functioning.

People who have trouble breathing are often placed in oxygen tents. Here the patient breathes in air that is from 40 to 60 percent oxygen. The patient thus uses little energy to get the oxygen he needs.

While oxygen is continually being removed from the air, the supply of oxygen never seems to get used up. Plants give off oxygen as they make food, and this helps keep up the supply of oxygen.

HOW IS BODY TEMPERATURE CONTROLLED?

A thermostat controls the temperature in a room or building by controlling the amount of heat the furnace produces. There is a part of the brain called the thalamus, which acts like a human thermostat. It controls the amount of heat in the body and keeps it at about 98.6 degrees Fahrenheit.

The body burns fuel and oxygen to make energy, which is mostly heat. Since the body makes heat all the time, it must have ways of letting some heat off, or it would keep getting hotter and hotter. The job of the thermostat is to control the amount of heat let off so that the body temperature stays at about 98.6 degrees.

Air from the lungs carries off some heat. Waste passing out of the body also carries off heat. The body lets off much more heat through the skin. It always lets off some heat this way, which is why the skin is warm to the touch.

But the thalamus can make the skin give off more—or less—heat as needed. If the body is getting too warm, more blood than usual flows to the surface of the skin; it gives off heat to the skin surface, which gives off heat to the air. If the body is getting cold, the capillaries under the surface of the skin become smaller; less blood passes near the skin and so less heat is given off.

When the body becomes very warm, we begin to sweat. Sweat is a salty liquid produced by the sweat glands. Little tubes lead from the sweat glands to the pores in the skin. From the pores sweat spreads over the skin. Sweating speeds up the escape of heat from the body because the liquid evaporates.

The liquid changes to a gas and is carried away by the air. At the same time, it carries away heat. That is why you feel colder when you are wet than when you are dry.

WHY DO WE HAVE EYEBROWS?

All mammals have hair on various parts of the body. For most mammals it acts as an insulating layer, to keep the body warm and cool, and to protect the body.

Human beings have less hair on their bodies than animals. The development of the "hair coat" in adult human beings is regulated by the sex glands. The male sex hormone promotes the development of the beard and the body hair, and inhibits the growth of hair on the head. The action of the female hormone is just the opposite. It inhibits growth of hair on the body and promotes growth of hair on the head.

While scientists know this, they still cannot fully understand the purpose behind all the hair on the body. One thing seems clear: hair grows in certain places as a kind of protection against dust and insects. This is why there is hair in the ear and the nose. And the purpose of eyebrows and eyelashes is to help protect the eyes against dust.

Charles Darwin believed that the fine hairs of the body are intended to serve as "gutters" for perspiration and rainwater. And it is believed that the reason men have beards is that it helped render the difference between man and woman evident at a distance, to indicate the sex of the person, and to give the male an appearance of power and dignity.

Altogether, man has 300,000 to 500,000 hairs in his skin. Blond persons with finer hair have somewhat more than this, and dark persons with coarser hair have one-quarter less.

WHAT IS ENDOCRINOLOGY?

Certain organs in the body produce chemical substances that keep the body in proper working order. These chemical substances are called hormones. The group of organs that produce hormones is called the endocrine system. And the study of these organs and hormones is called endocrinology.

The organs of the endocrine system are called "glands of internal secretion" because they send their substances directly into the bloodstream to be distributed throughout the body.

The endocrine glands are: the pituitary, the thyroid, the parathyroids, the adrenals, the testes, the ovaries, part of the pancreas, and the thymus. Some of these produce many hormones and others produce only one.

The endocrine system is responsible for regulating many functions of the body. For example, the rate of growth and final size of the body, the body contour, the distribution of hair, total weight, and the masculine or feminine aspect of the body are all influenced by hormones.

They also regulate the amount of urine produced, the body temperature, the rate of metabolism, the calcium and sugar levels in the blood, the transformation of proteins into energy-giving substances. How they are able to do all this is still not fully understood by experts on the subject.

The reproductive system is especially affected by hormones. And they are also a great factor in the personality of the individual. A person's mental and physical alertness, and masculinity or femininity, are influenced by hormones.

WHAT IS HEMOGLOBIN?

Most of the cells in the blood are red corpuscles. Millions and millions of red cells circulate in the bloodstream.

The red corpuscles contain a protein called hemoglobin. Hemoglobin is a pigment (coloring matter) containing iron. Our blood is red in color because of the combination of hemoglobin and oxygen.

But hemoglobin has a more important function than just giving the blood its color. It has the ability to combine loosely with oxygen. It is this ability that makes it possible for the red corpuscles to deliver oxygen to the cells of the body.

Oxygen is part of the air breathed into the lungs. The red corpuscles in the bloodstream pass through the lungs, where the hemoglobin picks up oxygen. The red corpuscles, traveling through the bloodstream, release oxygen to the body's cells.

When the oxygen is released, hemoglobin takes up carbon dioxide from the cells. This gas is waste that is formed when the cells burn food. The red blood corpuscles, loaded with carbon dioxide, return to the lungs.

Here an exchange takes place. Carbon dioxide is dropped (to be breathed out) and fresh oxygen is picked up. Then the red corpuscles continue on their way, carrying oxygen to cells throughout the body.

This is why foods containing iron are important to our health. Iron stimulates the production of red blood cells and increases the amount of hemoglobin in those cells.

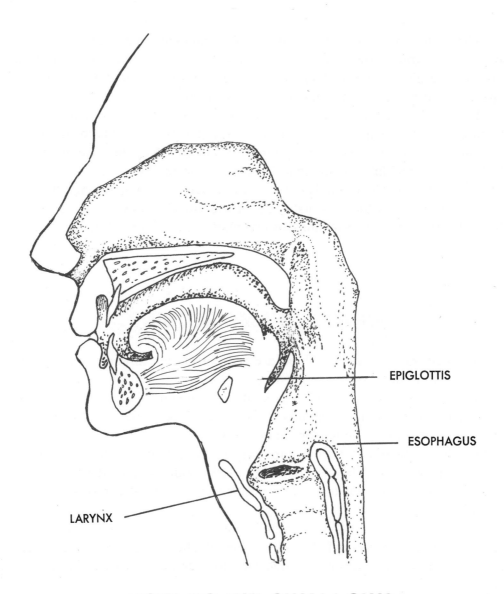

EPIGLOTTIS

ESOPHAGUS

LARYNX

HOW DO WE SWALLOW?

The act of swallowing food is quite a complicated process. It is done by nerves, muscles, ligaments and glands. Included in the process are the larynx, the uvula, the epiglottis, the soft palate, the tongue, lips, nose, lungs, diaphragm, the abdominal muscles, and the brain!

First our teeth cut and grind the food, which is moistened by saliva. The tongue kneads the food into a bolus (a large pill). In the act of swallowing, the soft palate in the back of the mouth is raised so that food won't enter the nose.

Then the food enters the larynx. Here the windpipe is open on top. To prevent food from entering the windpipe, the epiglottis, which is at the root of the tongue, comes down to cover the entrance to the windpipe. The bolus then passes into the gullet, or esophagus, which is about ten inches long.

The walls of the gullet consist of muscle fibers, and the food is pushed through the gullet by the contractions of its walls. Liquids pass quickly down the esophagus; a bolus of food takes about eight seconds to go through. So swallowing of food is not a matter of having it fall down into the stomach. It requires muscular action. That's why it's actually possible to eat and drink while hanging with one's head downward.

What makes the muscles contract during swallowing? In the wall of the alimentary canal are nerves which react to the presence of food. The food touches the wall of the canal, stimulates the nerves, and the nerves cause the muscles to contract—pushing the food through.

HOW DO WE GET OXYGEN?

Man cannot live without oxygen. We need it to keep our life processes going. Oxygen is all around us. It makes up about one-fifth of the air.

We have special groups of cells to enable us to take in oxygen. These cells are in the lungs. We breathe in oxygen through the lungs, and from the lungs the oxygen passes into the bloodstream and is carried to all parts of the body. The breathing process supplies the cells with oxygen for respiration.

The oxygen that the blood carries is part of the air we breathe. Air is usually taken in through the nose and is warmed and cleaned on its way to the throat. From the throat air goes through the voice box, into the windpipe, and then to the lungs.

In the chest the windpipe splits into two tubes called the bronchial tubes. Each tube leads to one of the body's two lungs. Here the tubes begin to branch into smaller and smaller tubes. Each of the tiniest tubes opens into a cluster of thin-walled air sacs, bunched like grapes and covered with a fine net of capillaries.

Waste-carrying blood is pumped from the heart into the capillaries of the air sacs. Here a quick exchange takes place. The waste gas—carbon dioxide—passes through the thin capillary walls into the air sacs. Oxygen from the air sacs passes into the capillaries and the red blood cells. Now the blood has oxygen and it moves to the left side of the heart. From there the heart pumps the blood with the oxygen to all the cells of the body.

WHY DO PEOPLE SMOKE?

Millions and millions of people know that smoking is believed to be harmful and even dangerous to the health, yet millions and millions continue smoking—or even start smoking. Why?

Experts in various fields say that the beginning of smoking, and the process by which it becomes a habit, are complex and not fully understood. Of course, certain things can be pointed out, as those that get people started on smoking, and others that keep them at it—but the point is that it isn't just a simple matter.

For example, we know that most people start smoking because other people around them do it. Do you know that in the 12th grade, from 40 to 55 percent of children are smokers? By the age of 25, about 60 percent of men and 36 percent of women are smokers. Children feel it makes them seem ''adult'' to smoke, and other children urge them to smoke, and they see their parents smoking—so they start smoking, too.

The effect that smoking has on a person then acts to strengthen the habit. For example, nicotine has an effect on the heart and the nervous system. Smoking one or two cigarettes causes an increase in the heart rate and a slight rise in blood pressure. The effect on the nervous system is chiefly tranquilizing and relaxing. People want these effects, or feel they need them, or come to depend on having them at certain times and in certain situations—and so they go on smoking.

And because the reasons for smoking are complex, and vary so much, there is no one way that works for everybody to give up smoking.

WHAT ARE PHAGOCYTES?

In the body there are millions of lymph nodes, which are balls of cells surrounded by connective tissue and muscle fibers. The cells that come from the lymph organs are called lymph cells.

But they also have several other names. They are called white blood cells. They are called leucocytes, because they float in the blood as colorless bodies alongside the red blood cells. They are called wander cells, because they wander about through the body.

And they are called phagocytes, which means "scavenger" cells, because they have the ability to ingest foreign bodies. There are about a thousand times as many red blood cells as white cells.

The number of white cells in the blood increases during digestion, after strenuous exercise, during fever, and in the course of various infectious diseases. This is why every complete medical examination includes making a white blood cell count.

The white blood cells, or phagocytes, can be compared to policemen, soldiers, street cleaners, firemen, and first-aid men of the blood. Whenever there is a foreign substance in the body, a dying cell, or some vital activity is disturbed, they go into action.

For example, if a splinter penetrates the skin, it is attacked by a whole army of these cells. They gnaw at it. They secrete digestive substances around it and try to dissolve it. They eat into the tissue around the splinter so it will become liquefied.

This liquefied tissue is called pus. If we have a wound that gives off pus, it is a sign that there is something there which the body wants to remove. A large collection of pus is called an abscess.

WHY DO CHILDREN GET CHICKEN POX?

Chicken pox is usually considered to be a disease of childhood, but adults can get it, too. The reason we see it so rarely in grownups is that once a person has had an attack of chicken pox it ordinarily makes him immune to the disease. So if somebody has had chicken pox as a child, he's through with it.

Chicken pox is a very contagious disease. It is believed that a virus causes the disease. It is usually transmitted directly from person to person—and not by contact with clothing or other articles soiled by an infected person. A person who has chicken pox can be considered infectious for about 14 days.

This is why doctors say the patient should be kept isolated from members of the family who have not had the disease, especially young children. They are also kept from school and all other public places.

One of the problems in connection with this has to do with symptoms of the disease. Some of the symptoms are a slight rise in temperature, loss of appetite, headache and backache. But sometimes the first sign of chicken pox is a rash or eruption of the skin. Since a person with chicken pox can infect another person about two days before the rash appears—you can see how a whole group of children could become infected before anything was done to prevent it.

While chicken pox is usually a mild disease that requires little special treatment, it is important to have a doctor make a diagnosis and observe the patient to see if there are any complications.

WHY DO WE NEED SO MUCH SLEEP?

If we think of the human body as a "machine," it has one big weakness compared to other machines. They can work around the clock. The human machine must have a chance, at regular intervals, to restore tired organs and tissues of the body, to do repair work, and to get rid of wastes that have accumulated during the day. This is done during sleep.

When the body is asleep, everything slows down. The rate of metabolism is at its lowest. The blood pressure drops. The pulse rate is slower. Breathing is slowed down. Even the temperature drops a little.

So the body needs sleep just to "keep going." But how much sleep does a person need? The surprising thing is that it varies with the individual. Of course, babies need more sleep than grownups. But as one grows older, less sleep is required. The one thing that matters is that we should have enough sleep so that when we wake up we are rested and refreshed.

There are some people who say that four hours of sleep a night is all they need, but this is not enough for most people. There are some who are "long sleepers" and seem to need ten or more hours. The great German philospher Kant needed so much sleep that he had his servant wake him up after seven hours and force him to get out of bed—or he would sleep on and on!

By the way, a short sleep—which may last only 15 minutes or a half hour—may be more restful than a long sleep. This is because it is a deep sleep, when our body really relaxes and goes to sleep.

WHAT MAKES THE RATE OF HEARTBEAT CHANGE?

Each beat of the human heart lasts about 0.8 seconds. The heart beats about 100,000 times a day. It also rests an equal number of times between beats. In one year, the heart beats about 40,000,000 times.

The beating of the heart is really a wave of contraction that takes place in the heart to send blood circulating through the body. So the rate of the heartbeat (or pulse rate) depends on the body's need of blood.

Change in the heartbeat is most often caused by work. Here is how this happens. When a muscle begins to function somewhere in the body, it produces carbonic acid. The molecules of carbonic acid are carried by the blood to a certain part of the heart, the right atrium, within ten seconds.

There are cells there that react to the presence of the carbonic acid molecules. And the reaction adjusts the rate of the heartbeat to the carbonic acid content of the blood. If the muscle stops working, and the carbonic acid content of the blood becomes lower, the action of the heart becomes slower.

But the action of the heart is related to the needs of the body as a whole. Mental excitement stimulates a nerve which makes the heart beat faster. When we are depressed or frightened, a different nerve is stimulated, which makes the heart beat slower.

The ordinary person cannot change the rate of his heartbeat by just wanting to do it. But there have been certain people who had this ability. There is the case of one man who was able to make his heart "stand still" so that people thought he was dead—and then was able to make it beat again.

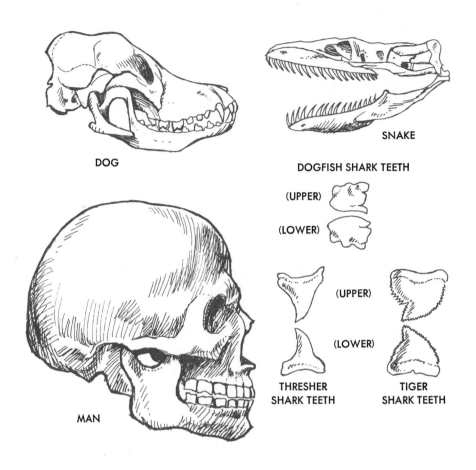

DOG

SNAKE

DOGFISH SHARK TEETH

(UPPER)

(LOWER)

(UPPER)

(LOWER)

THRESHER
SHARK TEETH

TIGER
SHARK TEETH

MAN

WHY DO WE HAVE TWO SETS OF TEETH?

Every creature that has teeth, whether man, horse, cow, dog, cat, or mouse, has the kind of teeth that fit in with its way·of life, nutrition, and general nature.

Among the lower vertebrates, there is a succession of teeth during their whole life. For example, in sharks, when the teeth are fully developed and used up,they fall out, like hairs, and new ones take their place. Among higher animals, the number of teeth they have, and how often they get new sets of teeth, is much less. In man there is only a single replacement, the permanent teeth following upon the milk teeth. Man's development has brought him to the stage where he needs only two sets of teeth.

At birth a human infant has no teeth. After six months the first teeth appear in the center of the lower jaw. In the course of about two years a total of twenty teeth appear. These are known as the milk teeth.

Beneath these milk teeth rest a second series of teeth that begin to erupt after the age of six. So the first set is replaced between the ages of six and twelve. In addition, three more teeth, the molars, erupt on each side in the back part of the jaw. An adult has thirty-two permanent teeth in place of the first set of twenty milk teeth.

Man also has what is called a "collective" dentition. This means that various types of teeth, incisors, canines, premolars, and molars, all appear alongside each other. In man, also, all the teeth are of equal height and arranged in regular rows.

WHY DO ALCOHOLIC BEVERAGES MAKE YOU DRUNK?

Alcohol is a narcotic, which is how we describe a substance which enters the nerve cells quickly and tends to paralyze them. But before any narcotic paralyzes, it stimulates nerve cells, putting them in a state of excitement. So alcohol first acts as a stimulant.

How does alcohol affect the brain? The first effect is a feeling of stimulation. Action and speech seem to be speeded up. The skin gets redder, blood pressure rises, the heart beats faster, and breathing is quickened.

But alcohol soon exerts a depressing effect on the brain. Our ability to observe, think, and pay attention is affected. As the higher functions of the brain are paralyzed, the power to control moods is lost.

Another serious effect is that inhibitions are relaxed. In our body nerve fibers called inhibitory fibers act as brakes in the nervous system. They are developed as the result of education and training, and make us disciplined, restrained people.

Under the influence of alcohol, these inhibitory fibers are paralyzed. Our controls become relaxed, our judgment is unclear, and we are ready to say and do things that we would never do if our minds were normal. Alcohol has produced a state of drunkenness!

Since alcohol does first act as a stimulant, if it is taken into the body in weak solutions, it will continue to act as a stimulant rather than as a narcotic.

WHAT CAUSES GOUT?

Gout is a disease that has been known since ancient times. At one time it was thought of as a "rich man's disease." This was because it was believed that gout was caused by eating too much and drinking too much wine—and, of course, this couldn't be done by poor people.

Gout is a condition of having too much uric acid in the blood. A person who has gout is unable to metabolize, or break down, certain proteins taken into the body. These proteins are called "purines" and are obtained from the diet of the person.

Among the foods with a high purine content are: sweetbreads, liver, kidney, sardines, anchovies, turkey, pork, beef, and many others. So a person with gout is usually advised by his doctor to avoid such foods.

Gout is a very painful disease, and the pain seems to come very suddenly. In 70 per cent of the cases, the first attack is in the large toe, and in 90 per cent of the cases the large toe is involved eventually.

Within hours, the joint swells, becomes hot, red, and tender. It hurts so much that a person with gout is very much afraid of being touched on the painful part. This feeling is typical of a patient with gout.

The acute condition lasts a few days or weeks, and then disappears completely—until the next attack. A person who is subject to attacks of gout may have them brought on not only by his diet, but by such things as physical strain, overwork, emotional strain, and allergy.

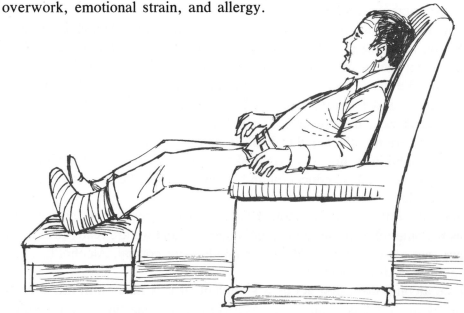

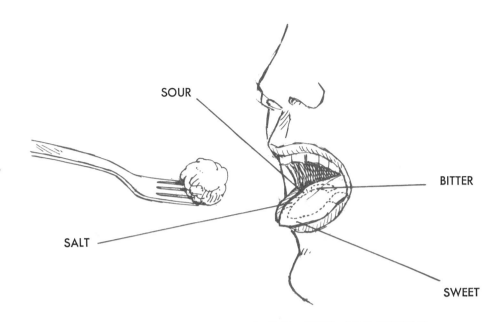

SOUR

BITTER

SALT

SWEET

WHAT GIVES FOOD ITS TASTE?

The whole process of tasting is actually quite a complicated thing. First, we start with the taste buds, tiny wart-like bumps on the tongue called "papillae." An individual has about three thousand taste buds.

We taste when the molecules in a fluid strike the hairs in the taste buds and produce a reaction. Only substances in solution, where the atoms move about freely, can be tasted. A glass ball, for example, has no taste.

Anything that makes atoms move faster intensifies taste. Heat does this, and that's why hot coffee has a more bitter taste than cold coffee, why salt pork is saltier when it is warm, and why meat tastes better when it is hot.

Our taste buds register three or four different sensations: sweet, salt, bitter, and perhaps also sour. Different parts of the tongue are more sensitive to different tastes. The back of it is more sensitive to bitter, the sides to sour and salt, the tip to sweet.

Since almost all our foods are composed of various substances, they produce mixed sensations of taste. An apple is sour and sweet. And the taste sensation itself is a mixed sensation. There is no pure taste. We experience pressure, cold, heat, odor impressions as we taste. The combination of many sensations results in what we call the taste of food. And at least half of what we think of as "taste" is really odor! Coffee, tea, tobacco, apples, oranges, lemons, and other things really stimulate the sense of smell, as we enjoy them more than the sense of taste.

WHAT IS A RETARDED CHILD?

A person whose mind stops growing before it has reached its full powers is mentally retarded. Retardation is not a single disease. It is a symptom, or sign, that something is wrong. It has many causes, not all of which are understood. This condition must begin before the 17th year of life, since that is when the mind of the average person reaches its full growth.

Although there is no complete agreement among experts, many believe that a person's intelligence may be measured with certain tests. The results of these mental-ability tests are known as the Intelligence Quotient, or IQ. An IQ of 100 is considered average. A person whose IQ is below 70 and who does not seem to understand how to get along in everyday life is considered mentally retarded.

There are four classes of retardation: mild, moderate, severe, and profound. The IQ's of the severe and profoundly retarded are below 35. Their mental ability is not above that of a normal five-year-old. They cannot care for their personal needs or protect themselves from common dangers. Someone must always take care of them.

Moderately and mildly retarded persons have less difficulties. They can learn useful skills, work in special workshops, do simple jobs. They have difficulties in reading, writing, and arithmetic, though the mildly retarded can learn elementary-school subjects.

Retardation can be caused by something going wrong in the mind, the body, or the surroundings in which the child grows up. About two hundred specific causes of mental retardation have been identified so far. These include injuries to the brain at birth, brain tumors, an unusual blood condition, infection with certain viruses, and a few types of inherited mental retardation.

WHY IS WATER GOOD FOR YOU?

If you asked a biologist to list the most essential things for life, water would be right at the top. Water is absolutely essential to every form of life that we know. Every living cell—of plant and animal alike—depends on this substance.

As you may know, of every ten pounds of your weight, about seven pounds is nothing but water. Much the same is true of other living things. Without water to drink, human beings die in a short time.

Why is this so? Why is water necessary to life? The reason every living

things needs a certain amount of water is because the cells—the basic units that make up living things—have water molecules in them. Without water these basic units would be very different and of no use to life as we know it.

In the course of a day, an adult human being takes in about two quarts of water as fluids, and one quart in what we call solid foods, such as fruit, vegetables, bread, and meat. These are really not dry, since they are thirty to ninety per cent water.

Besides these three quarts that enter the body from outside in the course of a day, about ten quarts of water pass back and forth within the body between the various organ systems.

There are about five quarts of blood in the vessels of the body, and three quarts of this is water. And this remains unchanged. Even if a person feels "dried out" after a long hike in the summer heat, or has drunk four quarts of beer, his blood vessels still contain three quarts of water. No matter how much water you drink, you cannot dilute the blood.

WHAT MAKES HAIR CURLY?

Hair is the slender, threadlike strands that grow out of the skin. There are many kinds of hair. Hair may be thick or fine, long or short. It may be white or colored. It may be straight, wavy, or curly.

Scalp hair is not the same among the many peoples of the world. Oriental people generally have hair that is quite straight. The Negro has tightly curled hair. The hair of Caucasians, or members of the white race, can be straight, slightly curly, or very curly.

So the color, curliness, and thickness of a person's hair are inherited. A person is born with a certain structure and type of hair. But there is something about the structure of hair that determines whether it will be curly or not.

Imagine that you cut across a shaft of straight hair and a shaft of curly hair, as you might cut across two tree trunks. If you were to look at the cut section of straight hair under the microscope, you would see that it is round. The cut section of curly hair is oval or flat. The flatter the hair is, the more easily it bends and the curlier it is.

The color of a person's hair depends largely upon a substance called melanin. Melanin is a pigment, or coloring matter. It is contained in the hair cells at the time they are formed in the root. It is the amount of this coloring in the cells that makes hair dark or light.

As people grow older, there is less and less melanin in the newly formed cells. That's why the hair gradually turns gray or white.

HOW DOES THE BRAIN SEND MESSAGES TO THE BODY?

The brain can get signals, add them up, and signal back for action in a split second. Different parts of the brain do different things.

The medulla, at the top of the spinal cord, controls nerves that are in charge of certain muscles and glands. The medulla keeps your heart beating, your lungs taking in air, and your stomach digesting food.

The cerebellum controls body movement and balance. The cerebrum is where thinking, learning, remembering, deciding, and awareness take place. The sensations of seeing, hearing, smelling, tasting, and touching are centered here. So are body feelings.

Scientists still do not understand how the brain does its work. But they have learned that the messages that travel through the nervous system—to and from the brain—are weak electrical charges.

Nerves are made up of nerve cells. A nerve cell consists of a central cell body with a number of threadlike parts reaching out from it. Messages are passed from cell to cell through these threads.

The billions of nerve cells in the body form a huge network that leads toward the spine. Along the way nerves from different parts of the body come together in thick bundles. A thick cable of nerves runs up the hollow of the spine to the brain. One set of nerves in the cable carries messages from the senses to the brain. Another set carries messages from the brain to the muscles and glands. The brain sorts out the signals and makes the right connections.

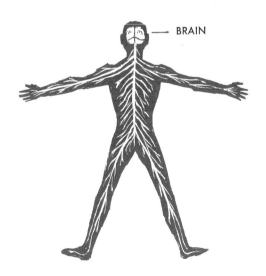

BRAIN

HOW FAST DOES OUR BLOOD FLOW?

Blood doesn't flow through the human body the way water flows through a regular series of pipes. The vessels through which blood is pumped out of the heart to all parts of the body are the arteries. But the arteries that are some distance from the heart keep on dividing and dividing until they become tiny vessels called capillaries. And the blood flows much more slowly through these vessels than it does through arteries.

Capillaries are fifty times thinner than a human hair, so that the blood corpuscles pass through them in single file. It takes a quantity of blood about one second to flow through a capillary.

Blood is constantly flowing through the heart. It takes about 1.5 seconds for a given quantity of blood to pass through the heart. Blood flows from the heart to the lung and back to the heart. This takes about 5 to 7 seconds.

Blood flows from the heart to the brain and back to the heart. This takes about eight seconds. The longest trip the blood has to make is from the heart through the trunk and the legs to the toes and then back to the heart. This takes about 18 seconds.

The time required for the blood to circulate through the entire body—that is, from the heart to the lung to the heart to the body to the heart—is about 23 seconds.

But the condition of the body has an effect on how fast the blood flows. For example, fever or work can increase the number of heartbeats and make the blood flow twice as fast. A single blood cell makes about three thousand round trips through the body's circulation in one day.

WHY DOES YOUR TEMPERATURE RISE WHEN YOU'RE SICK?

The first thing your doctor, or even your mother, will do when you don't feel well is take your temperature with a thermometer. They are trying to find out whether you have "fever."

Your body has an average temperature of 98.6 degrees Fahrenheit when it is healthy. Disease makes this temperature rise, and we call this higher temperature "fever." While every disease doesn't cause fever, so many of them do that fever is almost always a sign that your body is sick in some way.

Your doctor or nurse usually takes your temperature at least twice a day and puts it on a chart, showing how your fever goes up and down. This chart can often tell the doctor exactly which disease you have, because different diseases have different patterns or "temperature curves."

The strange thing is that we still don't know what fever really is. But we do know that fever actually helps us fight off sickness. Here's why: Fever makes the vital processes and organs in the body work faster. The body produces more hormones, enzymes, and blood cells. The hormones and enzymes, which are useful chemicals in our body, work harder. Our blood cells destroy harmful germs better. Our blood circulates faster, we breathe faster, and we thus get rid of wastes and poisons in our system better. So fever helps us fight off sickness.

But the body can't afford to have a fever too long or too often. When you have a fever for 24 hours, you destroy protein in your body. And since protein is necessary for life, fever is an "expensive" way to fight off disease.

DO WE KEEP THE SAME
SKIN ALL OUR LIFE?

The skin consists of two tissue layers. One is a thick, deeper layer of fibers called the corium. On top of this is a delicate layer of cells called the epidermis.

The epidermis contains no blood vessels. In fact, it is made up of dead cells. Only the bottom layer of these cells receives nutrition and is alive. These cells are very busy. It is their job to produce cells. The growth of the epidermis takes place as a result of the cells that are being produced by the cells of the deeper layers.

The new cells are pushed upward by the other cells, and so are removed from sources of nutrition and die. As a result, a chemical change takes place in them and they become a horny material. So the lower half of the epidermis consists of cells that produce cells, the upper half of cells that have died and have been changed into horn.

The top layers of cells are detached at the same rate at which the lower layers produce new cells. So our skin manufactures many billions of new cells daily and sheds as many billions of dead horn cells. Have you ever noticed how when you take off a pair of black stockings at night they are covered with these tiny dead cells?

This process goes on without interruption and is why our skin continues to look young year after year. So we do not actually keep the same skin all our life—we are always getting a new skin.

This is also why stains on our skin, such as ink, grease, iodine, tar, or rust, all disappear very soon. The top layer of cells is removed, a new one takes its place. And there are thirty layers of these horn cells, and when one is rubbed off, a new one pushes up from the lowest layer. We can never run out of layers of these cells.

WHAT VITAMINS DO WE NEED?

The answer is simple: we need them all. When we don't get a particular vitamin, the conditions that result are known as deficiency diseases.

Vitamins are very different from each other in structure. But each vitamin is a substance that the body cannot manufacture, but must have. So a vitamin is essential for some vital function of the body and must be supplied by food.

Here is a brief description of what vitamins do for us. Vitamon A is essential for growth, for vision, and for healthy skin and mucous membranes. It is supplied by milk and milk products, eggs, liver, fruits and vegetables.

Vitamin B1 (thiamin) makes possible the proper use of carbohydrates and is required by the nerves. It is found in whole-grain bread, milk, vegetables, beans, nuts, and pork. Vitamin C prevents scurvy and is essential for healthy teeth, gums, and blood vessels. It is obtained from fresh fruits and vegetables.

A vitamin called niacin is needed to prevent pellagra, a disease that causes great suffering in undernourished people. It is supplied by meat, vegetables, and whole-grain cereals. Vitamin D prevents rickets. It is manufacutred in the body through the action of sun on skin. Vitamin D is now made synthetically in chemical factories and is often added to the milk you buy.

Other vitamins such as E and K and riboflavin have been isolated. Each one has a special duty to perform. That's why one should have a well-balanced diet to ensure an adequate intake of all vitamins.

WHY IS HAIR DIFFERENT COLORS?

Our hair has a very interesting structure. It develops from the horn layer of the skin, actually growing downward. It strikes root and then shoots upward through the layers of the skin.

Hair, like the epidermis from which it is derived, has a tissue of cells which form the "soil" in which it grows, and a horny shaft which is nourished and pushed upward by this "soil."

Among the cells at the root of the hair are cells that contain a pigment called melanin. These cells (like the others) multiply and move upward with the hair shaft as it grows. They die and leave the granules of pigment in the hair.

The pigment granules are all shades of brown, from a reddish color to a deep black-brown. The horn substance of the hair, in which the pigment is embedded, is yellow. The color of the horny material and that of the pigment granules mix together. And that's how all the different colors of human hair develop, from blond to black. Our genes, which we inherit, help decide what shades the pigment granules will be, and so what the color of our hair will be.

The average person has from 300,000 to 500,000 hairs in his skin. Blond persons have finer hair and more hairs than others. Dark persons have coarser hair and about a quarter less hair. Red-haired persons have the coarsest hair and the fewest hairs.

Your hair grows at the rate of about half an inch a month. And it grows at a different rate at various times of the day.

WHY DO PEOPLE GET ALLERGIES?

What is an allergy? It is any condition in which a person reacts in a hyper-sensitive or unusual manner to any substance or agent. That seems to cover a lot of ground, and the range of allergies is very broad.

People may become allergic to various foods, drugs, dusts, pollens, fabrics, plants, bacteria, animals, heat, sunlight, or even many other things! The symptoms that result from an allergy may be of many different kinds, too. Generally, however, they affect the skin and mucous membranes. They are the result of changes that take place throughout the body.

Whenever foreign material invades the tissues, the body reacts to fight it. The body produces certain materials called antibodies. The antibodies combine with the foreign material and render it harmless. But when the foreign material enters the body a second time, the antibodies are torn away from the body tissues to attack the substance. This causes a chemical substance called histamine to be released, and when histamine reaches the skin and mucous membranes it produces the disorders which are symptoms of an allergy.

While many facts about allergy are still not fully understood, it is believed that allergies may be inherited in some cases. Certain weaknesses in the structure and function of parts of the body make the allergies possible.

It is also believed that the adrenal glands are involved, making certain people more likely to have allergies. And it is believed that even mental attitudes play a part in producing allergies in some people.

WHY DO WE GET SUNBURNED?

Most of us have no idea of the many ways in which light from the sun affects us. For example, sunlight destroys fungi and bacteria that may have settled on the skin. The action of sunlight on the skin produces a substance which contracts the blood vessels of the skin and thus raises the blood pressure. Ultraviolet light from the sun produces vitamin D in our bodies.

And one of the other things sunlight does to our skin is create the condition we call sunburn. There is a substance in the skin called histidin. Ultraviolet light from the sun transforms histidin into a substance that dilates the blood vessels, causing the skin to become red.

How do we get a "suntan"? The skin also contains a substance called tyrosin. Ultraviolet light acts on tyrosin and transforms it in the brown pigment called melanin. This melanin is deposited in the outside layers of the skin and makes it look "tanned." The melanin acts to protect the skin against further action of the light rays.

Because sunlight affects our skin and our body in so many ways, a person should be very careful in taking "sun baths." Did you know that if you expose only your feet to the sun's rays, you can raise the blood pressure, produce vitamin D that will go to the bones of the body, and so on?

Most people can't be bothered to do it right, but the healthiest way to take sun baths is very gradually. This would be exposing only one-fifth of the body for five minutes the first day, another fifth of the body for ten minutes the second day, and so on.

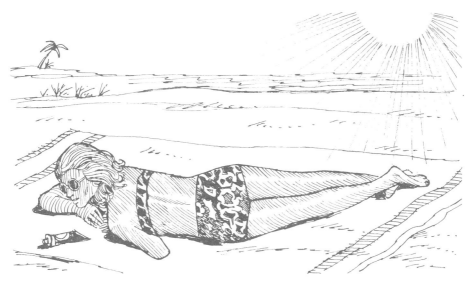

WHERE DO WARTS COME FROM?

Many people have superstitions about warts. They believe that if you handle toads, you get warts. Or that certain animals can pass them on to you.

None of this is true. You can't get warts by handling toads, and while dogs and cattle do have warts, there is no animal that passes warts on to human beings.

Warts are caused by a virus, which is a very small germ. This virus may be picked up by contact with others who have the virus.

A wart is usually a small raised area of the skin which is quite rough or pitted on the surface. It is flesh-colored or slightly darker than the normal skin. Since the wart is caused by a virus, it can be spread by scratching it and spreading the virus on the skin. That's why there are sometimes many warts on the skin.

Most warts disappear after a year or two. But there is really no guarantee that they won't spread or continue on and on. That's why it's a good idea to see a doctor about the warts.

In treating the patient for warts, the doctor usually uses some form of local medication, or he may inject special preparations into each wart. When there is constant pressure on a wart, such as those on the palms or soles, the problem becomes a bit more serious. The wart may become quite hardened and have to be removed.

WHAT MAKES A BOY'S VOICE CHANGE?

To produce what we call a "voice," three things are used in the body. One is the vocal cords, which vibrate. The second is air, which normally serves for breathing, as a source of energy to set the vocal cords vibrating. And the third is the cavities of the throat (pharynx), mouth, and nose to reinforce, or resonate, the sounds.

The vocal cords are located in the larynx, or voice box. A voice has volume, pitch, and quality. Volume is related to the energy of the stream of air and to the type of resonance provided. The vibration of the cords produces vocal tone. The pitch is related to the tension, length, and thickness of the vocal cords.

Now that we see how a voice is produced, we can understand what makes a boy's voice change. A child has a small larynx (voice box) with short vocal cords. When the vocal cords vibrate, they produce short air waves, and this results in a high-pitched voice.

At puberty the larynx begins to grow and the vocal cords become longer. And this is what makes the voice change; it becomes deeper. In boys the growth is so rapid and the difference in size of the whole voice mechanism in the throat is so great, that boys cannot get used to it quickly and often lose control of the voice. This is what people sometimes call "the breaking of the voice." This happens with boys and not with girls because in an adult male the vocal cords are about 50 per cent longer than in the adult female. Girls' vocal cords don't grow as fast nor as long.

While the general pitch of the adult voice depends on the length of the vocal cords, each voice has a certain range which decides to which class it belongs, such as bass, baritone, tenor, soprano, and so on.

WHAT IS AMNESIA?

Amnesia is a state of total loss of memory by a person. He cannot recall his identity or anything about his past. Amnesia may be permanent or temporary.

One type of amnesia may result from an injury to the head. The person cannot recall the accident or events following the accident. But he still may be able to carry on his activities and be aware of his surroundings. Unless there has been serious damage to the brain, memory usually returns within a few days.

There is another kind of amnesia called hysterical amnesia. It may happen when a person tries to remove himself from a situation he can't bear in his personal life. The anxiety has become so great that the person is forced to forget it. This amnesia often arises when the person feels he must suppress many of his natural impulses and feelings.

By forgetting his anxiety, he also forgets a great many other things, even including his identity. He may still act in a normal manner, but be unable to recall anything about the past.

He acts so normally that he may move about without attracting notice. Or he may wander restlessly from place to place. Or he may assume a new identity. Then he may suddenly recover his memory.

Where this doesn't happen, psychiatric help may enable him to do it. When he does regain his memory, he doesn't recall events which took place during his period of amnesia.

Chapter 4

HOW THINGS ARE MADE

WHAT CAUSES CEMENT TO HARDEN?

Cement is one of the most useful materials in modern building. By itself, it is a soft powder. But when it is mixed with water and allowed to harden, cement can bind sand or gravel into a hard, solid mass.

Cement is used chiefly as an ingredient of mortar and concrete. Mortar is a mixture of cement, sand, and water. Concrete is the same mixture with gravel or broken stone added to it.

Modern cement is made by heating a mixture of limestone and clay or slag to a very high temperature. This mixture is heated until large, glassy cinders—called "clinkers"—are formed. The clinkers are then ground to powder.

When water is added to the cement powder, a very complicated chemical reaction takes place. The result is a durable artificial stone that will not dissolve in water.

What is this chemical reaction? What takes place that enables the cement to harden?

Chemists are still not sure of the exact answer. There are four major compounds in the cement, and it is believed that each of these compounds, when water is added, becomes crystals. These crystals interlock—and the result is the hardened cement.

The kind of cement that will harden under water is called hydraulic cement. An amazing thing is that the Romans discovered how to make a type of hydraulic cement in the 2nd or 3rd century B.C. by mixing volcanic ash with lime. This discovery was one of Rome's outstanding achievements.

HOW CAN A DIAMOND BE CUT?

If a diamond is the hardest substance known, how can a diamond be cut? It is possible to do it because of two things: the structure of a diamond, and the way the cutting is done.

A diamond is highly crystallized carbon. The carbon atoms that make up a diamond have a geometrical arrangement. This means it is possible to cleave a diamond parallel to the planes in which the atoms are arranged and get smooth flat faces.

To cleave a diamond, a small diamond fragment is used as the cutting tool. A small groove is cut into one of the edges of the crystal. Then a thin, blunt-edged knife, or "cleaving iron," is positioned in the groove. A sharp blow is struck on this and the diamond crystal breaks apart. This is often done with large diamonds in order to remove flaws, or get a shape that provides more brilliancy, or to get more usable weight from the original stone.

In sawing or cutting a diamond, it is also necessary to go only in certain directions. A diamond is sawed by a thin phosphor bronze disk with its edge impregnated with diamond dust mixed in oil. In other words, it takes diamond to cut diamond. The saw revolves very fast, but it cuts the stone slowly.

The "facets," or little faces of a diamond, are ground on a high-speed cast-iron wheel impregnated with the same combination of diamond dust and oil.

Diamond cutting is a very skillful art which requires years of training.

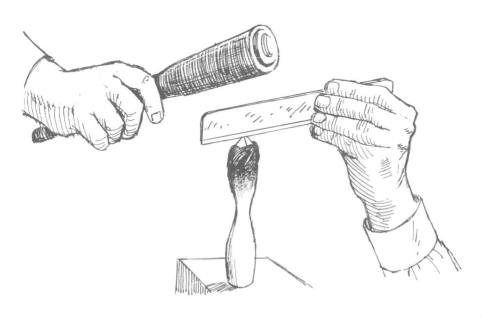

WHAT IS BEER?

Beer is a mild alcoholic beverage that man has made and used for thousands of years. The brewing of beer starts with grain. The chief grain for brewing is barley, though corn or rice is sometimes used as well.

The grain is mixed with water and kept in a warm room until it begins to germinate, or sprout. After a week of germination, the grain is roasted in a furnace and germination stops. The partly sprouted grain is known as malt.

The malt is mixed with water and boiled to form a sweet-tasting liquid called wort. Then the dried seed cones of a plant called the hop vine are added to the wort, and the mixture is boiled again. The seed cones, called hops, give beer its tangy flavor.

All the solid matter is then filtered out, and yeast is added. As the yeast organisms feed on the sugars of the wort, they give off alcohol as a waste product. This change from sugar to alcohol is called fermentation. During fermentation, carbon dioxide is also given off. This gas gives beer its bubbles.

The beer is pumped into closed storage tanks where it ages for about 6 weeks. Then it is filtered again before it is put into barrels, bottles, or cans. From start to finish, the brewing process may take as long as 3 months. Bottled and canned beer is pasteurized to keep it from turning sour.

The most popular kind of beer in the United States is lager beer. This beer originated in Germany and gets its name from the German word for "storage" (Lager), because beer is stored for some time before it is used.

WHAT IS A PHOTOELECTRIC CELL?

There are many types of photoelectric cell, and they are used for many things. One of the most familiar ones is when a door seems to open by itself when we approach it, as we often see at airports. This happens because our body blocks a beam of light and a photoelectric cell makes the door open.

Light is a form of energy. When light strikes certain chemical substances, such as selenium and silicon, its energy causes a push on the electrons in the substances.

If two different substances happen to be touching one another, some of the electrons may leave one substance and enter the other. Suppose an outside wire is attached to these substances so as to make a path for the electrons. Then, as long as light shines on the chemical substances, a continuous flow of electrons will take place through the substances and the wire.

Such a flow of electrons is an electric current. The entire path that the electrons travel along is called an electric circuit. A device that produces or increases the strength of an electric current when light shines on it is called a photoelectric cell.

Photoelectric cells are used in many ways. For example, solar batteries, placed in satellites and spacecraft, are a number of photoelectric cells connected together. In an exposure meter used on cameras, a dial is connected to a circuit that has a tiny photoelectric cell. The dial registers the amount of current flowing through the circuit. This tells how much light is shining on the cell.

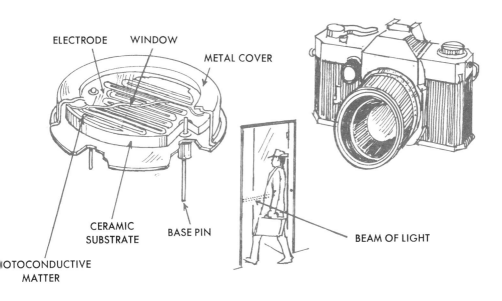

ELECTRODE WINDOW METAL COVER

CERAMIC SUBSTRATE BASE PIN BEAM OF LIGHT

PHOTOCONDUCTIVE MATTER

HOW IS WHISKEY MADE?

Whiskey is an alcoholic beverage that is distilled. Not all alcoholic beverages are distilled, as, for example, beer and wine are not. Distillation is the process of separating different kinds of liquids by boiling them.

All liquids have a different boiling point. The temperature in a still is regulated so that the liquid that is boiled off is mainly alcohol. The escaping vapor is trapped and condensed—that is, turned back into liquid.

Whiskey and most other distilled beverages are made from grain, which is composed mainly of starch. This starch must be changed to sugar, and the sugar will then be fermented into alcohol. Tiny plants called yeasts go to work on the sugar, breaking it apart into alcohol and carbon dioxide.

To change the starch into sugar, so that the yeast plants can feed on it, malt is added to a cooked mash of grain mixed with water. The malt contains enzymes which convert the grain starch into sugar.

When the sugar has been fermented into alcohol, the alcohol is separated from the mash by distillation. We now have alcohol that has been obtained from the grain, and this might be called "raw whiskey."

Whiskey is stored in wooden barrels for aging. This eliminates any unwanted impurities and gives the whiskey a smooth, mellow taste. The wood for the barrels may first be charred, to give the whiskey a nutty flavor and help absorb impurities.

HOW DOES ETHER WORK?

Ether is used as an anesthetic. Anesthetics affect the nervous system and keep a person from feeling pain. Some anesthetics prevent the nerves from sending messages of pain. Others affect the brain. In either case, no pain is felt.

There are two main types of anesthetics: general and local. A general anesthetic causes the patient to lose consciousness. All senses are temporarily cut off.

A local anesthetic affects only part of the body. It leaves the patient awake and conscious. His only loss of feeling is in the anesthetized area.

Ether is a general anesthetic. It is the chemical ethyl ether or diethyl ether. It is a colorless liquid that quickly changes into gas. When the gas is breathed in, the blood carries the drug to the central nervous system.

Once there, the anesthetic acts on the nerve cells of the brain. These cells lose their ability to send and receive messages. No sensations are felt, and the patient loses consciousness.

While ether was one of the first and most common anesthetics, it is now being replaced by newer ones. Ether has a strong odor and it irritates breathing passages and lungs. It also leaves the patient feeling sick after an operation.

Since there is no single all-purpose anesthetic, doctors choose one that seems best for the patient and the kind of operation. In some cases they may even use several together.

WHAT IS A DETERGENT?

A detergent is a substance that makes things clean. So soap is really one kind of detergent. But when we say "soap," we usually mean a cleaning agent made from natural materials. And when we say "detergent," we usually mean a detergent made of synthetic materials.

Synthetic detergents are put together from many different chemicals by complicated processes. Petroleum, fats, coal tar, and other materials go into the complex formulas of these detergents. They are manufactured in chemical plants with special equipment. The ingredient in the detergent that does the actual cleaning is called the surface-active agent—surfactant, for short.

Surfactants can be made from a wide variety or raw materials, including petroleum, animal fats, and vegetable oils. The chemical processes involved are quite complicated. For example, animal fat may be treated with a series of different chemicals—an alcohol, hydrogen gas, sulfuric acid, and an alkali—to make one surfactant that is being used.

The surfactant must be mixed in a crutcher with other chemicals that help it remove dirt more thoroughly and keep the dirt from settling back on the cleaned material. Special bleaches, coloring, and suds stabilizers may also be added.

What has made synthetic detergents popular is that they produce suds in any kind of water, hard or soft, hot or cold; and they don't produce the curds that cause "bathtub ring." Today, about 90 percent of the packaged dishwashing and laundry products used in homes in the United States are synthetic detergents. Soap is still the most popular type of detergent for personal uses.

HOW ARE COLORS FORMED?

Light from the sun or from any very hot source is called white light. But that white light is really a mixture of light of all colors. This can be seen when light passes through a glass prism and is dispersed. We then see all the colors—red, orange, yellow, green, blue, and violet.

What creates the different colors? Color is determined by the wavelength of light. The wavelength of light corresponds to the distance between one crest and the next in a wave traveling on water. But the wavelengths of light are so small, they are measured in millionths of an inch.

The shortest visible waves are violet, with a wavelength of about 15 millionths of an inch. The longest are red, with a wavelength of about 28 millionths of an inch. In between are all the colors of the spectrum, and each shade has its own wavelength.

Most of the colors we see are not of a single wavelength, but are mixtures of many wavelengths. Purple is a mixture of red and violet; brown is a mixture of red, orange, and yellow. Different shades of any color can be made by adding some white light; for instance, a mixture of red and white is pink.

Why does a piece of cloth have a certain color when we look at it? When white light falls on an object, some wavelengths are reflected and the rest are absorbed by the material. A piece of red cloth absorbs almost all the wavelengths except a certain range of red colors. These are the only ones that are reflected to our eye—and so the cloth looks red.

WHAT IS MUSIC?

Suppose you hit a wooden table with your hand. It makes a sound. Now suppose you hit a bell. It makes a sound. The second sound is called a tone. A tone is a single musical sound.

Music is the art of organizing tones into meaningful patterns of sound. We might call it the language of tones. Sometimes the language of music speaks to us in tones sounding after one another in melody. Or the tones could be sounding together in harmony.

When tones clash with one another, it is called dissonance. But this clashing is often full of meaning. What we call melody is given meaning by its rising or falling or moving straight ahead. It is also given meaning by its rhythm of beats and phrasing, its speed or tempo, and how loud or soft it is at any moment.

All of this sounds very technical, or mechanical. But it doesn't have to be understood or thought about for us to enjoy music. What music means to us can often not be put into words. We can feel that the music expresses joy or sorrow, gaiety, tenderness, love, anger—all kinds of things and feelings that words alone could never do.

Music can also be enjoyed just for its beauty, and not for what it is saying. We can get pleasure from even a single tone of voice, violin, horn, or some other instrument. We may love a beautiful melody for many years of our lives and always enjoy hearing it.

There are, of course, many forms of music, from the anthem to the symphony; and many types of music, from folk music to opera.

WHAT IS IRRIGATION?

Irrigation is the artificial application of water to land in order to increase the growth and production of plants.

In ancient times, irrigation was a natural process. For example, the annual flooding of the Nile River spread a thin layer of silt (mud) across the land. At the same time, the land received enough water so that crops could be grown.

Where irrigation was a natural process, people sometimes built canals, reservoirs, and drainage ditches. Floodwaters could then be directed where needed or stored for future use. This was the earliest form of man-made irrigation.

Today, in order to supply enough water for irrigation, costly dams and reservoirs are needed. Irrigation water may be so expensive that only good land can be irrigated profitably. Only such crops as vegetables and fruits can produce enough income to cover the costs.

The kind of irrigation used depends on the type of crops grown. Occasional

flooding may be enough for hay, pasture, and the small grains. Furrow distribution (spreading water in ditches between rows) may be required for such crops as sugar beets and vegetables. In some cases, underground pipes with overflow standpipes are used.

Irrigation is not done only in dry lands. In Asia, irrigation is needed to raise rice, because rice fields must be covered with water at all times, until the rice crop is ready to harvest. In some parts of the world, supplemental irrigation is used. Pipes and sprinklers carry water to where it is needed most. This may save a valuable crop from serious damage by drought.

HOW IS CARBON-14 USED TO DATE OBJECTS?

All living things contain carbon. They also contain small amounts of carbon-14, a radioactive variety of carbon. Using carbon-14, scientists can determine the age of wood and clothing—in fact, anything that was once alive. Dating an object by means of carbon-14 is called radiocarbon dating. Radiocarbon dating is used to date objects up to 50,000 years old.

The rate at which a radioactive element breaks down is described by its half-life. An element's half-life is the time in which half the element's atoms break down.

Carbon-14 has a half-life of about 5,500 years. This means that about 5,500 years after a plant or animal dies, half the carbon-14 atoms present at the time of death are left. After 11,000 years, one quarter of the original carbon-14 atoms are left, and after 16,500 years, about an eighth of the original amount, and so on.

Suppose an old piece of wood is found in an ancient tomb. In the laboratory it can be heated and turned to carbon, or burned to release various gases, including carbon dioxide. The carbon or the carbon dioxide contains a few carbon-14 atoms. These atoms of carbon-14 are breaking down. With each breakdown a tiny particle is sent speeding out of the atom.

The carbon or the carbon dioxide is placed in a sensitive instrument—called a Geiger counter—which detects the particles given off by the atoms of carbon-14. From the number of particles given off, scientists can determine the amount of carbon-14 in the sample.

Scientists know how much carbon-14 is contained in an equal amount of wood from a living tree. From the amount of carbon-14 left in the ancient sample, scientists can tell its age. For example, if the ancient sample contained half the original amount, it would be about 5,500 years old.

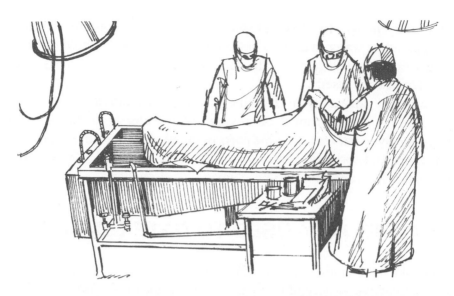

WHAT IS AN AUTOPSY?

Quite often we read in the papers that an autopsy has been performed on a person who died from a disease, or from unknown causes, or who was murdered.

An autopsy is the examination of the body after death. Its purpose is to try to determine the cause of death. It is done by inspecting the organs of the body, and by making microscopic and chemical studies of pieces of tissue removed from the body.

Permission for an autopsy must be granted by the nearest of kin. It is similar to a surgical operation and is performed by medical personnel. An autopsy is performed in such a way that there will be minimal disturbance of the body. There is no visible evidence of an autopsy when memorial services are held for the person.

Why are autopsies done? Sometimes a doctor doesn't know the exact cause of a person's death. An autopsy can clarify this problem and might save someone's life in a future situation of the same kind.

An autopsy might reveal something about a disease that could be important to save the lives of surviving relatives. Sometimes an autopsy is done to identify a dead person who cannot be identified in any other way. An autopsy can help establish the time of death, which can be important when the person died from unknown causes or because of an act of violence.

Autopsies performed hundreds of years ago enabled man to begin to know about the human body and started the science of anatomy.

228

WHY DO GOLF BALLS HAVE HOLES?

To begin with, those are not "holes" in golf balls. They are small indentations, called dimples.

Like any sport, golf has certain rules and regulations. These also apply to the balls used. A golf ball is about half the size of a baseball or tennis ball.

But it just can't be any size. United States rules provide that a golf ball shall not weigh more than 1.62 ounces nor be less than 1.68 inches in diameter. In Great Britain and most other Commonwealth nations, the rules allow for a slightly smaller ball.

Early in the history of golf, the balls were made of heavy leather, stuffed with feathers. Today the ball is made by winding strip rubber tightly around a core and covering it with a hard, rubberlike composition material.

Since one of the objectives of the game is to be able to hit the ball a long distance, and do it accurately, the cover of the ball is usually marked with the small indentations. It has been found by experts that these indentations (or what some people call "holes") make the ball fly straight when struck properly. It is also supposed to lessen wind resistance, and thus give greater carrying power to the ball.

The strongest and best players can hit a golf ball 300 yards or farther, but drives of 200 to 250 yards are considered long.

HOW IS WINE MADE?

Wine can be made from many fruits and plants that contain natural sugar. But most wine is made from grapes. The grape is nature's most suitable product for wine making. Grapes have enough natural sugar to ferment properly. And grapes carry the yeasts that begin the wine-making process when the juice is released.

As grapes ripen on the vines, they produce more sugar and less acid. The grapes are picked when they reach the exact stage of ripening necessary for the wine that is to be made. Mechanical grape crushers break the fruit and release the juice gently, so that the seeds are not broken. Natural wine yeasts on the grape skins ferment the juice, changing the grape sugar into alcohol and carbon dioxide.

White wines are made by fermenting the juice of the grapes without the grape skins. Red wines are made by fermenting the juice with the grape skins.

The color of wine comes from the skins of the grapes. When the wine is the right color, the skins are removed and the wine continues to ferment without the skins.

If a wine maker wants a sweet wine, he stops the fermenting process before the sugar is all turned into alcohol and carbon dioxide. If a dry wine is wanted, the wine is allowed to ferment until almost all the sugar is gone. At the end of the fermenting process the wine is put into a cask or tank to begin aging.

The aging is divided into two stages. In the first stage wooden casks or barrels are used. In the second stage, the wine is placed in bottles. The length of time it takes for a wine to age to perfection depends on the type. Aging makes a new, harsh-tasting wine into a smooth-tasting wine.

WHAT IS FERMENTATION?

Fermentation is a chemical change in which certain chemical compounds are broken down into simpler forms. The change is caused by substances called enzymes, which are produced by tiny living plants or animals. Yeasts, for example, are one-celled plants which produce enzymes.

There are three main kinds of fermentation: alcoholic, acetic, and putrefactive. Each is caused by the presence of bacteria—yeasts or molds—which produce the particular enzyme responsible for the chemical change. Fruit syrups become alcoholic when yeast, containing an enzyme called zymase, is added.

Wine or cider turns to vinegar when certain bacteria, called "mother of vinegar," are present. This is acetic fermentation. Meat and animal matter decay in putrefactive fermentation after certain molds have formed on them.

Fermentation helps in the digestion of food. An enzyme called ptyalin in saliva changes the starch of foods into soluble sugar—the first step in digestion. Enzymes are also present in the stomach, the intestines, the pancreas, and in various other organs.

Yeast is put into dough to make bread light by producing bubbles of carbon dioxide which form as the enzymes attack the starches and sugars present.

Sometimes fermentation is harmful. To keep foods from spoiling, they are kept in cool places or refrigerators where the low temperature checks the growth of bacteria, yeasts, and molds. Food can be preserved by killing the fermenting agents with heat and then sealing it. This is done in canning.

WHAT THINGS ARE MADE FROM OIL?

Petroleum, or crude oil, is one of the world's most important substances. Through a process called refining, petroleum can be changed into more than 2,000 useful products. Here we can give only a general idea of what some of these are.

The best-known petroleum products are the high-energy fuels—gasolines, kerosenes, and diesel and fuel oils. Bottled gas is derived from petroleum. Much of the food we eat and the clothes we wear depend on substances from oil. Oil is used to prevent bread from sticking when it is being mixed. Petroleum-derived plastic film wraps much of our food. Many of our garments are made with synthetic fibers derived from petroleum.

Over a thousand different kinds of oils and greases are made from petroleum. The lubricants are used for everything from watch and machine parts to locomotives and electric generators.

From oil comes asphalt for roads and rooftops. Wax obtained from oil is used in making candles, waxed paper, and cellophane. Other products that come from oil are used in making carbon paper, ink to print books and newspapers, and detergents.

On farms, synthetic ammonia, made from petroleum, is used as a fertilizer. Oil-based sprays kill insects and weeds. And petroleum is used to manufacture petrochemicals. These are raw materials from which other chemical products, such as plastics and synthetic fibers, are made.

From petrochemicals the products made include such things as synthetic foam rubber, plastic tile, plastic film, and detergents.

ARE HORSES USED TO MAKE GLUE?

An "adhesive" is any sticky substance that holds things together. Adhesives are made out of a great variety of materials. The most modern kind of adhesives are synthetic resins, which are made from chemical raw materials.

Now, "glue" is also an adhesive, and it is made in a very special way. But many people call all adhesives "glue," and technically speaking, that is not correct.

Glue is an adhesive that is made from the protein "collagen." This protein is the chief thing found in the connective tissues of animals and fish. The chief way of obtaining the raw material for glue is by boiling animal hides and bones. And so that would include the bones and hides of horses (as well as other animals) when the animals have died. Actually, the bones of the animals make one kind of glue, and the hides make another.

The need for adhesives by man goes back to very ancient times. Primitive man used resins and plant gums to stick things together. But glue—the animal kind—has also been known for thousands of years. As far back as 1500 B.C., the Egyptians used glue to join pieces of wood.

The biggest change in the history of adhesives came with the development of the synthetic resins in the 1930's. They proved to be stronger and more durable than the natural adhesives, and they stood up against water, mold, and fungi as well. (Animal glue dissolves easily in hot water.) Today's synthetic adhesives are so strong that they are used in bonding the metal skins of some airplanes and missiles.

HOW CAN THE DISTANCE
TO A STAR BE MEASURED?

Most stars are very large, yet to us they look like points of light. This is because they are so far away from the earth. In fact, while we can measure the distance to stars, we cannot really imagine how great that distance is.

The stars are so far away that the distance to them is measured in light-years, not in miles. One light-year is the distance that light travels in one year—nearly 6,000,000,000,000 (trillion) miles.

The closest star that can be seen with the unaided eye is just over four light-years away. Its name is Alpha Centauri. If the sun (which is a star) were as far away from the earth as Alpha Centauri, the sun would also look like a point of light.

Here is one way astronomers can estimate the distance to a star. They observe the star from two positions that are a known—and very large—distance apart. For example, they may observe the star from opposite sides of the earth. Or they may make observations a half year apart, when the earth is at opposite sides of its path around the sun.

When they do this, the star appears to have changed its position. This apparent change in position is called parallax. By measuring a star's parallax, an astronomer can calculate how far away the star is.

Because the stars are far away, they must be studied with telescopes. Through telescopes astronomers have observed and photographed hundreds of millions of stars. The most distant objects that can be seen through telescopes are thousands of millions of light-years away.

HOW ARE RAISINS MADE FROM GRAPES?

Raisins are small, very sweet grapes that have been carefully dried in the sun. There aren't too many regions in the world where grapes can be produced. The reason is that when the grapes are ripe, there must be many weeks of hot, rainless weather in which the grapes can dry.

There are regions near the Mediterranean, parts of Spain and Greece, and areas in Asia Minor that have the required climate; so do parts of southern Australia.

The San Joaquin and Sacramento valleys of California are ideal for making raisins, and lead the world in production. The drying season, from August to

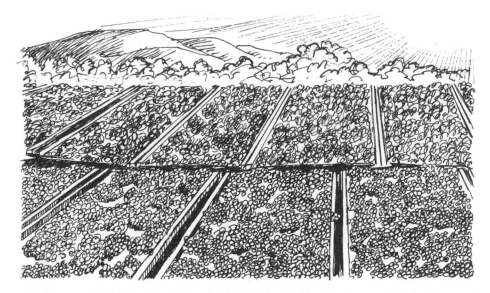

November, is hot and rainless, while the nearby mountains provide water for irrigation during the growing season.

In California, the grapes ripen in August. They are cut from the vines and allowed to lie in trays between the rows for from two to three weeks. Then they are put in boxes and allowed to dry some more. Then they are taken to the packing plant.

Here they are carried on conveyors to go through the process which prepares them for market. Special machinery removes stems and dirt from the grapes. Then the grapes are washed, steamed, or soaked in special solutions. Then they are dried and packed. About three-fourths of the original weight of the grapes is lost in drying them to make raisins.

Seedless raisins are made from the Sultana grape and from the Sultanina, both of which types grow in California.

WHAT IS LEATHER?

Leather is an animal hide or skin that has been tanned, or treated. The word "hides" is usually used to denote skins of large animals, as in cowhide or horsehide. The word "skins" is usually used for the smaller animals, as in goatskin or pigskin.

Cattle hides are the single most important source of leather raw materials. Calfskin leather is finer grained and lighter in weight that cattle hide. It is used for the most expensive shoes and handbags. The skin of any goat, old or young, is known as kidskin. Most suede leathers are kidskins buffed on the side that originally was next to the flesh.

The hide of the horse is used for shoes, jackets, and sports equipment. Pigskin leather is produced from hogs. The kangaroo provides the strongest of all leathers. It is used for track and baseball shoes. Alligator leather is used for shoes, handbags, wallets, and luggage. Even the skins of snakes and lizards are used as leathers for shoes, bags, and luggage.

Tanning turns animal hides and skins into soft, flexible leather. Tannin, the bark extract used in tanning, causes a chemical reaction. Different types of leathers are produced by slight changes in the chemical processes.

Before the hides are tanned, they must be preserved, or "cured." This is done in the packing house by salting the skins to prevent rotting. After the leather has been tanned, waxes, resins, shellac, or other chemicals are applied to make it shinier. Dyes are used to add color. The application of enamel paint called japan, or of plastics, gives patent leather its shiny surface. Suede leather is made when the underside of the leather is buffed or sandpapered to produce a nap.

BUFFING LEATHER

HOW CAN A HELICOPTER
STOP IN SPACE?

A helicopter can fly in any direction: forward, backward, to the side, or straight up. It can even hover over a single spot. To understand how this is done, we must understand how a helicopter flies.

As the rotor blades of a helicopter slice through the air, the air beneath the blades has greater pressure than the air above them. This pushes the blades up and creates lift.

The wings of an airplane create lift in the same way. In fact, the rotor blades of the helicopter are really moving wings. The difference is that the whole airplane has to move forward in order to get lift, while the helicopter needs only to move its rotor blades through the air. This is what enables a helicopter to go straight up or down or hover over one spot.

In front of the pilot in a helicopter there is the "cyclic stick" or go-stick. He moves it in the direction he wants to go and the helicopter flies that way. The cyclic stick works by changing the pitch of one blade at a time as it passes one side of the helicopter. This means that one side of the disc—the circle made by the whirling blades—has more lift than the other, and the disc tilts.

When the disc is flat, the helicopter hovers because all the lift force is straight up, keeping the helicopter in the air. If the disc is tilted, most of the force is still up, keeping the helicopter in the air, but some of the force pushes slightly forward, backward, or to the side, and the helicopter moves in that direction as a result.

HOW IS SYNTHETIC RUBBER MADE?

Natural rubber is made from latex, a white fluid of the rubber tree. The latex is held in a network of tiny tubes under the bark of the tree. When the bark is cut, the white, milky juice oozes out. Tiny particles of rubber float in this liquid.

Man has learned to manufacture latex by combining chemicals in certain ways. This rubber is called synthetic rubber. The kind of synthetic rubber produced in the largest amount is known as general-purpose rubber. Its two main ingredients are butadiene and styrene. Butadiene is a gas made from petroleum, and styrene is a liquid made from petroleum or coal.

The butadiene and styrene are pumped into a large tank containing a soapy mixture. The soapy solution makes it easier for the rubber particles to form. A catalyst (a chemical that speeds up the reaction) is added. As the mixture in the tank is stirred, it gradually changes to a milky white liquid. This is synthetic latex.

Synthetic latex is very similar in appearance to the natural latex that comes from the rubber tree. When the synthetic latex has developed to the proper state, a chemical is added to stop the reaction.

The latex is then pumped into another tank with acids and brine (saltwater). The mixture is stirred to coagulate it. The coagulated piece of synthetic rubber looks like gray crumbs. After being washed to remove any extra chemicals, the synthetic rubber is dried and pressed into bales. Basic synthetic rubber can be varied by adding other ingredients or combining them in different ways.

WHY DOES SILVER TARNISH?

Silver is a precious metal with remarkable qualities. It has been known and used by mankind before the dawn of history.

Silver conducts electricity and heat better than any other metal. Silver is the whitest of all metals. It reflects light better than other metals, which is why it is used as the backing material for mirrors.

Silver is also very easy to shape. Only gold can be worked with greater ease. Pure silver is very soft. Therefore, to increase its usefulness, small amounts of other metals are added to it. Sterling silver is 92½ percent silver and 7½ percent copper.

People who own objects made of silver often get annoyed because the silver begins to tarnish. The reason for this is that silver reacts very strongly to sulphur and many sulphur compounds.

With sulphur and hydrogen sulphide it forms black silver sulphide—and we notice this as the tarnishing or blackening of our silverware. The sulphur may be contained in certain foods, such as eggs, or by the tiny amounts of sulfurated hydrogen in the air. When buildings are heated by coal or oil, this can produce that effect in the air.

Silver is sometimes found in nature as native, or solid, metal. But more often it is combined with other metals and non-metals in mineral ores.

HOW DO ESKIMOS BUILD IGLOOS?

To most of us the word "igloo" means a house built from snow. But "igloo," or "iglu," is the Eskimo word for shelter. An igloo need not be made of snow. It can be a tent, a schoolhouse, a church, or even a railroad station. Only the Eskimo of Canada and northern Greenland ever build snow houses, and these are used only in winter.

A snow igloo is called an "apudyak." It is made of frozen snow—not ice—which is carved into neat blocks. Snow has hundreds of air spaces, and this is what provides excellent insulation against cold weather.

An Eskimo can build a snow house quite quickly. Blocks of snow are cut about two feet long, eighteen inches wide, and five inches thick. These are set on edge slanting inward to form a circle ten or twelve feet across. The blocks spiral upward and inward to form a dome. A small "breathing hole" is left open at the top of the igloo. Snow and ice platforms inside the igloo are covered with animal skins.

Sometimes several snow houses are built together with connecting tunnels. Eskimo families can visit each other without stepping out into the cold.

Eskimos of Alaska never built snow houses. Their winter houses were partly underground. A white settler in Alaska once showed his young daughter how to build a snow igloo. His Eskimo neighbors were all amazed—they had never seen a snow igloo before!

During the summer almost all Eskimos do what many campers do—they live in tents.

HOW ARE SYNTHETIC FIBERS MADE?

Some fibers, such as cotton, wool, silk, linen, and hair, are natural. They are produced by plants and animals. Others, such as rayon, nylon, Dacron, Saran, are man-made. To understand how man-made, or synthetic, fibers are made, we have to know something about fibers.

Most fibers are made up of organic (carbon-containing) chemicals, such as are found in all living things. Some organic chemicals have a special quality. Their molecules (groups of atoms) attach themselves to one another somewhat like the links of a chain. This is called polymerization. Each fiber consists of millions of such molecular chains held together by natural forces called chemical bonds. Different fibers contain different numbers of each kind of atom in their molecules, and the atoms are arranged differently.

In making synthetic fibers, chemists take atoms of carbon, hydrogen, oxygen, and other elements, and combine them in such a way that new substances are created. The raw materials for synthetic fibers are coal, oil, air, and water.

Atoms from these raw materials are combined and arranged into long molecular chains called polymers. In other words, the polymerization is created by the chemists, instead of by nature.

These polymers are liquid when they are hot. They can be cast into solid plastics and films like Saran wrap, or they can be extruded through spinnerets (nozzles with tiny openings) to form filaments. From these filaments fabrics are made.

Of all the fibers produced every year, about one-fifth are synthetic fibers.

HOW IS BUTTER MADE?

Most butter sold in the markets today is made in creameries that buy milk and cream from many farmers.

After the cream is unloaded, it is pasteurized. Most butter is made from sweet cream. Sometimes a starter—lactic-acid-producing bacteria mixed with other organisms—is added to the cream. The starter causes the cream to ripen. Some coloring is usually added, too.

Then the churning begins. It is done by a revolving drum that shakes the cream back and forth until it is a grainy mass. Churning takes about an hour. The buttermilk is then rinsed off by spraying the butterfat with water. What is left is butter.

The churn is filled with water and rotated for a few seconds to wash the butter. Salt is sometimes added. The butter is then kneaded mechanically until it has the right texture and the proper amount of moisture. The butter is then smooth and firm and ready for packaging.

Butter is usually packed in bulk containers weighing about sixty pounds and shipped to central markets. There it is repackaged into smaller pound or quarter-pound boxes or bars.

Butter has been made by man since the earliest times. It is mentioned in the Bible many times. In Proverbs 30:33: "Surely the churning of milk bringeth forth butter." The Hindus used butter as long ago as 900 B.C., and it was often a part of their religious ceremonies.

In the United States, butter was made by the very first settlers.

WHY DOES SWISS CHEESE HAVE HOLES?

We enjoy different kinds of cheeses because they have different flavors. The flavor of most cheese develops while it is curing. Curing takes place when the cheese is held in storage under carefully controlled conditions of temperature and moisture.

During curing, harmless bacteria, yeasts, and molds are allowed to grow in or on the cheese to develop its flavor and odor. For example, many different microorganisms grow in cheddar cheese to give it a distinctive cheddar taste. Other kinds of bacteria and yeasts produce the special flavors of brick, Limburger, and Liederkranz cheese.

In the making of Swiss cheese, a special kind of bacteria is also used. It is called propioni-bacteria, and it gives Swiss cheese its sweet, nutty flavor.

It is the action of these bacteria that also gives Swiss cheese its odd appearance. While the cheese is curing, the bacteria give off gas. The gas bubbles form the round holes, or "eyes," of the cheese.

Other cheeses get their special appearance and flavor from certain molds. The blue veins in Roquefort and blue cheeses come from the mold *Penicillium roquefortii*, which produces the flavor and smooth body. A grayish-white mold, *Penicillium camemberti*, grows on the surface of Camembert and causes the creamy texture and that special flavor.

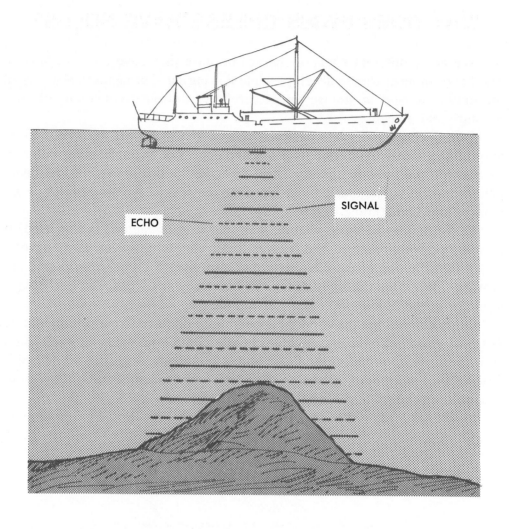

ECHO

SIGNAL

HOW DO SCIENTISTS DETERMINE OCEAN DEPTHS?

Finding the depth of water is called "sounding the depth" or "taking a sounding." In the old days, a weight was attached to one end of a rope. The rope was marked by a knot at every fathom (six feet). By counting the number of knots that went over the side before the weight hit bottom, one could determine the depth.

Today an echo sounder uses echoes of sound to explore the ocean floor. A device on board the ship sends out a sound signal which travels through the water at nearly one mile a second and is reflected—or echoed—back to an instrument. The deeper the water, the longer it takes for the echo to reach the ship.

In a modern echo sounder, high-frequency sound waves are beamed down from the ship. The instrument then records the echo as a dark mark on special paper. The paper is usually printed so that the depth can be read off in fathoms right away.

The echo sounder does more than just find the depth of the sea. It produces a continuous profile, or line, showing exactly what the ocean floor is like beneath the ship.

The soundings are so close together that the depth changes very little between one sounding and the next. If the ship passes over an undersea mountain, the echo sounder records the exact shape of the mountain. And if the bottom is flat, the record shows it as flat. The sounder does not miss a bump even a few feet high.

WHAT IS VIRGIN WOOL?

Soft woolen cloth is a favorite material for clothes and coverings all over the world. It keeps people warm, wears well, keeps its shape, and it can absorb moisture and still not feel damp to the skin.

The source of this fine fabric is chiefly the hairlike coat of the domestic lamb and sheep. This coat, like the fabric made from it, is known as wool.

The hairlike coat, or fleece, of some other animals also is wool, but usually has another name. Mohair comes from Angora goats and cashmere from Cashmere goats. Alpaca, llama, and vicuna come from animals of those names.

Wool is so valuable and useful that it is often used more than once. Manufacturers recover wool fibers from old clothing, rags, and manufacturing waste. They clean these and use them again.

To protect buyers, the United States government passed a Wool Products Labeling Act, which requires that products containing wool carry a label showing the amount of wool; the percentage of new, reprocessed, or reused wool; and the percentage of any fiber other than wool.

According to this act, "wool" means the fiber from the fleece of certain animals and not reclaimed. "Reprocessed wool" has been reclaimed from unused woolen materials. "Reused wool" has been salvaged from used woolen materials. And "virgin wool" means wool not used before in any way.

WHAT IS A SATELLITE?

In astronomy a satellite is a body that revolves around a larger body and is held captive by the larger body's attraction. Our moon is a satellite of the earth. The earth is a satellite of the sun.

Today when we say "satellite" we usually mean a man-made spacecraft circling the earth. Artificial satellites are sent into space for many purposes. Some are used for scientific research. Some send back information concerning the weather.

Some satellites relay television and radio broadcasts over long distances. Satellites may be used in navigation and map-making. Manned satellites give scientists information about how the human body reacts in a spacecraft.

Satellites can be of any size, from a tiny package of instruments to a huge balloon more than a hundred feet in diameter. They can weigh a few pounds or many tons. They can be shaped like balls, hatboxes, tin cans, bell buoys, and cigar boxes.

A satellite is launched at a velocity of 18,000 or more miles an hour. If no outside force acted on the satellite, it would travel off into space in a straight line. But the satellite cannot continue in a straight line because the earth's gravity attracts it, so the satellite is pulled into a curved path around the earth. The satellite is then in orbit.

Some satellites have orbits as near as 110 miles from the earth. Some have orbits as far as 22,300 miles from the earth. A satellite's orbit is chosen by scientists in advance, according to the task the satellite must perform.

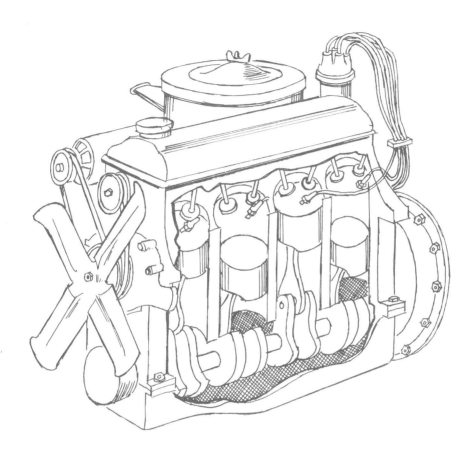

WHAT MAKES GASOLINE BURN?

Gasoline is very important in our lives because it is used as a fuel to make our automobiles go. Gasoline is a liquid fuel. It burns so rapidly and with such heat that it explodes.

Gasoline is a mixture of hydrocarbons or compounds made of hydrogen and carbon. These compounds are light liquids which boil at low temperatures. Carbon and oxygen are attracted to each other almost the way a magnet and iron are. When carbon combines with oxygen, burning takes place. This burning produces heat energy. When gasoline burns, the hydrogen joins with oxygen to form water vapor. The carbon and oxygen form carbon dioxide.

245

How does the burning of gasoline make a car go? The liquid gasoline is changed into a vapor and mixed with air by the carburetor of the engine. This mixture then flows into a cylinder where it is compressed by the piston moving up in the cylinder.

When the mixture of the gasoline vapor and air is compressed, a spark from a spark plug ignites the fuel. A great deal of gas is produced by the explosion (rapid burning). The pressure of the gas pushes hard on the piston and drives it down in the cylinder. The piston is connected to a crank which is free to turn. Thus, the push produced by the burning gasoline makes the crank go around. The crank is connected to the wheels and makes them turn.

The gasoline we use comes from crude oil or petroleum. In a refinery the oil is distilled, or separated into different parts, one of which is gasoline.

WHY IS THERE LEAD IN GASOLINE?

Gasoline is a mixture of hydrocarbons. These are substances composed of hydrogen and carbon atoms.

The gasoline sold as motor fuel is usually a blend of several different hydrocarbon liquids. Special substances, called additives, are mixed with the gasoline to make it burn better.

At temperatures about 70 degrees Fahrenheit, gasoline turns from a liquid into a vapor. In an automobile engine, the gasoline is mixed with air and sprayed into the engine. The heat in the engine turns it into a vapor. A spark plug then sets off a spark that burns the mixture.

Sometimes the gasoline mixture may be ignited too soon. When this happens, the engine makes a sound, usually called a knock. There are two ways to reduce engine knock. One is to use a slow-burning gasoline.

The other is to put a chemical into the fuel to slow down the burning. The best-known chemical used for this is called tetraethyl lead, or simply ethyl. And that's why there is "lead" in gasoline.

Different kinds of gasoline are classed according to how much they are likely to knock in an engine. They are rated by an octane number. A gasoline with a high octane number will produce less knock than a gasoline with a low number.

Gasolines with an octane rating of 85 or more are considered good enough for most modern engines. Airplane fuel has an octane rating of 115 or more.

WHAT IS A LASER BEAM?

The word "laser" is formed from the first letters of some long scientific words. The first two letters stand for "light amplification." The *s, e,* and *r* stand for "stimulated emission of radiation."

So a laser amplifies light. The laser can take a weak beam of light and make it into a strong beam. So lasers produce beams so strong that when they are focused, they can burn tiny holes in strips of steel in less than a second.

Laser beams can travel long distances through space without spreading out and growing weaker. Because of this, they may become an important means of communication in the space age. Many uses have already been found for lasers in medicine, science, and industry.

Scientists think of light as traveling in waves. The distance from the crest of one wave of light to the next crest is called a wavelength. Light from the sun or from a lamp is a mixture of many wavelengths. Each different wavelength produces a different color.

A laser beam is made up of rays that are all exactly the same wavelength. Light rays in ordinary light are all traveling in different directions. The rays in a laser beam move in exactly the same direction. A laser beam does not spread out and grow weak.

All the rays in a laser beam are in step. That is, the crests of one light ray are lined up with the crests of all the other rays. When light rays are in step like this, they strengthen one another. That's why a laser beam is very powerful. A laser beam is started in the laser by a weak flash of light that has the same wavelength as the beam.

WHERE DO WE GET WAX?

Many fruits and vegetables and the leaves of many plants have a thin protective coating of wax. Waxes are also produced by animals and are found in minerals and petroleum. And there are synthetic, or man-made waxes. So you see, we obtain wax from many, many sources.

Carnauba wax is obtained from the leaves of the carnauba palm tree of Brazil. This wax is hard and gives an excellent luster when it is used in floor and furniture polishes. Candelilla wax comes from a plant of the same name that grows in Mexico and the southwestern United States. It is a brown wax used in phonograph records, floor dressings, and candles.

Bayberry wax, from the berries of this shrub, is used for making candles. Worker bees secrete wax that they use in making their honeycombs. This wax, beeswax, is used for making cosmetics, church candles, polishes, crayons, and artificial flowers.

Wool wax from wool-bearing animals is called lanolin when it is purified. It is used in some ointments, cosmetics, and soaps. More than 90 percent of all commercial wax used today is petroleum wax. Petroleum wax has a wide variety of uses, because it is odorless, tasteless, and chemically inactive; that is, it does not react easily with most other substances.

A hard sort of petroleum wax is called paraffin. Paraffin's most important use is as a coating for paper products. Soft petroleum waxes, such as petroleum jelly, are used for medicinal purposes. Synthetic waxes are chemical combinations of hydrogen, carbon, oxygen, and sometimes chlorine. They are tailor-made to have definite properties.

WHAT KEEPS YOU UP ON A MOVING BICYCLE?

Of course, when you go spinning down the street on a bicycle, you don't think of what forces are at work to keep you balanced upright. But there are at least two things that enable you to stay up on a moving bicycle.

One is the gyroscopic force. A gyroscope is a heavy-rimmed wheel-and-axle mounted so that its center stays in one place no matter how the gyroscope is turned. When the wheel is set spinning, it holds its position in space until an outside force changes it.

Your bicycle wheels, when they start spinning, react in the same way. They

will stay in the same plane unless considerable force is used to change the direction. So gyroscopic forces tend to keep the bicycle upright.

The second thing is centrifugal force. Centrifugal effect pushes things away from the center of a rotating body. It is the force that pushes you against the side of the car when it turns sharply.

As you start to fall just a little bit on the bicycle, you turn the front wheel in the direction of the fall. The centrifugal force pushes you upright again. The path of the bicycle curves first to the right and then to the left as you compensate for each tendency to fall. In other words, you move the wheel, without thinking, in such a way that the centrifugal force will keep you upright.

WHAT IS INCENSE MADE OF?

Incense is a compound of gums and spices which produces a fragrant smoke when burned.

A resin is a substance that exudes from plants. A gum resin called frankincense, which comes from a certain tree, is the base of most incense, but other gum resins are used, too.

Incense has also been made from many other substances, including the bark, wood, and roots of trees, aromatic herbs, and plants, seeds, flowers, and fruits that give off an odor.

The custom of burning incense is ancient and found all over the world.

One of its earliest uses was in religious ceremonies, to fumigate and purify animal sacrifices and fruit offerings at the altar. Among the Jews, following the Exodus, the burning of incense was a rite that was ordered to be done. It was part of the memorial worship.

Incense has been used by many peoples, including the ancient Egyptians, Romans, Hindus, Chinese, Persians, Aztecs, and Incas. The Catholic Church began to use incense extensively about the 5th century.

Today, both the Latin and Greek churches use it in worship. Among Roman Catholics, it is used chiefly at High Mass, and in processions, funerals, and the consecration of churches. The Anglican Church at one time stopped the use of incense, but then began doing it again in the middle of the 19th century. So the burning of incense has played a significant part in the religious ceremonies of man.

HOW DOES HEAT INSULATION WORK?

Heat insulation slows down the flow of heat from one place to another. This can be very useful and important. For example, heat insulation keeps a house comfortable in winter by keeping the heat in. It also keeps a house cool in summer by keeping the heat out.

It is also used on hot pipes and tanks to keep them from losing heat; in refrigerators and cold-storage rooms to keep heat out; and it is used in refrigerated freight cars and trucks.

One form of manufactured insulation—that is, not natural insulation, but insulation made by man—is called mass insulation. It works by preventing the movement of heat. This is done by using materials that conduct heat poorly. These materials are filled with tiny closed-in spaces of air or gas, which are also poor conductors.

Different materials conduct heat differently. Some materials allow heat to flow through them easily, while others prevent the movement of heat. For example, silver is a good conductor of heat. It conducts heat about 19,300 times better than air does.

One of the best and most commonly used insulating materials is rock wool. The fibers of this material are made by dropping a certain kind of molten rock onto a whirling wheel. The wheel tosses droplets of molten rock into a current of air, which cools them into thin fibers.

Rock wool prevents the movement of heat (that is, it insulates) about 44 times better than glass, seven times better than wood, and even four times better than asbestos.

WHAT IS A DAM?

A dam is a barrier that holds back or controls the flow of water. Dams create lakes (called reservoirs) for storing water and supplying it as needed.

Dams help man to preserve and use water and land resources. A dam built in the right place can help prevent floods. The reservoirs behind dams store up drinking water for people and livestock. Dams provide water for irrigating dry fields. Electric power is produced at many dams by harnessing the power of falling water to turn machines called turbines, which drive generators.

There are several types of modern dams. Solid concrete gravity dams are designed so that the sheer weight of the solid concrete is enough to keep the dam from sliding or being overturned by the pressure of the water behind it. They are called gravity dams because they depend on the force of gravity to hold them in place.

Hollow concrete dams are made of concrete reinforced with steel. They require less concrete than solid dams, so they may cost less. Embankment dams are made of piles of earth and rock. They are also called earth-fill or rock-fill dams. Dikes and levees, which control floods along coasts and rivers, are embankment dams.

For almost every dam a spillway is important. A spillway is a sloping ramp or tunnel that is used to let water out of the reservoir gradually. Spillways are used to control the water level in the reservoir and to prevent water from suddenly overflowing the top of a dam.

Dams have been built on rivers and streams all over the world for thousands of years. The earliest known dam in Egypt is over 4,500 years old.

WHERE DO THEY GET
IRON TO MAKE STEEL?

Basically, steel is an alloy of iron and carbon. Other ingredients may be included to give the steel different characteristics, such as hardness, toughness, and resiliency. But the most important material for steelmaking is iron. Iron does not usually occur in nature as a pure metal. Most of it is found combined with other elements in the form of iron ore.

In the United States, the area around Lake Superior—which includes Michigan, Minnesota, and Wisconsin—is the chief source of iron ore. This region at one time supplied about 80 percent of the iron ore used in the United States and Canada. Today, imports of iron ore from abroad have increased.

Lake Superior ores average about 51 percent iron. These high-grade ores are mostly near the surface of the earth. They can be mined simply by stripping away the covering layer of earth and scooping up the ore. The high-grade deposits have been running low, however.

The richest sources of iron are iron ores, such as magnetite, hematite, limonite, and siderite. Magnetite contains a higher percentage of iron than any of the other iron ores, sometimes as much as 72 percent. It is a black mineral in which three parts of iron are combined with four parts of oxygen. Sizable deposits of magnetite are found in the Adirondacks region of New York, in New Jersey, and in Pennsylvania. Magnetite is also found in Sweden, Norway, Russia, and Germany.

Hematite is the most common iron material now used as a commercial source of iron. It is a soft, sandy or earthy, red-colored ore. The best grades of hematite contain 70 percent iron.

HOW ARE BRICKS MADE?

Did you know that bricks are one of man's oldest permanent building materials? They were first used over 5,000 years ago.

All bricks are made from clay. Clay is a common mineral substance composed of very small rock particles. Some types of clay are formed by the disintegration of rocks by weathering. Clay is found over most of the earth's surface, often in lake and river beds.

Clay becomes slippery and plastic (easily molded) when it is wet. When it is dry, it becomes hard and stony. When clay is heated to a high temperature (about 850 degrees Fahrenheit), it changes chemically so that it no longer becomes plastic when it is wet.

This means that bricks of baked clay will not soften and lose their shape when they become wet. Bricks are baked, or burned, at 1600 to 2200 degrees Fahrenheit. At about 1000 degrees Fahrenheit the brick turns red and its color becomes darker as the temperature increases.

Basically, the manufacture of bricks has changed little since ancient times, except that machines now do most of the work. The clay is dug by power shovels. After drying, it is ground in mills and screened to get particles of uniform size. The clay is mixed with water into a stiff paste, then forced out under pressure through shaped nozzles, like a giant square-cornered strip of toothpaste. The strip is automatically cut into pieces of the proper size by knives or wires. The soft brick is then dried in heated tunnels and finally carried in small railroad cars to the kilns for firing.

The average brick can take a load of about 5,000 pounds a square inch before it is crushed.

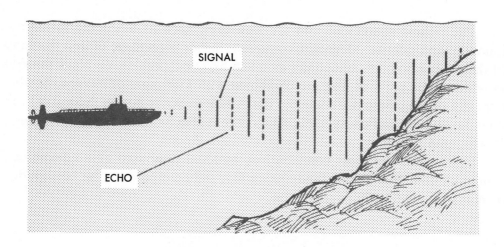

SIGNAL

ECHO

WHAT IS SONAR?

Let's start with an echo. When a sound bounces back from a large object, we call the returning sound an echo. When a radio signal is bounced back from an object, the returning signal is called a radio echo. Producing and receiving radio echoes is called radar.

A radar set produces radio signals. It radiates (sends out) the signals into space by means of an antenna. When a radio signal strikes an object, part of the signal is reflected back to the radar antenna. The signal is picked up there as a radar echo. A radar set changes the radar echo into an image that can be seen.

The word "sonar" comes from the first letters of "sound navigation ranging." Sonar is very much like radar. Sonar can detect and locate objects under the sea by echoes. Since radio signals cannot travel far underwater, sonar sets use sound signals instead.

Compared with ordinary sounds, sonar signals are very powerful. Most sonar sets send out sounds that are millions of times more powerful than a shout. These outgoing sound signals are sent out in pulses. Each pulse lasts a short fraction of a second.

Some sonar sets give off sounds that you can hear. Other sonar signals are like sounds from a dog whistle. Their pitch is so high that your ear cannot hear them. But the sonar set has a special receiver that can pick up the returning echoes. The echoes are then used to tell the location of underwater objects.

Sonar is used in searching for oil on land. A sonar pulse is sent into the ground. Echoes come back from different layers of soil and rock underneath. This helps geologists predict what may lie deep in the earth.

Chapter 5

OTHER CREATURES

DO HYENAS REALLY LAUGH?

There is actually a kind of hyena that is called the laughing hyena. It is the spotted hyena and is the largest member of the hyena family.

When this creature is on the prowl, or becomes excited by something, it utters a kind of eerie howl and chuckling gurgle that sounds like a laugh. But, of course, it is not "laughing" in the sense that human beings laugh. It is just making a shrieking noise that—to us—sounds like it is laughing.

The laughing hyena is a fierce-looking animal that stands about three feet high at the shoulder and is about six feet long. A big one may weigh as much as 175 pounds.

By day this hyena sleeps in a burrow or cave. When darkness falls, it comes out to seek food. Hyenas often hunt alone, but they may gather in packs around the remains of a kill left by lions or other beasts of prey. Their keen senses lead them to the kill, and they clean up all the remains.

The hyena is usually cowardly and sneaky, and it prefers to eat what others have killed and left. But it also lingers around camps and villages and sometimes attacks people sleeping in the open. It often follows herds of cattle or antelope. Closing in for the kill, it attacks a sick or crippled animal or else a very young or very old one.

The spotted, or laughing hyena, is an African species and it ranges from Ethiopia to the Cape of Good Hope. An unusual thing about the spotted hyena is that, unlike most animals, the female is larger than the male.

WHAT ARE EELS?

Eels are fish. Like all other fishes, they have backbones, live in water, and breathe through gills. They are cold-blooded—that is, their body temperature varies with the surrounding temperature.

Most kinds of eels live in the sea. A few kinds live in fresh water for long periods of time, but they too spend part of their lives in salt water. All eels shed their eggs in salt water.

The eels most familiar to North Americans are the freshwater eels. They live in lakes, ponds, and streams from the Atlantic to the Mississippi River. Conger eels and moray eels, which live only in salt water, are found along the rocky coast of southern California and along the coast of the Gulf of Mexico, and along the Atlantic coast of the United States.

Eels eat many things, including dead fish and small living creatures. Eels are most active at night. Sometimes in late afternoon you can find tiny eels feeding in shallow salt water. When disturbed, they burrow rapidly into the sand.

The skin of eels feels smooth, for it is slimy with mucus. But there are tiny scales in the skin of freshwater eels and some others.

Freshwater eels migrate a long distance to spawn (shed their eggs) and they spawn in salt water, even though they live in fresh water. Few other fish can go from the ocean to fresh water, or from fresh water to the ocean, without dying. Biologists think that the body mucus helps protect eels against damage from this change.

Freshwater eels, moray eels, and some others, have a remarkable ability to recover from wounds that would kill other fish. A substance in their blood prevents possible infection.

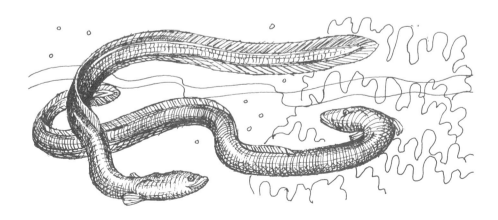

WHY DOES A BABY KANGAROO STAY SO LONG IN THE POUCH?

Pouched mammals form one order of mammals, the marsupials. Marsupials differ from all other mammals in the way their young develop and are cared for.

At birth, baby marsupials are tiny and only partly developed. The reason is the short time spent within the mother's body. It may be as little as 8 to 12 days with some of the smallest species; with the largest it is usually no more than 30 to 40 days.

At birth, a baby kangaroo is hardly an inch long and not even fully formed. Its tail and hind legs are like tiny stumps. Its eyes are closed, and its ears are not fully formed. Its mouth is just a tiny hole. Only its front feet are well developed, with toes and nails.

As soon as the tiny baby kangaroo is born, it begins to climb through the mother's fur toward the opening of her pouch. It seems to be guided by instinct. The mother, however, licks a path for it through her fur. Climbing hand over hand, the baby reaches the opening of the pouch and pops in.

Once inside, the baby quickly searches out a nipple and hangs. The little kangaroo remains firmly attached there for a number of weeks, nursing and developing. It grows, becomes covered with fur, its eyes open, and its ears form. Finally, it can let go of the nipple and peer out of the pouch.

When it is several months old, it starts to venture outside. But if danger threatens, it pops right back. By the time the baby is six months old, it is too big to fit into the pouch.

Now it eats grass and vegetable matter, like its mother. It is well on the way to growing up and taking care of itself.

WHY DO BIRDS SING?

The bird songs and calls we hear in the spring are part of the courtship that precedes mating.

The male uses his song to attract a mate. When male and female have found each other, the male woos the female by more singing. In some species of birds, the females respond with songs of their own.

Not all birds sing. And there are even some birds, such as the stork and the pelican, that seem to have no voice at all. Birds have vocal organs that are a bit different from ours.

In man, the vocal chords are located in the larynx at the upper end of the windpipe. Birds have simple membranes which are located at the lower end of the windpipe in a structure called the syrinx. These membranes vibrate.

The reason different families of birds are able to produce different songs is that the shape of this structure, and the number of muscles which control the membranes, varies with different birds.

Birds make other sounds besides singing. There are notes, signals from one bird to another of the same kind, and there are alarm calls, which all species of birds recognize as meaning danger.

If a snake approaches a nest too closely, this alarm call will be used, and birds of many kinds in the area will arrive and try to help. Notes and calls are used by birds throughout the year, but the songs are usually heard during the nesting season only.

Bird songs differ from each other in pitch, pattern, rhythm, and quality. The thrushes are supposed to have the greatest ability to sing true songs.

WHERE DO DOGS COME FROM?

All the living members of the dog family are descended from a wolflike creature called *Tomarctus*. This ancient canine, called "the father of dogs," roamed the earth's forests perhaps 15,000,000 years ago.

The characteristics and habits of the wild dogs are all shared by the domestic dog. Domestic dogs are brothers under the skin to wolves, coyotes, and jackals—the typical wild dogs. All belong to the branch of the dog family called *Canis*.

All are so closely related that domestic dogs can mate with wolves, coyotes, or jackals, and produce fertile offspring. But none of these species will interbreed with foxes. The foxes belong to another branch of the canine family.

At some time long ago early man tamed a few wild dogs. These dogs may have been wolf cubs. Or they may have been jackals or some other member of the wild dog family. Man found that these animals could be useful. He used them to help him catch other animals and birds for food and clothing.

As man became more civilized, he found that the dog was a good friend and a helpful guard for his home and cattle. In time, different breeds of dogs were developed for special purposes. Dogs with long noses, like setters, pointers, and beagles, were bred to track the scent of game, birds, and rabbits. Others, like greyhounds, chased rabbits and deer. Strong, heavy dogs like the mastiff pulled carts. Other dogs were bred to use for guard work and to scent the enemy in war. In addition to hunting and working dogs, other breeds came to be used in sport and as pets.

CAN SNAKES HEAR?

Snakes have no ears on the outside of their heads. This means that they do not hear airborne sounds as you do.

But snakes are sensitive to vibrations through the ground. So when a snake seems to "hear you coming," it is really feeling the ground shaking under your footsteps. Although a snake seems to have no sense of hearing, it more than makes up for it with other senses.

Most snakes can see very well. The eyes of snakes are always open, for snakes do not have movable eyelids. Snakes notice their prey more by movement than by shape or color. Snakes have a very keen sense of smell. They can recognize prey animals, enemies, and each other by odors.

Snakes also have another sense, related to both smell and taste, that human beings don't have. A snake can pick up chemical particles from the air, from the ground, or from some other animal or object, with the tips of its long forked tongue. The snake then thrusts these tips into a pair of openings in the roof of its mouth. These openings contain some highly sensitive nerve cells. And with these the snake can identify the chemical particles as food, enemy, friend, or whatever.

In fact, snakes have such a highly developed chemical sense that they can follow the trail of another animal like a well-trained hound. In addition, certain snakes—pit vipers and some boas and vipers—have a sense that no other animal has developed. They can sense a prey animal that is a little warmer or a little cooler than its surroundings.

This is a heat sense, and it enables these snakes to locate and strike a prey animal in the dark without ever seeing it!

WHAT IS AN ORGANISM?

Scientists speak of all living things as organisms. A human being is an organism. So is a mouse, a fish, an insect, a tree, a daisy. So are bacteria and other tiny creatures.

All these living beings share some important features. That is one reason why scientists use the word "organism," thus giving each living being a name in common with every other living being.

The word "organism" also suggests that each living thing is organized. That is, its parts are arranged in certain ways and do certain work within the organism as a whole.

To be alive, a substance must be active. The activity of an organism is chemical and it takes place inside the organism. This chemical activity is a continuous process. Without it the organism would not be alive.

Energy must continually enter an organism so that the living machinery keeps going. Matter must also be continually flowing through an organism. A living organism has shape and substance (material). New material is continually flowing in to take the place of older material which is being pushed out or used up. The flow of energy and matter through an organism is called metabolism.

An organism must grow until it reaches its full size. And an organism must reproduce—make small, new organisms which replace larger, older organisms. So we can say an organism is alive if it can metabolize, grow, and reproduce.

WHAT DO HORNETS USE TO MAKE THEIR NESTS?

Several large members of the wasp family of insects are called hornets. They have thick bodies, usually black or dark brown, marked with brilliant white or yellow. This is why some of them are called "yellow jackets."

Hornets are social insects. They live together and build nests. If their nests are attacked, they become so angry that they sting the enemy very painfully. No wonder we have the expression "as mad as a hornet."

Hornets build large nests, sometimes a foot long, with a hole at or near the bottom. These nests are attached to branches of trees, or on bushes, or sometimes under the projecting roofs of buildings.

What are the nests made of? Paper. Yes—paper! We might say the hornets were the first paper-makers on earth. The paper is produced from wood pulp. The hornet collects it from boards or trees that have had the bark removed by accident or other means.

In collecting the pulp, the hornet goes backward, scraping off the pulp with its jaws and moistening it as it goes. This forms a round ball of paper pulp. The pulp is then spread into a sheet in building the nest.

Most people don't like hornets because they are afraid of their sting. And hornets do some damage to fruit. But, actually, hornets are a friend to man in destroying flies and other harmful insects.

HOW DO WORMS CRAWL?

There are many different kinds of worms, but we will discuss the earthworm, the kind most familiar to us.

The body of the earthworm is divided into little rings, or segments, separated by grooves. So an earthworm belongs to the group known as "annelids." The name annelid means "little rings."

An earthworm stays underground most of the time, tunneling through soft, damp topsoil and feeding as it goes. It produces a slime that makes travel easy. An earthworm burrows along, using two sets of muscles.

One set of muscles runs around the body, with one muscle in each segment. When the segment muscles tighten, the body becomes longer and thinner. The front end is pushed forward. The second set of muscles runs lengthwise along the body. When these muscles tighten, the segments are pulled up close together. The body shortens.

An earthworm is like a tube within a tube. The long, segmented body is one tube. Within this is the long digestive tube through which the food passes. The digestive tube is open at both ends. Food passes in at one end, and the undigested remains pass out at the other.

In heavy or deep soil a worm tunnels by swallowing the soil. This method of moving is also a way of eating, for there are decaying bits of plants and animals in the soil. These are digested as the soil passes through the digestive tube.

This activity of swallowing soil and bringing it up to the surface plays an important part in turning over and enriching the soil. Scientists say that in each acre of land earthworms turn over ten to eighteen tons of soil each year.

HOW DOES A CATERPILLAR SPIN A COCOON?

The larvae or young of butterflies and moths are called caterpillars. A caterpillar is really an insect in the making.

When a caterpillar hatches from the egg laid by the mother butterfly or moth, it is usually very small. But it grows rapidly, and all kinds of changes begin to take place.

The change caterpillars undergo is called metamorphosis. The first step for many moth caterpillars is to build cocoons. They spin them with threads of sticky fluid that flows from an opening in the lower lip. This fluid hardens in the air and becomes the thread we call natural silk.

Some caterpillars form bags of silk that entirely enclose them. Others roll up a leaf, fastening the edges with the silk. Many of the hairy kinds of caterpillars pad the cocoons with their own hair. Some caterpillars, including most of those in the butterfly group, do not build cocoons.

But all caterpillars go through a resting stage, and in this stage it is called a pupa. The pupa does nothing except rest. This stage may last two weeks; it may last a whole winter. During this period the caterpillar changes into a full-grown butterfly or moth.

In its new and adult form, it emerges wet and shaky from the cocoon. As blood flows into the veins of the wings, the adult flutters its wings and dries them. In a few hours, when the wings are strong and dry, the butterfly or moth flies off to live as an adult.

WHY CAN'T THE OSTRICH FLY?

In the air the force of gravity is felt even more than when standing on the ground. This is because air gives little support to a creature's weight. Only small birds are able to fly by flapping their wings, because very large breast muscles are needed for this purpose.

A large bird does not have room for such muscles. And so the real giants among birds cannot fly at all. These include the ostrich, the rhea of South America, the emu of Australia, and a few others. All are much too heavy to fly. No bird can be truly a giant and still fly.

Is the ostrich really a giant? It certainly is! It is the largest of living birds. A full-grown ostrich is seven, and sometimes eight, feet tall. It weighs from 150 to more than 300 pounds!

But birds that cannot fly in some cases make up for this by having tremendous running speed. The ostrich is believed by some experts to be the fastest running bird. It has long, strong, thick legs and it can speed across the desert faster than the swift Arabian horse.

Some people claim they have seen ostriches run as fast as 50 miles an hour. But biologists believe that the fastest an ostrich can run is from 28 to 37 miles per hour—which is very fast, indeed.

The stride of the ostrich as it runs, moving one foot and then the other, can cover as much as 28 feet in a single leap.

HOW ARE FISH ABLE
TO SMELL THINGS?

It probably surprises many people to learn that fishes can smell things just as other creatures can. Fishes smell with their noses.

There are two pairs of nostrils in a fish. That is, each nostril has two openings, which are called pits. One opening is in the front. The other is directly behind it. The two are separated by a small flap. The nostril can be in a number of different locations on the face. As is true with everything about fishes, there are many variations.

A current of water enters and leaves each pit. It flows in the front one and out the rear one. As the water flows, it stimulates the sense cells that tell the fish about odors. Many fishes have a keen sense of smell. They can detect the very smallest traces of substances.

In fact, the sense of smell may be important to fish in helping them find their way home. As we know, salmon return to their original home to spawn. How do they do it? Scientists believe that perhaps salmon can tell their childhood stream by its odor.

Researchers have trained salmon to distinguish 14 different kinds of colors. Some fish could tell the difference between water from two creeks. But if their noses were plugged up, they couldn't tell.

In other experiments a large number of salmon were taken out of their home stream. One half had their noses plugged; the other half didn't. Those with plugged noses got lost. The others found their way home again.

DO ALL FISHES LAY EGGS?

Most fishes lay eggs and these eggs are fertilized outside the body. Fishes that emit eggs are described as oviparous. But some fishes give birth to living young. These are described as viviparous.

Among the viviparous fishes are guppies, platies, swordtails, and mollies. The eggs are fertilized inside the body of the female and grow into baby fish there. At the appropriate time, they are born. In platies it is 21 days after fertilization.

The number of eggs that are laid and fertilized vary a great deal from one kind of fish to another. Some fishes expel their eggs and then abandon them, showing no more interest in them. These kind of fishes lay great numbers of eggs. Those fishes that watch over their developing young lay far fewer eggs.

Fishes also lay two types of eggs. One type floats and the other sinks. Eggs that float are called pelagic eggs. They are usually tiny and transparent and do not have much yolk. Eggs that sink are called demersal eggs. They are usually heavier and yolky.

As an example, herring lay demersal eggs and show no care for these eggs. They may deposit 20,000 to 40,000 eggs. Cod, on the other hand, lay pelagic eggs. An average-sized cod can lay one hundred million eggs!

Mackerel lay 400,000 to 500,000 eggs in a season, but they never lay more than 50,000 at a time. Large halibut can lay over two million eggs!

Eggs vary in size, too. Herring eggs are 1/25-inch in diameter. Cod eggs are about 1/15-inch. Halibut eggs are ⅛-inch. Eggs that are guarded until the young are larger have greater chance for survival. But billions and billions of fish eggs are eaten by other creatures.

HOW DO ANIMALS GET RABIES?

Viruses cause certain diseases in man and in animals. A virus is a germ which is too small to be seen with the ordinary microscope.

The virus which causes the disease known as rabies can infect all warm-blooded animals. Man most often receives the disease from a dog infected with the virus. In the country, wild animals such as wolves, foxes, skunks, bears, and bats may also become sick with rabies virus. Even domestic animals, such as cows and cats, become infected. In other words, the rabies virus enters the animal's body, an infection is started, and the animal has rabies.

After infection, the disease will not show up for some time, usually four to six weeks. Dogs at first are quiet, have fever, and are not interested in food. Then they become excited. Saliva froths from the mouth. They growl and bark, and are likely to bite. The dog will die in about three to five days after these symptoms appear. Since the virus is in the saliva, the disease is passed on by biting. Very seldom is it passed on in any other way.

The disease begins in man much as it does in the dog. He is quiet and has fever and strange feelings. Soon his muscles draw strongly together. When he tries to drink, the muscles of his mouth and throat tighten as in a spasm. That's why another name for this disease is hydrophobia, which means fear of water. But the muscle spasms are due to changes in the nervous system. Death comes when the breathing muscles go into spasm.

Once the disease appears in man or animals, death is almost certain. That's why the disease must be prevented. The bite area is cleaned thoroughly. If the man or animal can be treated within three days of being bitten, a serum is used. The serum acts against the virus before it can increase and attack the brain. Injections are given each day for a period of two or three weeks.

WHEN DID HORSES COME TO NORTH AMERICA?

This question should really be: when did horses come *back* to North America? The horse developed into its present form in North America millions of years ago.

From time to time during their long history, horses traveled over land bridges from their North American homeland. They spread into South America, Asia, Europe, and Africa. On all these continents they evolved into numbers of different species. But during the Ice Age all the horses living in the Americas became extinct. At the dawn of recorded history there were no horses in North America. Horses then lived only in Europe, Asia, and Africa.

It was the Spanish conquistadores who brought horses back to America. In 1519 Hernando Cortes carried 16 horses with him when he sailed from Havana for the conquest of Mexico. De Soto brought more than two hundred horses with him when he landed in Florida in 1539. He still had most of them when he pushed on across the Mississippi River in 1541. And Coronado, exploring the Southwest at the same time, had one thousand or more horses in his expedition.

Spanish missionaries and settlers followed the explorers, bringing still other horses with them. At first the Indians were frightened by the horses, for they had never seen such beasts. But they quickly discovered how useful horses could be. Soon they began to steal horses from the Spaniards and to capture runaways. Tribe after tribe acquired horses.

Possession of the horse changed the whole way of life for many western Indian tribes. Horses made it possible for them to move from one campground to another quickly and easily. Horses also allowed them to follow the bison herds and kill all they needed. Plains Indians also used horses in warfare against one another and against the invading white man.

HOW DO SCIENTISTS KNOW
ANIMALS ARE COLOR BLIND?

To find out whether animals can see colors, scientists have conducted certain experiments. All they can say is that, according to the results of these experiments, certain animals cannot see colors.

Let's consider dogs, for example. Dogs were able to be trained so that their mouths watered (salivated) when definite musical notes were sounded. This was because when those notes were sounded, the dogs would be given food. Then the same kind of experiment was tried with different colors. It was impossible to make dogs tell one color from another as signals for food. Conclusion: dogs are color blind.

A similar type of experiment was made with cats. An attempt was made to train different cats to come for their food in response to signals of six different colors. But the cats always confused their color with shades of gray that were shown. So it is believed that cats are color blind.

We know that monkeys and apes can see colors because certain experiments prove it. They have been trained to go for their meal to a cupboard, the door of which was painted a certain color, and they wouldn't go to doors painted with other colors—and which had no food.

But even scientists say that the evidence that most animals are color blind is not complete. Maybe more tests will reveal things we don't know about animals. For example, tests were made that showed that horses are able to tell green and yellow from any shade of gray and from one another. But they don't seem to be very good at recognizing red or blue as colors.

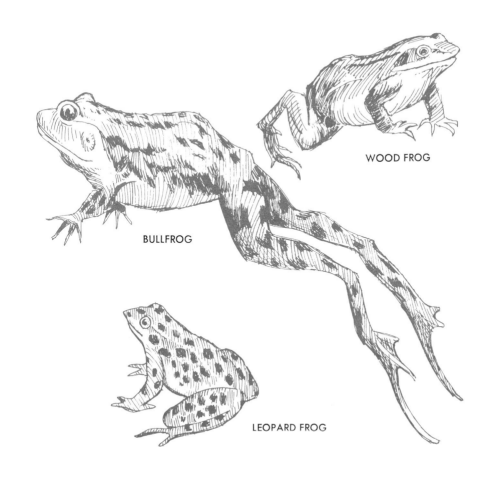

WOOD FROG

BULLFROG

LEOPARD FROG

WHAT HAPPENS TO FROGS IN WINTER?

There are about 17 species of frogs that live in the United States. The most common are the bullfrog, leopard frog, and the wood frog.

Frogs vary considerably in shape, color, and size. Some little tree frogs are no more than one inch in length. Leopard frogs are about two to four inches long. Bullfrogs often reach eight inches and have legs that are ten inches long. A fully developed bullfrog is usually dark green or brown in color so that it can hardly be seen on a muddy bank or among the weeds.

What do these frogs do in the winter? In northern countries, when cold weather sets in, some frogs dive into a pond, bury themselves in the mud and stay there all winter. Ponds do not freeze solid, even when winters are very cold, so the frog does not freeze either.

But it does become very cold. The frog is an amphibian, belonging to that group of cold-blooded creatures that live both in water and on land. When an amphibian becomes cold, it needs very little oxygen because it is burning little food. This explains why the frog can stay under water all winter without breathing air.

There is some oxygen in water, and what little the frog needs during the winter it gets from the water through its skin. The frog sometimes spends the winter in a hole in a soft bank or buried under loose stones and earth.

Did you know that there are some frogs that live in trees? These tree frogs are usually quite small and have suckers or sticky disks on their feet to help them in climbing.

HOW CAN FLIES WALK UPSIDE DOWN ON CEILINGS?

We see the housefly around so much that it is hard for us to realize what a remarkable creature this is. There are so many parts of the housefly that are unusual, that it doesn't matter where we start.

The body of the housefly is divided into three parts: the head, the middle section, or thorax, and the abdomen. The thorax has three pairs of legs attached to it.

The legs are divided into five parts, of which the last is the foot. The fly walks tiptoe on two claws that are attached to the underpart of the foot. Under the claws are pads, and these pads secrete a sticky liquid. It is because of this sticky liquid in the pads that the fly can cling to practically any surface. It can walk upside-down on the ceiling or even on the underside of a glass skylight.

Another amazing thing about the fly is the way it sees. Its eyes are two big brown balls on either side of the head. Each eye is made up of thousands of lenses. Each lens contributes one bit of the picture which the fly sees. These two big eyes are called compound eyes. The fly also has on top of the head, looking straight up, three simple eyes that can be seen only through a magnifying glass.

The feelers, or antennae, of the housefly are used as organs of smell, not of feeling. These antennae can detect odors at a great distance. A housefly will appear pretty quickly when some good-smelling food is around.

WHAT MAKES A RATTLESNAKE POISONOUS?

Scientists think that there are between 3,000 and 3,500 kind of snakes now living. Of these, 10 to 15 percent are poisonous kinds. They stun or kill their prey with venom. The rattlesnake happens to be one of the poisonous kind.

Rattlesnakes belong to a group of snakes called vipers, all of which are venomous. Rattlesnakes are pit vipers, and they get this name because of the two large pits on their heads. These pits are sensitive to the slightest change in temperature. They enable a viper to detect the presence of a warm-blooded animal even in the dark.

Vipers have a complicated type of venom system. Their fangs are very long. Each fang is set on a very short upper jawbone that can rotate. When a viper closes its mouth, the jawbone is rotated so that the fang lies lengthwise in the mouth and the mouth can close. When the mouth is opened for a strike, the jawbone is turned forward, bringing the fang at right angles to the throat.

The venom that vipers put into their victims with their fangs affects mainly blood cells and blood vessels. It may cause great swelling and bleeding. The venom of a few species, such as the South American rattlesnake, affects the nerves also.

There are 15 kinds of rattlesnakes, of various sizes and colors, in the United States and Canada. All of them have rattles at the tips of their tails. The "rattle" is made up of dry, horny rings of skin that lock loosely onto one another. When the snake shakes its tail, as it does when excited, these horny pieces of skin rub against one another. This results in a rasping or buzzing sound. This rattle helps the snake warn other animals away.

WHERE DO BACTERIA LIVE?

Bacteria are probably the most common form of life on earth. They are microorganisms, which means they can be seen only under a microscope. A bacteria consists of only one cell, and they have some features of both plants and animals.

There are at least two thousand species of bacteria, and they live practically everywhere and anywhere. Some live in the mouths, noses, and intestines of animals, including man. Others live on fallen leaves, dead trees, animal wastes, and carcasses.

Bacteria live in fresh and salt water, in milk, and in most foods. They live in dust, soil, and sewage. Some bacteria are able to use as food such substances as hydrogen gas, ammonia, iron compounds, and paraffin. A few feed on acids and gases that are poisonous to man.

Although most bacteria are killed by extreme heat, some live in hot springs. Freezing may check their growth, but does not ordinarily kill bacteria. They can remain inactive for long periods of time. Bacteria have been found frozen in salt deposits that are hundreds of millions of years old. These bacteria have become active in the laboratory.

If bacteria can survive under practically any conditions, isn't man in great danger from them? Luckily, most bacteria are either harmless or actually helpful to other forms of life. Bacteria cause the decay of dead plants and animals. Bacteria play an important part in the digestive processes of man and other animals. They are a vital link in the food chain that supports life. They are used in the fermentation processes which produce certain foods, drugs, and many products in industry.

DO INSECTS HAVE HEARTS?

It is hard for us to believe that tiny creatures like insects have organs like hearts and brains. But insects do have them. An insect has nerves and a brain. A large nerve center in the head is the insect's brain. The brain receives sensations and sends messages to certain muscles to make them work. This is done automatically, because an insect's actions are automatic.

An insect's blood is not red like ours. It doesn't carry oxygen, so it has no hemoglobin, which is what makes blood red. The insect's heart is part of

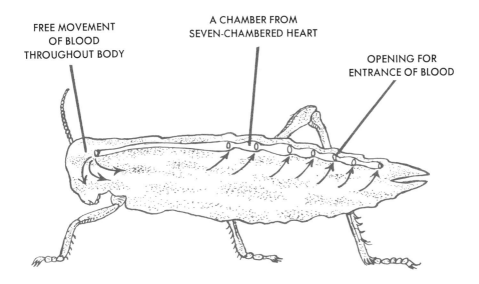

FREE MOVEMENT
OF BLOOD
THROUGHOUT BODY

A CHAMBER FROM
SEVEN-CHAMBERED HEART

OPENING FOR
ENTRANCE OF BLOOD

a long tube running along the top of the body, right under the skin. The tube opens just under the brain.

There are tiny openings with valves along this tubelike heart. Blood is sucked into the heart through these openings. The heart contracts and forces blood to flow toward the head.

In the head the blood pours out over the brain and then flows backward through the body. As it flows backward it bathes the body organs, muscles, and nervous system. It brings digested food and takes away waste material.

You can see an insect's heart in some living specimens. If you look carefully at a cutworm, a mosquito larva, or some caterpillars, you can see the tubelike heart along the back. Watch it beat. You may be able to notice that the heart beats faster when the insect is warm than when it is cold.

Another interesting thing about insects is their strength. Considering their size, they are remarkably strong. This is because of the thickness of their muscles, and because they have so many. Man has about 800 muscles. A grasshopper has about 900!

WHAT IS A VULTURE?

The vulture is a large bird of prey. The word "vulture" has become a kind of symbol for creatures that feed on other animals.

Vultures belong to the same order of birds as the falcons, hawks, and eagles. There are five vultures to be found in North and South America. They are the turkey vulture, the black vulture, the king vulture, the California condor, and the South American condor.

All vultures feed on carrion (dead animals), which is why most people don't like them. Actually, these large birds are very graceful in flight, and one can admire the way they glide about in the air. But when a vulture discovers a dead animal, it swoops down, is joined by other vultures, and the birds tear the animal apart with their hooked beaks.

The South American condor is the only member of the vulture family that sometimes kills animals for food. It eats eggs, young sea birds, and young mammals. It also eats any dead animals that it can find.

How do vultures discover dead animals they eat? Many experiments have been made to get the answer. It is known that vultures have much better eyesight than human beings have. They can see small things from great distances. But they have hardly any sense of smell. So we still don't know exactly how they do it.

By the way, the North American vultures are quite welcome during stock-killing time on western ranches. They gather in numbers and save the rancher the labor and expense of getting rid of the unused parts of the animals killed.

HOW DO OWLS HUNT?

Owls are birds of prey, and they are among the finest hunters for prey to be found anywhere. It's as if everything about the owl is designed to help it in its hunting.

The owl has powerful, needlelike talons (claws) that it closes over its prey like the jaws of a trap. The talons have one toe which the owl can change from a forward to a backward position.

In most species of owls the large eyes help it to see better during the evenings and moonlit nights than during the daytime. The owl has better ears than any other bird. Its two ears may be of different shapes and are hidden in the head feathers.

The owl has soft "furry" edges to the flight feathers of its wings. This makes the flight of the owl almost noiseless—and so helps it in its hunting. Not even the owl can see in complete darkness, but it can see on nights that people would call completely dark.

The owl hunts best at dawn or dusk, or on moonlit nights. It can hear a mouse scamper over the ground many yards away. When an owl is listening from its hunting perch, it spreads out the feathers and skin which cover its ears. This forms a large funnel which collects even the faintest sound. After it locates the prey by sound, the owl attacks swiftly and directly on noiseless wings and captures its prey with talons.

Owls eat mammals such as mice, squirrels, and rabbits. They also eat reptiles, frogs, birds and even fish. They are better at catching mice than most man-made mousetraps.

HOW DO WE KNOW BATS USE RADAR?

Most bats are active only at night. They come out at night to find food. For centuries men who studied bats wondered how they found their way in the dark. How could a bat with no light to see by find a flying insect and catch it in flight?

Many people used to think that bats had unusually keen eyesight and could see by light too faint for human eyes to detect. Scientists now know that a bat's ability to navigate depends not on its eyes, but on its ears and vocal organs.

Way back in the 1780's an Italian zoologist named Spallanzani did an experiment. He blinded some bats and released them into a room crisscrossed with silk threads. The bats flew through the maze without touching the threads. When he plugged their ears, they became entangled in the threads. Spallanzani felt that bats used their ears rather than their eyes to find their way in the dark.

In 1920 a scientist suggested that bats sent out signals that were beyond the range of human hearing. Such sounds are called ultrasonic. In 1941, two other scientists decided to use a new electronic instrument that detected ultrasonic sounds in an experiment with bats.

The machine showed that the bats were uttering high-pitched cries, and that they were constantly squeaking as they flew through a maze of wires that had been set up in the dark. When they taped the bats' mouths shut, the animals blundered badly.

A bat sends out signals—high-pitched squeaks that bounce off anything in its path. A sound is bounced back, or reflected. It is an echo. The bat uses echoes to locate things in the dark.

Scientists call this echolocation, and it is like our systems of radar.

WHY DO OPOSSUMS CARRY THEIR YOUNG?

Opossums belong to a group of animals called marsupial. The females of this troup have pouches on the underside of the body in which the young develop.

An interesting thing about opossums is the fact that the young are so small. You could put all of the 5 to 18 babies in a tablespoon when they are born! At birth they are blind, hairless, and practically shapeless.

The babies climb into their mother's pouch, and attach themselves to the milk glands. When they are a month old they begin to poke their heads out of the pouch. A few weeks later they crawl out for short periods of time.

Because they are so small, and still quite helpless, the mother opossum carries her young. They ride on her back. She brings her tail up and they wrap their tails around it. When they are about three months old, they leave their mother; and at one year they are ready to raise families.

Opossums spend a lot of time in trees, hunting and eating. They like to eat upside down. To do this, they wrap their tails around a branch, hang down, and grasp their food by all four feet.

Opossums eat small mammals, insects, small birds, eggs, poultry, lizards, crayfish, snails, fruit of all kinds, corn on the cob, mushrooms, and worms. At night opossums invade orchards for fruit and henhouses for poultry and eggs. So man doesn't exactly like all their eating habits. But opossums do help farmers by killing mice and insects.

DO POLAR BEARS HIBERNATE?

The word "hibernate" comes from the Latin and means "winter sleep." Many people think that certain animals hibernate because the weather gets cold where they live. And since polar bears live where it's very cold, they must hibernate.

But animals who hibernate do it because their food supply becomes scarce in winter. They do not store up a food supply for the winter. Instead, they lay up a reserve supply of fat on their body. Then the hibernating animal sleeps through the cold winter, living on the fat it has stored up in its body.

During this sleep, all life activities nearly stop. The body temperature goes down, the breathing is slow, the heart beats faintly. Do polar bears do this?

The answer is no. They do sleep more in the winter than in summer, but their sleep is not the deep sleep of hibernation. Their temperatures and breathing remain normal. They sleep in hollows or caves in the ice or snow. During warm spells they may even venture forth for a day or so.

Female polar bears do more sleeping in winter than the males. They go into dens and are often snowed under for weeks. The cubs are born during this winter sleep. The cubs are often very small, weighing no more than six or eight ounces at birth. So the mother bear nurses them and cares for them for several months during the winter.

Hibernating animals are awakened in the spring by the change in temperature, moisture, and by hunger. They crawl out of their dens and start eating again.

DO FISHES EVER SLEEP?

Can you sleep with your eyes open? No, you have to close your eyelids to go to sleep. And that's why most fishes do not sleep as we do. They do not have eyelids that they can close. But they do rest when the light dims. Some fish, such as the triggerfish, even lie down on their sides to rest.

The eye of a fish is similar to ours in many ways. But there are differences because a fish sees in water, while we see in air. As in people, there is an iris that surrounds the lens in fishes. The opening in the iris is called the pupil. The pupil of the eye always stays the same size in most fishes.

This means it does not close in bright light or open in dim light, as ours does. So if we turn on a bright light, the fish may be dazzled. It can't close out some of the light, as we can. However, a few fishes do have pupils that can narrow. By the way, fishes can't shed a tear, for they have no tear glands. Their eyes are kept moist by the surrounding water.

In most fishes the eyes are placed on each side of the head. Fishes see different images out of each eye. They have a large field of vision on both sides. Their field is much larger than ours. They can see in front, behind, above, and below themselves. Just in front of its nose a fish can focus both eyes on the same object.

Experiments have shown that some fishes can see colors. They can also distinguish between red and green, and probably between blue and yellow. However, not many species have been tested. So we cannot say that all fishes can see color. Also, there are many differences among the species.

HOW DO BEES STING?

First of all, not all bees sting. There are hundreds of different species, or kinds of bees, and many of them don't sting at all. When it comes to stinging by bees, what most of us are familiar with is the sting of the honeybee.

At the rear of the abdomen of the bee is the sting and other organs that surround it. The sting is quite a complicated thing. For one thing, it is an egg-laying apparatus, and actually part of its job is to deposit eggs.

The spearlike sting is made up of three pieces which surround a central canal. Connected to the base of the sting are two poison sacs. There are also two very sensitive, fingerlike projections. These tell the bee when the tip of her abdomen is in contact with the object she wishes to sting.

In the act of stinging, the spearlike sting is pushed outward and the poison sacs force the poison into the wound. It is this poison, in addition to the pain of the sting itself, that people want to avoid, for that poison can be very harmful to some persons.

Once the bee has inserted the barbed sting into the skin, it cannot be taken out easily. So when the bee flies away, her sting and its attached organs are pulled from her body, and she eventually dies.

If a bee does leave its stinger in a person's skin, it should be removed by scraping the stinger out with a fingernail or knife. Trying to pull the stinger out by its end may produce a squeezing of the poison glands if they are still attached and thus force more poison into the wound.

HOW DO FROG EGGS HATCH?

Although frogs can live on land, many kinds go back to water when it is time to lay their eggs. This is usually done in the spring.

The frogs look for quiet places at the edges of ponds and small lakes, where the water is a foot or less in depth. In the night, or early morning, the female lays her yearly hatch of eggs. The eggs are enclosed in a mass of jelly that is attached to some kind of plant in the pond.

A small frog may lay two thousand to three thousand eggs; a large one, six thousand to eight thousand. Each egg is spherical, black above, light below, and about one-sixteenth of an inch in diameter. When first laid, the mass is as large as a teacup, but it swells up with water to several times this size by the time the eggs hatch.

After a few days or weeks, depending on the species of frog, the egg hatches. A tadpole swims out of the egg. It has a finned tail and gills, which look like small, furry branches.

At first the gills are outside the body. But in time, they are covered by a fold of skin. Inside the body lungs develop, and other changes take place. The legs develop. The hind legs are the first to show, and the front legs remain hidden until the last stages of metamorphosis. The tail is absorbed into the body. It has completely disappeared by the time the young animal—now a frog—is ready for life on land.

The whole change, from tadpole to frog, takes place within a week or less if the weather is warm. In cool weather it may take two weeks or more.

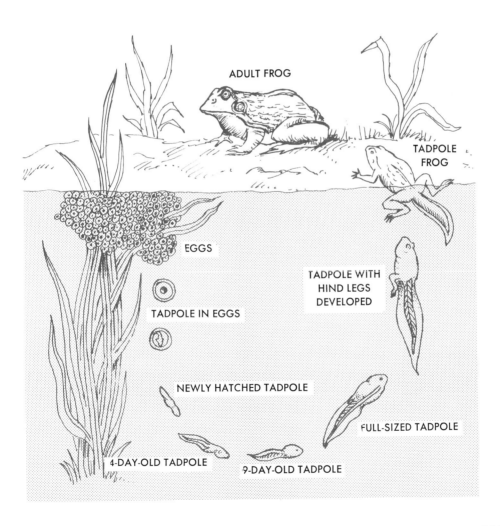

ADULT FROG

TADPOLE FROG

EGGS

TADPOLE WITH HIND LEGS DEVELOPED

TADPOLE IN EGGS

NEWLY HATCHED TADPOLE

FULL-SIZED TADPOLE

4-DAY-OLD TADPOLE

9-DAY-OLD TADPOLE

HOW OFTEN DO SNAKES
SHED THEIR SKIN?

There are over two thousand different kinds of snakes. They live on land, in the earth, in water, and in trees. So snakes vary quite a bit. But all snakes, young and old, shed their skins.

When they do this, even the film covering the eyes is cast off. During the process of shedding, the skin is turned inside out. The snake removes the skin by rubbing against rough surfaces. And snakes shed their skins several times a year.

The skin of a snake is scaly, and this is very important to them. In general, snakes have no legs, though a few types, such as the boas and pythons, have the remains of hind legs. These legs are imbedded in the muscles, and only spurs or claws show on the outside of the body.

It is the scales on the skin that enable snakes to move gracefully and even quickly. The broad scales on the underside can be moved forward in such a way that the rear edge of each scale pushes against some irregularity in the ground. When they are pushed back against these irregularities, the whole snake moves forward.

When the snake wants to move with great speed, it combines this with another method. This consists of swinging the body sideways into loops and, by pushing against any stone or plant it touches, gliding along the twisted path formed by the loops.

Snakes are related biologically to other cold-blooded vertebrates, such as lizards, alligators and crocodiles, turtles, and tortoises.

CAN A BUTTERFLY SMELL?

It may surprise us, but butterflies and moths have keen senses of sight, smell, and taste. The organs of taste in most butterflies are in the mouth, which is what you would expect. But most organs of smell in butterflies are on the antennae. And there are some butterflies that smell things through "noses" on their feet!

Many butterflies have odors, or scents, which they use for two purposes. One kind of scent is used to attract the opposite sex; the other is used to drive away enemies.

The scents of male butterflies come from scales in pockets on their hind wings. During courtship a male monarch butterfly may scatter these scent scales over the female. The scents of many male butterflies resemble those of flowers or spices and are often pleasant to humans.

Female butterflies produce their scents in special glands in their bodies. Most of these female odors are disagreeable to the human nose.

Did you know that the taste organs of a butterfly are far more sensitive in some ways than that of humans? They are far more sensitive to sweet things than our tongues are. Their chief food is flower nectar, which is a sugar solution, and they are easily able to find it. When a butterfly finds nectar in a flower, it uncoils its long, hollow "tongue" and sucks in the liquid.

Butterflies are able to see colors very well. They can even see certain ultraviolet colors that the human eye cannot see.

WHY DO WE HAVE MOSQUITOES?

Mosquitoes exist on earth like other creatures. Man may not want them around and wish to get rid of them, but that's his problem.

Mosquitoes are found all over the world. Some species are scattered in all districts, while others are found only in certain regions. About 70 species of mosquitoes are found in the United States.

It is because some types of mosquitoes carry disease that man has tried to get rid of mosquitoes. The mosquitoes that carry the virus of yellow fever, for example, are being wiped out of many tropical areas in which they were once found.

There are two other things about mosquitoes that are very annoying to man. One is the mosquito bite. When the female mosquito bites, it injects a poisonous liquid into the blood. This poison causes the pain and swelling of a mosquito bite.

The other annoying thing is the mosquito's hum. This hum is very important to the mosquito, for it is a sort of mating call. The males make a deep, low hum by vibrating their wings rapidly, while the females have a shriller note.

Can mosquitoes be of any benefit to man? The only such hope seems to be that certain types of mosquitoes can help us get rid of other, worse types. What happens is that the wigglers of some mosquitoes feed on the wigglers of other species. The first kind doesn't bite man, the second kind does. So they may be helpful in getting rid of the biting type.

WHY DO A CAT'S EYES GLOW IN THE DARK?

People who own and love cats consider them to be sweet little creatures and wonderful pets. Which they are. But cats are members of a family of animals of a very special kind. These include tigers, lions, leopards—and, of course, the domesticated cat.

No matter where they live, no matter what their size and appearance, all cats are alike in many ways. All have bodies adapted for hunting and killing. All are highly specialized beasts of prey.

One of the things that helps a cat to be a good hunter is its eyes. The cat's eyes are adapted for seeing in the dark, since it does most of its hunting at night. During the day the pupils contract to slits, or very small openings. But at night they open wide, letting in every bit of light possible.

The backs of the eyes are coated with a substance like polished silver. It reflects every bit of light that comes into the eye. That is why a cat's eyes shine like glowing lanterns if you point a flashlight toward them at night.

What are other things about the cat that make it a great hunter? In the front of its mouth the cat has four long, pointed canine teeth—deadly weapons for biting and tearing flesh. On its feet the cat has an arsenal of needle-sharp, curved claws. To follow its prey silently, there are soft pads cushioning the bottom of its feet. And the cat has unusually keen sight, hearing, and smell.

DOES THE MALE SEA HORSE HAVE BABIES?

Sometimes people who buy sea horses for their aquarium are told "the male is pregnant." There is a reason for this, even though it isn't true.

The sea horse is quite a strange creature. It has a head like a tiny pony and a body like a pigmy dragon. At times it swims upright through the water with the help of its single back fin.

But the sea horse is a fish. There are over 50 species of this fish found in temperate and tropic seas of the world. They range in size from two to twelve inches.

And the most peculiar thing about sea horses is the way they care for their eggs. The female lays about two hundred eggs. She places them in a pouch in the male's body just above his tail. After 40 to 50 days the male breaks the pouch open and the tiny baby sea horses come out. So you can see why people might get the mistaken idea that the male is giving birth to the babies!

Even after the young hatch out, they remain in the father's pouch for a time until they are old enough to take care of themselves. Sea horses eat small sea creatures and the eggs of other fishes. The refuse to eat dead things.

Sea horses were admired by man since ancient times. A sea horse was carved on a mummy case in Egypt. In ancient China they were ground up for medicine. In Italy a sea horse was considered good luck.

HOW DID THE HIPPOPOTAMUS GET ITS NAME?

There are many amazing things about this beast, including its strange name. The word "hippopotamus" means "river horse." The animal got this name partly because it spends much of its time in the water. And it may have been called a horse because of its great size or its wide nostrils or its little horselike ears.

Actually, the closest living relative of the hippopotamus is the pig! The hippo is far larger than any horse. A big hippo can be twelve feet long and weigh up to four tons.

The hippo has the biggest mouth of any mammal except the whale. It has two tusks in the upper jaw and four in the lower. When it attacks, it can kill a smaller animal with a single bite. Usually, however, the hippopotamus would rather hide than attack. Most of the time it will run to the water to hide.

A hippo can run as fast as a man. In the water it can drop out of sight like a stone or it can float. When the hippo floats, only its bulging nostrils and eyes and its little ears show above the surface. It is almost hidden, but it can still breathe, smell, see, and hear.

When it sinks, the hippo closes its nostrils to keep the water out. It can walk around on the bottom and gather the juicy water plants it likes to eat. It can easily stay under for eight or nine minutes!

The hippo has an appetite to match its size. A big hippo that lives in a zoo may eat about one hundred pounds of food every day. A herd in the wild will eat many kinds of river plants and grasses. Hippos usually feed at night and rest during the day.

DOES A COW HAVE FOUR STOMACHS?

The answer is no, a cow does not have four stomachs. But its stomach is divided into four compartments, which seems to be almost the same thing.

Cows, sheep, goats, camels, llamas, deer, and antelopes, all have the habit of swallowing their food and later bringing it back to the mouth. Then they chew it thoroughly at leisure. Such animals are called "cud-chewing" animals or ruminants.

The reason they developed this method of chewing their food is that their ancestors were easy prey to stronger, flesh-eating beasts. So, many thousands of years ago, to protect themselves, they began to swallow their food quickly and then go off to some more concealed places to chew at their leisure.

This is made possible by their complicated stomach with four compartments. They are the paunch, or "rumen"; the "reticulum," or honeycomb bag; the "omasum," or manyplies; and the true stomach, or "abomasum."

When the food is first swallowed, in the form of a coarse pellet, it goes into the paunch, the largest of the four compartments. It is softened there and goes into the reticulum. Here it is molded into "cuds" of convenient size. Later, these are passed up into the mouth by regurgitation, which is the opposite of swallowing. After chewing, they are swallowed again, passing into the third stomach or manyplies; then into the fourth compartment, or true stomach.

Cows, sheep, and goats have no front teeth in the upper jaw. Instead, the gums form a tough pad.

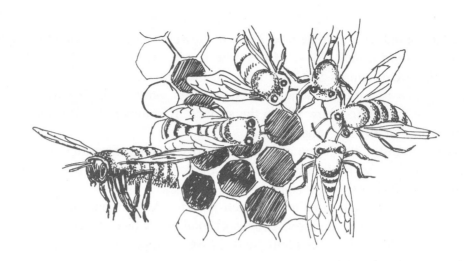

WHY DO BEES DO A DANCE?

Since all the bees who live in a hive together share their food, it is important for them to get all the food that can be found. So when foraging bees return to the hive, they get other bees from the hive to gather nectar and pollen from good flower sources.

They do this by performing dances on the combs of the hive. The bees around the dancing bees become excited and start to follow behind a dancer and imitate her movements. Then they leave the hive and—without the dancing bee to lead them—fly directly to the food source.

The dancing bees are able to tell the other bees, by these dances, the direction and the location of the food. If the bees do a round dance, then the bees fly out and look for food nearby. On the dancing bees is the odor of the nectar which tells the other bees which flowers to look for.

If the returning bees do a wagging dance, it means that the food is more than one hundred yards away. During this dance the bee goes in a straight direction for a short run, and this tells the other bees in which direction to look for the food.

If the straight run points directly upward, the feeding place is toward the sun; if it points downward, the feeding place is opposite the sun's position.

The speed of the dance tells the distance to the feeding place. If it is done quickly, the feeding place is near. The greater the distance, the slower the dance is. When the amount of food left at the source is very little, the returning bee does not do a dance, so other bees don't go there looking for food.

HOW DO SNAKES INJECT POISON?

In certain types of snakes, the venomous snakes, one of the saliva glands produces a substance that is poisonous to the snakes' prey. This substance is the snakes' venom. Some snakes have venom that is strong enough to kill an elephant. Others have mild venom; their venom can only kill small lizards. Probably only two hundred venomous snakes (out of 412 species that are known) can be considered dangerous to man.

Two of these are African snakes called the boomslang and the bird snake. Their fangs are in the rear of their mouths. The fangs are two or three rear teeth in the upper jaws that are greatly enlarged and have grooves running down one side.

Just above the fangs is an opening that leads to the venom-producing gland. When a rear-fanged snake bites, venom drips down the grooves into the wound made by the fangs.

Cobras have fangs at the front of the mouth, one on each side of the upper jaw. In most cobras the groove on the fang is closed over, forming a hollow tube. A muscle surrounds the venom gland. When the snake bites, the muscle presses on the gland. This forces the venom down into the fang and out through the fang tip directly into the prey.

The spitting cobra can spray venom from its fangs, the way water is sprayed from a squirt gun. These cobras aim at the eyes of a threatening animal. The spray goes about eight feet and causes almost instant blindness.

Vipers have a complicated type of venom system. Their fangs are very long and the fang lies lengthwise in the mouth so it can be closed. When the mouth is opened for a strike, the jawbone is turned forward, bringing the fang at right angles to the throat.

WHAT IS A MAMMAL?

Mammals are the most advanced of all the different classes of animal life. They are also the animals that we know best, and include dogs, cats, rabbits, horses, cows, pigs, elephants, bears, mice—and human beings. And there are hundreds and hundreds of other kinds of mammals.

Mammals have certain characteristics, some of which are shared by other creatures, some of which are not. Mammals are vertebrates—animals with backbones. (So are fishes, reptiles, and birds.) All mammals have lungs and breathe air. (So do birds, reptiles, and many amphibians.) All mammals are warm-blooded. (So are birds.)

All mammals, except two primitive types that lay eggs, give birth to living young. So do many fish, reptiles, insects, and other animals.

There are two important characteristics that set mammals apart from all other animals. They are the only animals that possess true hair, or fur. They are the only animals that produce milk. The word "mammal" comes from the Latin word *mamma,* which means "breast." All female mammals nurse their young with milk that comes from glands, usually called breasts, on their bodies.

Mammals have certain other characteristics. The mammal's lungs and heart are separated from its stomach and intestinal tract by a wall of muscle called the diaphragm. The mammal's lower jaw consists of a single bone on each side. And—most important of all—mammal brains are much more highly developed than the brains of any other animals.

HOW ARE INSECTS HARMFUL TO MAN?

In nature there are many insects that are helpful and friendly to man. But there are also insects that may sting and bite and insects that carry diseases.

Some insects are harmful at all times and should be avoided. Black widow spiders are in this group. It may be found from southern California to Chile, usually in damp, sheltered spots. The poison of the black widow spider causes great pain and stiffening of the muscles of the abdomen. Many victims of the black widow spider die.

Most insect bites and stings hurt for a time but are not serious. But some people are allergic to the poison in a bee or wasp sting. If they are stung, they should see a doctor right away to get medicine to prevent an allergic reaction.

Some kinds of mosquitoes carry germs that cause disease, such as yellow fever, malaria, and sleeping sickness. The germs that cause the disease are picked up by the mosquito and then passed on to another person it bites.

Typhus is a disease carried by the body louse. It is a serious danger whenever people must live in crowded conditions. Flies play a part in the spread of such diseases as cholera, dysentery, hepatitis, and typhoid fever. These diseases, like all those that are spread or carried by insects, are less apt to occur if an area is kept free of dirt—and if the insects are prevented from breeding.

WHAT IS A SLOTH?

When we say a person is a "sloth," we mean he is sluggish and lazy. What we are saying is that he takes after the sloth, an animal that is very sluggish and sleeps 18 hours a day

Sloths are strange-looking animals found in Central and South America from Nicaragua to Brazil. They live in trees and are never seen away from forest areas. Sloths are mammals and are related to anteaters, armadillos, and aardvarks.

There are two types: three-toed and two-toed sloths. The three-toed sloths have three toes on each foot. The two-toed have two toes on their front feet and three on the back.

They use their toes and claws to hang from branches in an upside-down position. At night they inch slowly along the branches in search of tree leaves and twigs, which they eat.

Sloths sleep in the trees, on the upper side of a strong limb. Sometimes they crawl over the ground, and where there is a stream or a lake they jump in without fear and swim easily.

Sloths are very low in intelligence, because their brain is very small. Their body temperature is also the lowest of any mammal, and in fact they sometimes behave more like cold-blooded animals than warm-blooded animals.

The fur of a sloth is gray and shaggy. Sometimes algae grow in the fur, and this gives it a greenish tinge. But this actually helps the sloth—because the green color helps them stay unnoticed by eagles, jaguars, and other animals that feed on them.

HOW DO JELLYFISH REPRODUCE?

One of the most common jellyfishes in the world is the moon jellyfish. It has long, milky-looking threads streaming down from its round, cuplike body.

On the upper side of a fully grown moon jellyfish there is a pink or orange pattern like a four-leaf clover. The four "leaves" are the reproductive organs. In male jellyfish they produce sperm cells, which are released through the animal's mouth into the water. In female jellyfish the reproductive organs produce eggs. The eggs remain inside the body until they are fertilized, or joined, by sperm cells from the water.

The eggs develop in four long, trailing folds that hang down from the mouth. When the eggs hatch, the young settle on the bottom of the ocean. They develop into a shape very different from the parent animal. They become polyps (which means "many feet").

The young polyp catches food with its tentacles and grows for several months. Then something strange starts to happen. The polyp begins to develop grooves. Gradually, the polyp begins to look like a stack of fringed saucers. One by one the saucers pinch off from the polyp and swim away. Each becomes a separate little jellyfish.

Apparently the jellyfish way of life and of reproducing works out quite well. Jellyfish have been doing this for more than 600,000,000 years! They are among the oldest forms of life on earth and have changed very little.

By the way, jellyfishes are not true fish. All fishes are vertebrates—animals with backbones. Jellyfishes are not vertebrates. Their bodies are bags of jelly with a hollow inside.

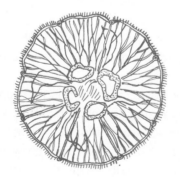
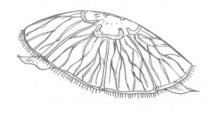

CAN ANIMALS COMMUNICATE?

The chief means of communication that humans have is words. No animals are able to communicate with words, of course, but many animals are able to communicate with one another.

Many animals communicate by making certain kinds of noises. When a horse, for example, neighs or paws the ground, this means something to other horses. A hen gives a warning noise to her chicks when danger is present.

Dogs communicate in a variety of ways: they bark, growl, snarl, whine, and howl. They bare their teeth or lift a paw. Other dogs understand these sounds and movements.

Bees have a fantastic ability to communicate. When they return to the hive, they do a dance that tells the other bees what kind of flowers they have found, how far away they are, the direction to go, and so on.

Birds, as we all know, have bird songs. And they are able to communicate in this way. In fact, there are "dialects" in bird songs. The song of the same kind of bird is slightly different in Switzerland than it is in England, and it even varies in different parts of the country.

Many people believe that their pet dog can understand human language. Actually, what dogs learn is what certain tones of voice mean, not the actual words. An interesting thing is that domestic animals, such as cats and dogs, have learned how to communicate with their masters. They beg for food, or mew until a door is opened. But wild animals do not seem able to express their desires, such as begging for food from each other.

But even when animals do communicate, the most they can express is feelings and intentions. They cannot have a "conversation."

WHERE IS A SNAKE'S HEART?

When we look at a snake we see a long and slender animal that has no legs and that seems to be all tail with a head stuck on the front.

But between the head and the tail of a snake is a long and complicated body. A snake has a backbone and a digestive system, a liver, a heart, and all the other muscles, glands, and organs that are found in most backboned animals.

A snake's most striking feature is its lack of legs. Another characteristic is the absence of movable eyelids, which gives the snake that glassy, unblinking stare. A snake's eyelid is a clear cover that protects the eye.

Most snakes have only one lung. As a result, there is more room in the slender body for the other internal organs. But pythons and some other snakes have two lungs.

Snakes have no ears on the outside of their heads. But they are sensitive to vibrations through the ground. And they have other senses that make up for the sense of hearing.

Most snakes can see very well. They notice their prey more by movement than by shape or color. Snakes have a good sense of smell and can recognize prey animals, enemies, and each other by odors.

Snakes can also pick up particles from the air or ground or some object and certain organs they have that possess a chemical sense will be able to identify the chemical particles as food, enemy, friend, or whatever!

WHEN DID REPTILES FIRST APPEAR?

The first reptiles walked on the earth about 300,000,000 years ago. In those days the largest animals on land were amphibians. Their eggs were laid in water.

The first reptiles looked like amphibians, but the big difference was that their eggs could hatch on land. The young had lungs and legs, and could breathe air. They walked on damp ground in forests, and probably fed on insects.

Later on, reptiles became larger and stronger. Some looked like lizards and some like turtles. There were also reptiles with short tails, thick legs, and large heads.

One group of early reptiles were very important because of their descendants. They looked like lizards that were about three feet long, but they walked on their hind legs.

From these creatures many new types of reptiles developed. Some were true reptiles with wings. One group developed feathers and warm blood—they became the first birds. Other types that developed were crocodiles and the first dinosaurs.

At one time, all the types of reptiles that existed dominated life on earth. But after millions of years, many of the ancient types of reptiles became extinct. There are many theories that try to explain why this happened. The chief explanation seems to be that changes in the earth and its climate made it impossible for them to live on. Swamps dried up and they couldn't live on dry land. Their food disappeared. Climates became seasonal, shifting from summer heat to frost in winter. Most reptiles could not adjust to these changes, and those that couldn't died out.

WHAT WERE THE FIRST FISHES?

500,000,000 years ago there were no fishes. Fossils show that the first fishes occurred in the Ordovician Period, which began about 460,000,000 years ago. But it is not yet known whether the first fishes evolved in fresh or salt water.

In the next period, the Silurian, there were jawless fishes, the most primitive of fishes. Their mouths were a simple opening, suited to feeding on the tiny animals that lay hidden in the mud.

During the next period, the Devonian, fishes spread throughout the waters of our planet. They were the common animals of the period, which is why the Devonian is sometimes called the Age of Fishes.

During that age jawless fishes and fishes with jaws became abundant. But eventually the jawless fishes became extinct because of the evolving of fish with jaws. Jaws allowed fish to explore various food sources and to feed more efficiently.

Early fishes with jaws are called placoderms. The jaws evolved from a set of gill arches that were present in the jawless fishes. Gill arches are the bony supports of the gills.

There were quite a variety of placoderms in these ancient times. Some lived in midwater, some at the bottom. One group had tremendous teeth with sharp blades. Some were probably 30 feet long.

From these Devonian placoderms came our present-day fishes, the sharks and bony fishes. Sharks have a skeleton of cartilage. Bony fishes have a skeleton of bone.

MOSASAUR

WHY DO PEACOCKS HAVE
SUCH BEAUTIFUL TAILS?

We often hear the expression "Proud as a peacock," or "Vain as a peacock." And that's because the peacock seems to take great pleasure in displaying its beautiful feathers.

There are some interesting things about this gorgeous display. First, it is done only by the male. The female doesn't have these beautiful feathers. And the male, the peacock, does it for the sake of the peahen and for her alone.

What the peacock does, many birds do during the mating season. The male bird puts on a display to try to attract a female bird. He practically goes through a dance as he tries to convince the peahen that he's very handsome.

Most people think it is the "tail" of the peacock that contains those beautiful feathers. But it actually isn't the tail. Those feathers are from the lower part of the back, the "train." The tail lies behind it and acts as support.

The peacock has been known and admired since ancient times. The Greeks and the Romans considered it a sacred bird. But in the days of the Roman Empire the Romans enjoyed eating this bird, anyway.

Peacocks are natives of Asia and the East Indies. There are only two species and they are related to the pheasant.

HOW DO TURTLES BREATHE UNDERWATER?

Many turtles spend all or most of their lives in fresh water. They may live in swamps, ponds, running streams. They come up on dry land to sun themselves or lay eggs. How do they breathe when they are in the water?

Turtles have lungs and breathe air. They do not get oxygen from the water as fish do. So turtles have to fill their lungs with air to enable them to stay underwater.

They cannot do this by moving their ribs, as we do. Their ribs are firmly fixed to their hard shells. Turtles fill their lungs in another way. A turtle has two special sets of belly muscles. One set pulls the other body organs away from the lungs. Then a second set of muscles pulls the organs against the lungs, forcing the air out. One deep breath may last a land or sea turtle several hours.

Some freshwater turtles may remain underwater for several days without surfacing. They can do this because they use up very little oxygen while lying still on the bottom.

A few kinds of turtles have a special lining in their throats or in the cloaca. This is the opening through which wastes and other substances leave the body. This lining can take oxygen from the water, as the gills of fish do. Such turtles still need to come up for air, however.

A soft-shell turtle can breathe without moving from its shallow river bottom. Its neck is long enough to reach up to the surface of the water.

HOW DO SNAILS GET THEIR SHELLS?

Soft-bodied animals that have shells are known as mollusks. There are many different kinds of shell-bearing mollusks.

Some have two shells, or valves, which are hinged together. These mollusks are called bivalves. This group includes clams, oysters, scallops, and mussels. Other mollusks have only one shell, which may be cap-shaped but is usually twisted into a spiral. These mollusks are called snails.

The snail builds its shell like all mollusks. The shell is a mollusk's skeleton. The shell is part of the animal, and the mollusk is attached to it by muscles.

The soft animal inside can never leave its shell and return to it. As the mollusk grows bigger, its shell increases in size and strength. The shell is made of a form of limestone and is built by the mollusk itself. Of course, the mollusk does not know that it is building a home for itself.

In the case of the mollusk, certain glands are able to take limestone from the water and deposit it in tiny particles at the edge of, and along the inside of, the shell.

As a mollusk grows, its home becomes larger and stronger. Some of its shell glands contain coloring matter. As a result, a mollusk's shell may be spotted, all one color, or marked with lines.

Most mollusks live in the sea. None of the bivalves live out of water. Many snails, however, are air-breathing. These land snails are generally found in moist wooded places.

Scientists estimate that there are more than 80,000 kinds of snails!

WHERE ARE BLUE WHALES FOUND?

First, what are blue whales? Well, to most of us, whales are whales. We are not aware that there are many different kinds of whales.

Scientists divide whales into two groups: Odontoceti and Mysticeti. Odontoceti means "whales with teeth." Mysticeti means "moustached whales." These whales have "moustaches" of baleen, or whalebone, hanging from the roof of the mouth. Baleen is a fibrous, horny substance, fringed along the inner edges. Using their baleen, these whales strain huge quantities of small food out of the water.

The baleen whales are the largest animals ever to live on earth. Bigger than the dinosaurs? Yes! The blue whale, which is the largest of this type, may be 100 feet long and weigh more than 120 tons—and even the biggest dinosaur didn't reach this size.

There are three families of baleen whales: the right whales, the fin whales, and the gray whales. Blue whales are the largest species of fin whales. The chances are that you will never see one swimming about—but, actually, these whales are found in seas the world over. There is no particular area or ocean which they prefer.

These huge whales feed mainly on small fishes and on shrimplike creatures known as krill. The whale takes a huge mouthful of water and closes its mouth. Slowly it presses its tongue against the blades of baleen, which hang down from the upper jaw. In this way the seawater is strained off, and the food remains in the whale's mouth.

Baleen whales differ in so many ways from toothed whales that they are believed to be only very distantly related.

CAN BIRDS SMELL?

Living creatures tend to have, or develop, those senses which are necessary for them to survive. How important would the sense of smell be to a bird? Apparently, not very important, since the sense of smell seems to be almost or entirely missing in most birds.

What senses are important to birds? Well, a large part of the brain and nervous system of birds is connected with the senses of sight and balance— because they are important in flight. Fine eyesight is vital for a flying animal, and birds have remarkable eyesight.

They usually have a wide angle of vision. Many birds are also "out-eyed." Each eye looks out at right angles to the bird and sees a completely separate area.

The ability of birds to see color is more-or-less like that of a human. Night birds also have large lenses. This type of eye (in birds like owls) is able to gather and concentrate dim light.

The sense of hearing is excellent in birds. So are the senses of balance and of place in and movement through space. All these senses are centered in the ears. Many birds also have a good sense of taste. They can select their proper food instantly.

Most of the habits of birds are the inherited abilities we call instincts. Birds are born knowing almost everything needed to know to carry out their normal lives. They have no need to learn very much.

WHY DO WOODPECKERS PECK ON TREES?

Most of us, when we hear a woodpecker at work on a tree, imagine that it is harming the tree. The fact is, the opposite is true! The woodpecker is actually helping keep the tree alive.

First of all, the woodpecker is an arboreal bird; that is, it lives in trees. And it eats in trees. Hidden down deep in the crevices of the bark of trees are many grubs and insects. The woodpecker finds them with a kind of instinct—even when they cannot be seen on the outside. Then he drills a hole straight down to them and eats them. Quite often these insects and grubs are the kind that are harmful to the tree.

How can the woodpecker reach down into the wood? For one thing, the woodpecker's beak is sharp and strong and has a chisel-shaped point. Then the woodpecker also has an amazing tongue. In some species it is twice as long as the head itself.

The tongue is round and at the outer end has a hard tip with tiny barbs on the sides. Inside the beak the tongue is curled up like a spring. When the woodpecker goes after insects in the tree, it is able to thrust that tongue quite some distance from the beak and go far down into the crevices of the bark.

Woodpeckers don't always peck away at live trees. They use their chisel-like beak also for cutting holes in decayed wood. This is to make a place for their nests. They like trees which are hollow part of the way up.

Sometimes woodpeckers make two openings, like a front and back door. This is to enable them to get away if an unwelcome visitor should show up.

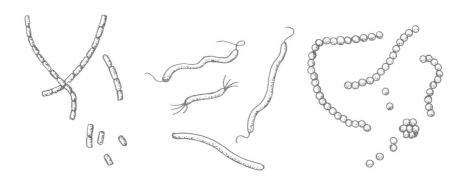

HOW ARE BACTERIA USEFUL TO MAN?

When you say "bacteria," most people think of germs that are harmful and cause disease. But the fact is that there are over two thousand different kinds of bacteria, and most of them are either harmless or helpful to other forms of life—including man.

Bacteria cause the decay of dead plants and animals, both on land and in water. Without such bacteria the earth would be covered with dead matter. While eating, the bacteria break down the complicated substances in these organisms into simpler ones. The simpler substances are then restored to the soil, water, and air in forms that can be used by living plants and animals.

Bacteria play an important part in the digestive processes of man and other animals. There are a great many in the human intestine. As the bacteria eat, they break down foods. At the same time, they make certain vitamins, which the body then uses.

Bacteria are a vital link in the food chain that supports life. Some bacteria, called nitrogen-fixing bacteria, live in the soil and help change nitrogen into substances that plants can use. Man depends on such plants for food.

Bacteria are responsible for the fermentation process by which such products as cheese and vinegar are made. The same fermentation is also used in industry to make substances essential for paints, plastics, cosmetics, candy, and other products. It is also used to make certain drugs. In other industries bacteria are used in curing tobacco leaves, in tanning hides, in eating away the outer covering of coffee and cocoa seeds, and in separating certain fibers for the textile industry. So you see in how many ways bacteria are useful to man. And there are still many more ways they are used and will be used in the future!

WHAT ARE LICE?

Sometimes when a person wants to describe something terrible he says, "It's lousy." "Lousy" is not a dirty word. It refers to the louse—which is a very obnoxious insect.

Actually, there are more than one thousand different insects that are called "louse" (plural: "lice"), but the one that people usually have in mind is the one that attacks human beings.

These are bloodsucking creatures. They are true parasites—their food is human blood. And these lice are more closely associated with man than any other members of the animal kingdom. This is because they exist upon his body during all stages of their development.

The "pediculus humanus" is typical of this kind of louse. It develops from eggs that are glued to the hair or clothing. In the hair, the eggs, or "nits" are sometimes easy seen. The body louse is passed from one person to another by wearing clothing from an infested person or by contact with bedding that is infested. The body louse is known to carry the disease typhus fever.

There is another kind of louse that attacks human beings and stays in hair in all parts of the body, including even the eyebrows. The control of these lice is done by dusting DDT powder or other insecticides under the clothing or in the hair.

An interesting thing about lice is that certain kinds attack other creatures as well. There are lice that live on birds, other mammals, and even lice that live on honey bees. There are also plant lice that suck the juices of plants.

WHAT IS THE 17-YEAR LOCUST?

There is no such thing! What is called the 17-year locust is really the 17-year cicada, an entirely different kind of insect. True locusts are grasshoppers, and calling the cicada a locust is a mistake that is commonly made.

The 17-year cicada is quite an unusual insect. It probably lives longer than any other insect (except perhaps the termite queen). Its life cycle goes like this: the nymphs, the cicada's young, hatch from eggs on the twigs of trees. Then they drop to the ground.

Then they burrow into the ground and attach themselves to rootlets. And

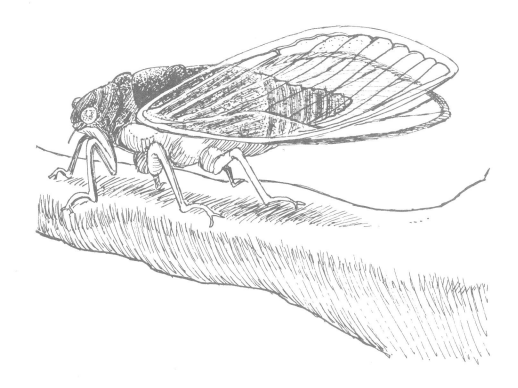

they remain there, without moving, as they suck the sap, for 17 years! Then some kind of mysterious instinct calls them out into the light.

Now they climb the trunk of a tree, and their skins split open. Out comes the mature cicada. For about five weeks they seem to live a happy life in the light of the sun. The males, and only the males, are able to make a piercing, metallic noise, the "voice" of the cicada. This sound is probably a mating call to the females.

The sound is made by one of the most complicated musical organs in nature. There are little drumlike plates at the base of the abdomen, and they are kept vibrating rapidly by muscles that seem never to get tired.

After the five weeks are over, the cicada dies. So it took 17 years to develop—for just five happy weeks of life. This 17-year cicada (in the South it matures in 13 years) is peculiar to the United States. Altogether, there are about one thousand species of cicada, and most of them live in the tropics.

WHAT DO SHARKS EAT?

There are about 250 different kinds of sharks, and they range in size from two feet long to the giant whale shark which is 50 or 60 feet long. Are there man-eating sharks? Yes, about 27 kinds are known to attack man. Among them is the white shark, the hammerhead, the tiger, the lemon, and the mako shark.

But no shark seeks man as food. Sharks feed mainly on bony fishes, squid, and crustaceans, such as shrimps and lobsters. Sharks also feed on turtles, dolphins, and birds. Some sharks eat other kinds of sharks.

The largest sharks, such as the whale shark, eat the smallest food. They eat tiny fish and other very tiny animals that feed on drifting seaweeds. To find its food, a shark relies mainly on its nose. The hungrier a shark, the more sensitive its nose.

Sharks usually circle about their prey before closing in for the kill. Thresher sharks use their long, curving tails to herd their prey. They sweep their tails from side to side, sometimes stunning the prey with their mighty strokes.

Often a group of sharks become so excited while feeding that they bite anything and everything. The more they bite, the more excited they become. In this state they will eat rubber tires, tin cans, logs, boats, or anything else that happens to be in the way. Scientists call this state a feeding frenzy. Even the smallest and most sluggish of sharks is dangerous during a feeding frenzy.

WHY DO CATS HAVE WHISKERS?

The cat family includes everything from the small domestic cats we keep as pets to Siberian tigers weighing 600 pounds or more. But no matter where they live, no matter what their size and appearance, all cats have bodies adapted for hunting. All are highly specialized beasts of prey.

A cat has whiskers to help it perform in this way. When a cat is on the prowl, and its eyes and ears are not receiving any information to help it, or are busy, whiskers help the cat learn more about its surroundings.

For example, when a cat puts its head into a dark hole, the whiskers touch the sides of the hole and tell the cat where the boundaries of the hole are. Or the whiskers may brush against the body of a mouse and tell the cat at once that its prey is there.

So the long hairs of the cat's whiskers are what it depends on to know where it is, what's there, when the other sense organs, such as sound and smell and sight, can't provide that information.

But cats do have very keen senses. Their hearing and sense of smell are highly developed. They have keen eyes and they are directed forward (as ours are). This allows the cat to focus both eyes on the same subject at the same time and to judge its distance.

The cat's eyes are also adapted for seeing in the dark. During the day the pupils contract to slits, but at night they open wide to let in every bit of light possible. The backs of the eyes are coated with a substance that reflects every bit of light that comes into the eye.

WHY CAN'T ANIMALS TALK?

Many animals are able to communicate with each other very well—but none of them can talk as we do. That is, no animals use words.

Birds cry out and make sounds that other birds understand. Smells, movements, sounds are used to communicate by animals, and they can express joy or anger or fear.

But human speech is a very complicated process, and no animals are able to perform it. One reason is the very special way we have to use a whole series of organs to produce the sounds we want to make when we utter words. The

way our vocal cords are made to vibrate, the way the throat, mouth, and nasal cavities have to be adjusted, the way the lips, teeth, lower jaw, tongue, and palate have to be moved—just to make vowel and consonant sounds—is something animals cannot do. They cannot produce a whole series of words to make a sentence.

And there is another, perhaps more important reason, why animals cannot talk. Words are only labels for objects, actions, feelings, experiences, and ideas. For example, the word "bird" is a label for a living, flying object. Other words describe its color, shape, flying, and singing. Still other words would be used to tell what the speaker thinks or feels about the bird or its actions.

So the use of words means the use of labels or symbols, and then organizing them in a certain way to communicate something. This requires a degree of intelligence that no animals have. So they can't "talk" the way people do.

DO BIRDS HAVE EARS?

Since birds are flying animals, practically everything about them is adapted to this very difficult activity. This covers their whole body, the outside and the inside. And it also includes their nerves and senses.

For example, fine eyesight is vital for a flying animal. It is one of the most important features of birds. In proportion to the size of the animal, bird eyes are much larger than those of most other backboned animals. Many birds are able to see a separate area with each eye. Other birds are able to see very small objects and great detail at long distances.

It is important for birds to have a good sense of hearing, and they have an excellent one. Birds do have ears, and the sense of hearing, the senses of balance and of place in and movement through space are all centered in the ears.

In spite of the hard, horny character of the beak and mouth, many birds also have a good sense of taste. They can select their proper food instantly. But it seems that birds do not have to be able to smell. The sense of smell seems to be almost or entirely missing in most birds.

Flying, of course, is an activity that requires large amounts of energy. So their metabolism (the living processes that produce and use this energy) is rapid. Bird temperatures are high, usually between 104 and 112 degrees Fahrenheit. Their pulse and rate of breathing is very fast. For instance, a sparrow's heart beats more than 500 times a minute!

WHY DO FLEAS LIVE ON DOGS AND CATS?

Fleas are parasites. A parasite is a plant or animal that lives with, in, or on another living organism. The other organism is called the "host."

The flea (the parasite) lives on dogs and cats (the host) by sucking blood. It has a small round head and mouth parts that are adapted to sucking. It has a tiny body, no wings, and three pairs of legs.

By the way, those long hind legs of the flea make it a wonderful jumper. In fact, it is the champion jumper of all creatures. This tiny insect can jump seven to eight inches into the air, and can jump forward at least 12 inches. For a man, that would mean being able to jump 450 feet into the air and make a broad jump of about 700 feet!

There are hundreds of species of fleas. In the United States there are more than 50 different kinds. The dog-and-cat type of flea is found almost everywhere in the world.

Fleas don't just live in dogs and cats. They also infest rats, rabbits, squirrels, tame and wild birds, and nearly all other warm-blooded animals. In the United States, the flea that lives on dogs and cats also lives on human beings.

During the Middle Ages flea-infested rats spread bubonic plague throughout Europe. The flea lived on the diseased rat until the rat died. Then the flea jumped to a human being, carrying with it the disease germs. Cases of bubonic plague are rare now, but they still occur.

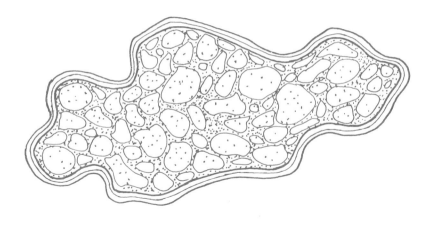

WHAT IS AN AMOEBA?

When we use the word "animal" we tend to think of pretty large creatures that move about on earth. But did you know that the amoeba is considered an "animal"?

It is a jellylike one-celled creature, so small that it can be seen only under a microscope. The common species of amoeba lives in freshwater streams and ponds, while other amoebas live on the bottom of fresh- and salt-water bodies, and in damp soils and foods.

The amoeba constantly changes its shape. It moves by pushing out one side and then another. As some of the jellylike substance is pushed out, it forms what are called false feet, or "pseudopodia." When the pseudopodia reach food, they wrap themselves around it and take it into the main body. This is the way the amoeba eats—it has no mouth.

The amoeba belongs to the Protozoa, which is the lowest division of the animal kingdom. It has no lungs or gills. But it absorbs oxygen from the water, gives off carbon dioxide, and digests its food, as more complex animals do.

The amoeba even seems to have feeling. If it is touched or disturbed, it immediately rolls itself into a tiny ball. The amoeba also tries to avoid bright light and water that is too hot or too cold.

In a full-sized amoeba, the nucleus, a tiny dot in the center of the protoplasm, divides into two parts. After this the amoeba itself divides, forming into new individual animals. When these become full-grown, each of them may divide again.

WHY DO PEOPLE HUNT WALRUSES?

The walrus, some experts think, may vanish from the earth if steps aren't taken to protect it. Why is this so, and what kind of animal is it?

The walrus is a huge mammal that lives in Arctic waters off both coasts of northern North America and also off northeastern Siberia. It measures from eight to twelve feet in length when full-grown, and weighs up to three thousand pounds.

Walruses have a thick hide which is tough and wrinkled and which has almost no fur. Both the male and female walruses grow tusks which are used in digging for mollusks and for fighting.

Walruses live together in herds. They stay in far northern waters during the summer. In the fall they drift southward with the ice, and in the spring they swim northward again.

Walruses are hunted by man for many reasons. Eskimos and other Arctic peoples have depended on the walrus to supply them with food, fuel, clothing, and equipment. Practically every part of the body is used.

The blubber supplies oil for fuel. The leathery hides are used for clothing. The flesh is used for food. And the ivory tusks are used to make many different kinds of objects. Eskimos have used these tusks to carve small decorative objects that can be traded or sold.

About ten years ago it was believed that the total walrus population was down to only 40,000 or 50,000.

WHERE DO PENGUINS LAY THEIR EGGS?

Penguins, as you know, live in the Antarctic, most of which is covered by deep snow and ice. Where can these birds lay their eggs?

During the Antarctic winter, February to October, the penguins live at sea. In October, which is early spring there, they come out of the sea and start a long trek to their rookeries, or breeding grounds.

The penguins may have to walk and slide, scramble and toboggan 60 miles across the sea ice to reach the rocky Antarctic coast. Usually the males arrive first and go directly to their nests of the previous year. The nests are made of stones. So you see, the penguins find a rocky area along the coast, where deep snow is not a problem, to lay their eggs.

The male and female penguin make a nest together before the eggs are laid. They go back and forth, collecting stones, carrying the stones in their beaks. They collect and guard the stones in turn. The stones are dropped by one partner; the other arranges them into a neat pile.

In mid-November the female penguin lays two bluish-white eggs. Now a very interesting process begins. The female and the male take turns guarding and hatching the eggs. After a certain period the female returns from the sea where she has been feeding and the male goes out to the sea to feed. Then he returns and she goes out to feed. But the timing is such that it is always the female who returns just as the chicks are coming out of their eggs. This taking turns in guarding and feeding goes on after the young are born for about four weeks.

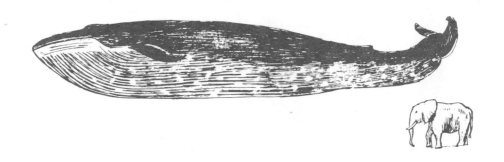

WHAT IS THE LARGEST
ANIMAL IN THE WORLD?

When we think of ancient times, when dinosaurs lived on earth, we think of huge creatures that were bigger than anything else that ever existed. Yet the fact is that even the biggest dinosaur did not reach the size of an animal that is found in the world today.

This is the baleen whale, the largest animal ever to live on earth. One kind, the blue whale, may be 100 feet long and weigh more than 120 tons! The heaviest of the dinosaurs probably weighed no more than 50 tons and was about 90 feet long.

The largest animal living on land is the elephant. The largest elephant of which we have records weighed about 12 tons and measured 13 feet 2 inches at the shoulder.

The next largest land animal is considered by some to be the rhinoceros. But there have been cases where a hippopotamus, which is a shorter animal than the rhinoceros, weighed more. One such hippopotamus weighed 8,600 pounds.

The largest fish is the whale shark. Some of them have reached a length of 60 or 70 feet and have weighed as much as 13 tons.

The largest snake is believed to be the anaconda. The biggest ones may be 35 to 40 feet long. A 40-foot anaconda snake would weigh about 1,000 pounds.

The largest living bird is the African ostrich. It may reach a height of over 8 feet and weigh more than 300 pounds.

WHY ARE DOLPHINS CONSIDERED INTELLIGENT?

Dolphins and porpoises are small whales, ranging in length from four to about twelve feet. Whether they are called "dolphins" or "porpoises" seems to be a matter of preference. Either name is correct.

There are several reasons why scientists consider the dolphin to be an unusually intelligent animal. Many of them have been known to imitate human speech quite distinctly—and without even being urged to do so. They can also learn to understand human words and respond to them.

Students of animal behavior have two other reasons for considering the dolphin intelligent. Dolphins are able to invent and play games. For example, suppose there is a feather floating about in a tank of water. A dolphin will get the feather and bring it near the jet of water entering the tank. The feather drifts into the jet and goes shooting off. The dolphin pursues it, catches it, brings it back, and again releases it into the jet.

Dolphins have invented games with small rubber inner tubes. They will toss the tube to someone standing by the tank and wait for the person to toss it back to them so they can catch it. This kind of play is considered a sign of intelligence.

Dolphins can also solve problems. If a piece of food is stuck under a rock, they can find a way to "blow" the food out from under the rock.

Just how intelligent dolphins are has not been tested. This is because there is no intelligence test by which animals as different as dogs and chimpanzees and dolphins can be rated.

HOW DO FISH REPRODUCE?

Most fishes lay eggs. They either sink or float in the water. The outside shell of the egg is a transparent membrane. Inside, the egg itself is made of yolk and of protoplasm. Protoplasm is the living matter that becomes the future fish. The yolk, like the yolk of a chicken egg, nourishes the developing fish.

The egg cell is fertilized by a sperm from the male. The sperm swims into the egg cell through the shell, or membrane. The membrane has a small opening in it, just above the cell. Sperm swimming to the egg can get into the egg only through this opening. If sperm pass through, the egg is fertilized by one of the sperm.

Then life within the egg begins. The cells begin to divide until they form a thin sheet that encloses the entire yolk. The sheet then gradually begins to take the shape of the future fish. There is a bulge where the head will be, muscles appear as small blocks, the tail bud appears, and so on.

This embryo fish continues to grow inside the egg. After a certain number of days, the shell softens. The embryo hatches out of it. It is free to drift and to grow into an adult fish.

We have been discussing eggs that are laid and fertilized outside the body. Fishes that shed eggs are known as oviparous. But other fishes are viviparous, which means that they give birth to living young. Among such fishes are guppies, swordtails, and mollies.

The eggs are fertilized inside the body of the female and grow into baby fish there. At the appropriate time they are born.

WHAT IS THE DIFFERENCE BETWEEN BACTERIA AND VIRUSES?

People usually link bacteria and viruses in terms of disease. But they are quite different from each other. Some bacteria cause disease, but most do not. There are at least two thousand species of bacteria, and most of them are either harmless or helpful.

A bacterium consists of only one cell. A single drop of sour milk may contain 100,000,000 bacteria. Bacteria are everywhere. Some live in the mouths, noses, and intestines of animals, including man. Others live on fallen leaves, dead trees, animal wastes, in fresh and salt water, in milk, and in most foods.

Since bacteria have some features of both plants and animals, scientists have not agreed on how to classify them. Most bacteria reproduce by fission—the cell divides in two.

Viruses are very small organisms, so small that they can only be seen in detail with an electron microscope. Viruses grow and multiply only when they are inside living cells. Outside living cells, viruses do not change in any way and seem lifeless. They cannot grow unless they are inside the cells of animals, plants, or bacteria.

Viruses that attack man and animals are called animal viruses. Those that attack plants are called plant viruses, and those that attack bacteria are called bacterial viruses.

The viruses that infect man and animals may be breathed in or swallowed, or enter through an opening in the skin. Some of them destroy cells simply by growing in them. Others cause the membranes separating two cells to dissolve, and still others cause cells to become malignant.

WHAT IS THE STORY OF THE ALBATROSS?

About two hundred years ago, Samuel Taylor Coleridge wrote a poem called *The Rime of the Ancient Mariner.* It is one of the most famous poems in the English language. It deals with the terrible things that happen to a sailor who had killed an albatross.

Since man first began to sail the seas, this giant bird has had a special meaning to sailors. They have believed that its ability to follow a ship for days and days, sometimes hardly moving its wings, was evidence that it had supernatural powers, and that it would bring bad luck to harm an albatross.

Of course, this is only a superstition, but the albatross is quite a bird! It has the greatest wingspan of any bird in existence. The body may be only about 9 inches wide, and it may weigh only 25 pounds, but its wings may measure more than 11 feet from tip to tip.

An albatross spends most of its life flying. When it is ready to eat, it floats on the water like a cork and uses its beak to scoop up small squids, fish, or scraps from ships.

The flight of the albatross is amazing. It can soar so high that it is out of sight. It can stand still in the air by balancing its wings delicately against the breeze. And when it has a favorable wind and wants to go fast, it can fly at more than a hundred miles an hour.

During the nesting season these birds go to barren antarctic islands. The mother lays a single egg in a nest of clay and grass. The parents take care of the baby bird until it is able to go off on its own.

HOW DO PARROTS TALK?

When we say that parrots and some other birds can "talk," we mean they can imitate the sounds that human beings make when talking. But the birds do not use words in order to share thoughts and feelings or to get something they want. They probably talk simply because they enjoy making the sounds.

Many kinds of birds mimic various sounds that they hear about them. Some can copy the songs of other birds, some can mimic certain man-made sounds such as musical tunes. But birds of only three families—the parrots, crows, and starlings—can mimic the sounds of human speech.

The voice equipment of talking birds differs from man's in position and structure. Birds have no vocal cords. Most talking birds do not sing, although many can whistle Talking birds, such as parrots, must be trained to talk while still very young.

Parrots and other talking birds do not learn human speech sounds easily. The words must be repeated slowly and clearly, many times over. Once the bird has mastered a word or phrase, it probably never forgets what it has learned.

But the words seldom seem to have meaning for the birds. Usually words are only sounds to them. A scientist tried to teach a parrot to associate words with feelings, but failed. The bird, an excellent talker, could not learn to say "food" when it was hungry, or "water" when it was thirsty. Even the phrase "Polly wants a cracker" does not mean that "Polly" is hungry.

But a good many parrots have learned to say "Good morning" at the right time of day and at no other time. So in such cases the words may be more than just sounds to these parrots.

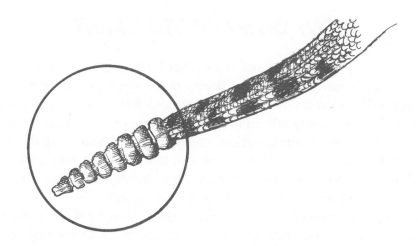

WHAT IS A RATTLESNAKE'S RATTLE MADE OF?

Rattlesnakes belong to a poisonous group of snakes called pit vipers. The pit vipers get their name from the two large pits on their heads, one on each side of the head, between the nostril and the eye. These pits are sensitive to the slightest change in temperature, so a viper can detect the presence of a warm-blooded animal even in the dark!

There are 15 kinds of rattlesnakes, and all of them have rattles at the tips of their tails. Even a young rattler has at least one round, shiny "button" at the tip of its tail.

The rattle is made up of dry, horny rings of skin that lock loosely onto one another. When the snake shakes its tail, as it does when excited, these horny pieces of skin rub against one another. This results in a rasping or buzzing sound. It serves to warn some other animal that it is too close for comfort.

Does a rattlesnake always give warning that it is going to strike by rattling? They usually do rattle when they become angry or frightened. But experts who have studied the habits of rattlesnakes report that this isn't always so. Many give no warning at all. So it isn't safe to depend on that warning rattle.

On the other hand, one can avoid being bitten by a rattlesnake by staying out of its range. A rattlesnake can only strike as far as it can raise its head. Even if it is coiled, it can strike only one-third to one-half its body length. And since rattlesnakes are rarely longer than six feet, one can be alert and stay out of its range.

Another interesting thing about rattlers—they give birth to living young.

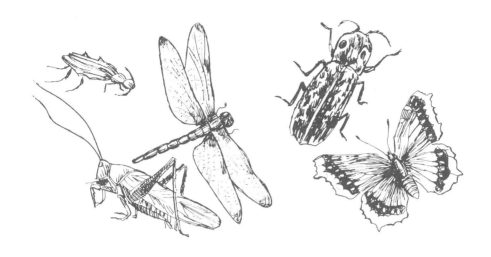

DO INSECTS BREATHE?

Because many insects are so tiny, it is hard for us to imagine their bodies performing all the functions of larger creatures. But like all animals, insects must breathe. They need oxygen from the air to burn digested food.

When the food burns, it gives the body energy. A waste product of this burning is a gas called carbon dioxide. The body breathes out the carbon dioxide together with the parts of the breathed-in air it did not use.

We breathe in and out through the mouth and the two nostrils in the nose. Insects have about ten pairs of "nostrils" along the thorax and abdomen (the two parts of the insect's body behind the head). Each segment of the insect's body has a pair of nostrils. They are little holes called spiracles.

Most insects breathe through their spiracles, but there are some exceptions. The water scorpion has a long breathing tube attached to the tip of its abdomen. It pushes the tip of this tube up through the surface of the water to get air.

Many insects that live in water have gills instead of spiracles for breathing. Gills are special kinds of organs for taking in air that is dissolved in water.

We shouldn't be surprised about anything concerning insects. First, there are so many of them. About 700,000 different kinds of insects are known to exist. And insects are able to live almost anywhere on earth—from deep underground caves to the tops of the world's highest mountains.

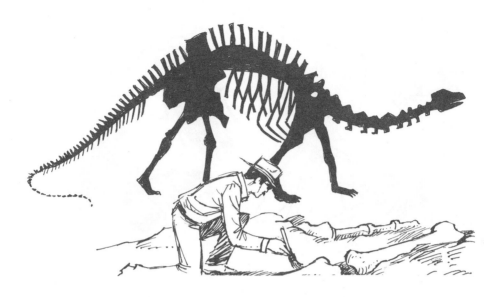

WHEN DID MAN FIRST FIND
OUT ABOUT DINOSAURS?

No human being ever saw a living dinosaur. Dinosaurs were animals that lived in most regions of the world, but they died out everywhere about 65,000,000 years ago. It is believed that the first kind of man appeared less than 2,500,000 years ago. So dinosaurs were extinct by the time man appeared.

We know about dinosaurs from their remains. These are bones, found either in skeletons or separately; footprints in rock; impressions of skin, also in rock; and eggs.

There is some doubt as to when the first recognizable dinosaur bones were discovered. Footprints have been known for many years. A dinosaur skeleton may have been seen at Haddonfield, New Jersey, toward the end of the 1700's.

The first bones that are still available for examination and identification are some that were discovered in England. One set was found in 1822 and is now in the British Museum of Natural History in London.

Another set of dinosaur bones, found about the same time, was the basis for the first scientific description of any dinosaur. This was done in 1824 by a professor at Oxford University.

So you can see that man has found out about dinosaurs quite recently. Dinosaur specimens have been found in great numbers in the United States, Canada, Argentina, Brazil, India, Africa, Australia, Mongolia, China, France, Germany, Portugal, and the Soviet Union. This indicates that dinosaurs really lived all over the world.

INDEX

327

328

331